The Collector's Encyclopedia of

Granite Ware

Colors, Shapes and Values

by
Helen Greguire

The Collector's Encyclopedia of

Granite Ware

Colors, Shapes and Values

by
Helen Greguire

COLLECTOR BOOKS
A Division of Schroeder Publishing Co., Inc.

Cover designed and photographed by Frederick Greguire III.

Items on front cover:

Coffee pot, cobalt blue and white, large swirl, unusual seamed bottom. Condition, good plus; rarity, 4 & 5; price, $350.00. **Pitcher,** old red and white, large swirl. Condition, near mint; rarity, 1; price, $950.00. **Pitcher,** green and white, "Emerald Ware," large swirl. Condition, good plus; rarity, 4; price, $285.00.

Additional copies of this book may be ordered from:

COLLECTOR BOOKS
P.O. Box 3009
Paducah, Kentucky 42002-3009

or

Helen Greguire
103 Trimmer Road
Hilton, New York 14468

@ $24.95. Add $2.00 for postage and handling.

When I think of dedication, I immediately think of all the people who love and cherish their Granite Ware, whether it's for its particular color, shape, or size.

I dedicate this book to all of you and future generations of Granite Ware collectors.

From the Author

Do You Love Granite Ware?

It was the fascination of granite ware and the need to know more about it that led me to write this book after years of research and study.

I have been collecting for a number of years along with doing articles and talks on granite ware all over the country. Still, each piece I collect is as exciting as the first. The need to share the knowledge I have acquired through the years with people who collect or those who just enjoy looking at and learning about granite ware, is most fulfilling to me. So many times, people would say, "Why don't you write a book on granite ware, because we have a need to know about what we are collecting."

I can't begin to tell you the hours it has taken to put this book together, but I do know that if I have helped to give people a better understanding of granite ware and its unending beauty, I will have accomplished what I set out to do.

Granitely,

Helen Greguire

Acknowledgments

I could not begin to put together the acknowledgments for this book without first giving "just due" to a number of people whose enthusiasm was the inspiration for the unending research into granite ware.

Special appreciation goes out to one of granite ware's first authors, Frances Thompson. We also respectfully acknowledge the early efforts of authors Fred and Rose Booher. To Vernagene Vogelzang and Evelyn Welch, collecting granite ware was never the same after your magnificent research books.

No collectable could obtain such broad nationwide acceptance without a network of enthusiasts. In 1978, on the 100th anniversary of the 1878 Paris Expostition, in which the United States firm, LaLance and Grosjean Mfg. Co., won the Paris Exposition Grand Gold Medal for its blue and white marbled granite ware, the American Graniteware Association was conceived. The American Graniteware Association was then officially created in July 1979. Again, special acknowledgments go out to the founders known as the "Granny Granites." After the American Graniteware Association disbanded, a new organization, The National Graniteware Society, 4818 Reamer Road, Center Point, Iowa, 52213 was organized on April 19, 1986. Granite ware collecting now took on a new fervor. Again, a special tribute goes out to all of those who have brought this current group to new heights. The combined efforts of the pioneer authors, researchers, and collectors, along with the nationwide organizations of enthusiasts, have made writing this book the next logical step.

Putting together a book of this magnitude requires the collective efforts of many people as well as the sharing of treasures from a number of collectors. I was fortunate enough to have the best of both!

To my husband, Fred, who so patiently helped construct shelves and backboards for the displays, a million thanks!

To my son, Fred, who did the photography, and to my daughter-in-law, Val, who aptly helped set up the displays, your efforts make the book!

To Carol Viterise, no words can express my appreciation for her great expertise in typing. Her efforts were tireless and her patience was unending!

To Phillip Dailey, for his special assistance!

To daughter, Marylou Prince; son-in-law, Paul Prince; and granddaughter, Paula Jean Prince.

Last but not least, my sincere thanks to:

Vikki and Gary Davis	Donald and Rita Maguire
Muriel DeFrank	Donald Mann
Lew DeFrank	Rose Schleede
Angel Diaz	Bob and Gail Scutt
Arthur G. Fraser	Betty and Bob Smith
Brenda Hutto	Jay and Joan Smith
Sharon Latka	Mary Ann and Stan Szambelan
Pat and Jim Lugert	Ruth Van Kuren
Boice Lydell	

My thanks go out to all of you for the loan of your granite ware and for your great moral support, all of which made this book possible.

Table of Contents

Introduction

When I look at granite ware today, my thoughts automatically go back to Grandmother's day; how she must have felt a sense of joy when she purchased her first piece of brilliantly-colored granite ware after cleaning her cast iron ware. It had to be a dream come true because a "new era" had begun with the appearance of this bright utilitarian ware called "Granite Ware." It was only the beginning of what was to come! Not only could she add beautiful colors to her drab kitchen, but her everyday chores would be made so much easier. "Granite Ware Ads" of the day stated it all: "It Cleans Like Glass." Even though granite ware did chip with careless use and could develop holes, the holes could be repaired temporarily with Mendets. When it no longer was repairable for its intended use, there was always a secondary use. We must remember that at the time, granite ware was not meant to be a collector's item. It was mass-produced for functional everyday use.

When people think of granite ware colors, they think of colors such as gray, blue and white swirl, and white trimmed with dark blue or black. Until collectors like myself started to "hunt out" the more unusual, we never realized there were so many colors and shapes in granite ware. In fact, this book could not begin to cover all the unique items which exist. Just since we completed photographing, many more great "unusuals" have turned up (see Section 27). This is what makes granite ware collecting so exciting.

This book is not meant to be a reference on companies or the history of companies, because extensive research on these subjects has already been covered in previous books on granite ware. What I am striving for in this book is a better understanding of the colors and shapes of granite ware and its intended use.

What is Granite Ware?

Granite ware is the adhering of different colored enamels to different metals and shapes at a high degree of heat, making a composition of a glass-like finish.

Pattern and Color Descriptions

Pattern and color descriptions refer to the predominant pattern and/or color (e.g. "Chicken Wire pattern," "End of Day" color.

Swirl - Marbled or ribbon-like effect. Can be small, medium, or large.

Mottled - Can be small, fine, medium, or large.

    Small Mottled - Small sponge-like effect.

    Fine Mottled - Smaller version of small mottled.

    Medium or Large Mottled - The color is more flowing thus predominates; in comparison with the lighter background.

Spatter - A splash effect.

Speckled - A flecked effect.

Snow on the Mountain - Usually heavy coats of white enamel applied over contrasting color giving the white a lumpy effect.

Confetti - Looks exactly like colored paper confetti.

Relish - Looks exactly like pickled relish but comes in a number of colors.

Chicken Wire - Looks like chicken wire. The wire effect is usualy the predominant colored part.

Feathered - Looks like feathers.

Checkered - Squared-type pattern.

Redipped - Colors applied over original color by the factory. The reason for the change may have been the lack of popularity of the original color, or the company may have wanted to experiment with another color variation. Often on redipped pieces the original factory color can be seen slightly through the redipped color. Sometimes when a piece is chipped, the original factory color can be seen clearly.

Solid Color - One overall color outside. It can be a light or dark shade, sometimes with a white or other color inside. It may be trimmed in another contrasting solid color.

Shaded - Gradual lightening of solid color.

End of Day - Combination of three or more colors, usually one color is more predominant. End of Day can also have a pattern. For example, some End of Day prices have a veining or chicken wire pattern with a number of colors in the veining, while others may have a swirl or mottled effect. This could have been a company's unique way of using leftover colors at the end of a day's production.

Decorated - Various decorations applied to the piece. Decorations may be in the form of decals, enameling in high relief, or impressed enamel decoration. Various metals may also be used for trimmings, such as pewter, e.g. pewter lids, bands, spouts, bottoms and feet of teapots or coffee pots, or cast iron handles on various items.

Lettered Pieces - Name and usage of piece such as "Bread." These may be in different languages. Another example of lettered pieces is a child's ABC plate. The letters can also be embossed.

Predominant Color - The predominant color is named first throughout the book when a color description is given.

Shades of Color

I have given a lot of thought on how to explain colors to the best advantage so that it is clear to everyone. I believe it would be more understandable to describe the shades of color, along with the manufacturer's and jobber's given name when possible, rather than using a color chart in the book.

Many times, I have had someone say, "I have a certain color," which doesn't mean much if you have never seen the color or had anything to compare it to. I believe more can be learned by identifying the shades of color as you are looking at the photos in the book. Any other way would cause mass confusion in attempting to describe the multitude of colors and their variations. For example, the shades of blue alone are so extensive that they could become confusing.

In summary, there is an old saying, "A picture is worth a thousand words."

Enameling Types

Single Coat of Enamel

Two Coats of Enamel

Three Coats of Enamel - Results in very high quality. (Some companies even boast of using four coats or more.)

Porcelain - A form of enameling usually found on kitchen table tops, appliances, and advertising signs, very often in white. Porcelain may also be applied over a ceramic-type base for such purposes as stoppers.

Granite Ware Names and Makers

Many names were given to granite ware such as Agate Ware, Enamel Ware, and Agate Iron Ware just to name a few. Even today in different parts of the country, collectors and dealers call it by different names.

In the 1800's, companies sprang up all over the United States and abroad. Many companies were short-lived. Some managed to become leaders in their field. It was the quality companies that survived for a number of years. A few of these were The LaLance and Grosjean Manufacturing Co., New York, NY, and The St. Louis Stamping Co., St. Louis, MO. Even though these companies do not exist today, they left behind a monumental amount of granite ware because their production was so extensive each day. Some companies were also called stamping and enameling companies. That is because the companies with stamping in their name also stamped out the metal shapes to be enameled.

Is Age Determined by Construction?

Most of the pieces I have seen that are riveted are of an early age. But rivets alone do not determine age. Some companies, in order to advertise a better quality product, felt that seams and extra bends in a certain area gave it more strength and appeal. Other companies advertised seamless ware, because they felt the seams would rust first, and they usually did.

Another factor determining age is when a piece has the company, brand name, and a date fired into the granite ware.

Construction of certain types of handles, knobs, spouts, and covers, (e.g. weld handles, wood handles, wood and spun knobs, and hinged covers) along with the shape of the piece itself, helps to determine age. The older pieces are usually heavier.

How to Determine the New Granite Ware

Paper labels on granite ware are one good source of age information. Some of the newer pieces have the name of the place where manufactured (e.g. Made in Hong Kong) lightly stamped on the bottom instead of fired into the enamel like the older granite ware. Generally, the newer pieces are of lighter weight and the texture of the granite ware seems to be applied thinly.

On some new granite ware, the swirl colors are applied both inside and out. Colors to watch for include red and white swirl, yellow and white swirl, blue and white swirl, brown and white swirl, brown and white mottled, green and white swirl, combination orange and red swirl, and a gray mottled (like a large relish pattern which was made in Romania).

In the red and white swirl, I have seen the mugs swirled on the outside only, and on both sides. The ones with the white inside are generally from the 1950's. This 1950's era red and white swirl has a black outline blending into the red swirl. After the 1950's, the red and white does not have this blending, and the red coloring is not as deep. On the other hand, the turn-of-the-century "old" red and white swirl also has a black blending into the red swirl. The main differences are that the "old" red and white swirl is usually very heavy, is white on the inside, and has more coats of enamel (e.g. triple coated with riveted handles and spout and a hinged cover).

Some newer blue and white swirl has been, and still is coming out of Hong Kong (C.G.S. International Inc. of Miami, Florida is the distributor). The coffee pot I have with this label looks like it might have been stamped out all in one piece except for the cover. Again, the cover is not hinged to the coffee pot. The piece is very lightweight.

There is also solid color enamel ware being made today that is heavy. I saw a collander in the solid red trimmed in black, but it had a modern look about it.

Some of the shapes made in newer granite ware are mugs, large wash basins, plates, sectioned plates, soup plates, large trays, coffee pots, teapots, utensils, collanders, handled butter melters, tumblers, cups and saucers, and sugar and creamers. These were made from the 1950's to the 1970's, and some are still being made today.

One of the best ways to sum this up is to check out stores and outlets in your area for what is being made today. Try to seek out experienced collectors when in doubt. When you are buying from a person you don't know, ask that person to mark your sales slip guaranteeing the item or items you have purchased as old.

Popularity Helps to Determine Desirability

Certain items are more popular among collectors for one reason or another. It could be for the color, shape, size, or rarity of a particular piece. Some of the most popular items in granite ware are coffee pots, teapots, and coffee biggins because these may be found in wide variety of colors, shapes, and sizes.

Hanging items such as dippers, muffin tins, and spoons are also popular because many collectors have only limited space to display their granite ware. Most of all, the rare pieces of granite ware are always at the top of the populartiy list.

How to Clean and Preserve Granite Ware

The best way I have found to clean granite ware is: If it is greasy and dirty, I first spray it with oven cleaner. I leave this on at least five or six hours or until I see the black grease start to roll off. I then rinse it with very hot water to remove the dirt and grease. If there is still a lot of dirt and grease left on the piece, I spray it again and leave it for as long as needed. I then rinse it in hot water again. After rinsing clean, use a hot soapy water to wash it thoroughly. Rinse again with hot water. Then if the piece has lots of stains, soak it in warm water and a liquid bleach combination until the stain is removed. Rinse again thoroughly. Wash again with hot soapy water. Rinse again and dry thoroughly, leaving all covers off or open to fully dry.

If a piece has a tin cover or other types of metal, it's not advisable to get the oven cleaner on the metal because it has a tendency to give the metal a spotty look. Also, wooden parts, painted or unpainted, should be covered with plastic because it will remove the paint when spraying with oven cleaner. Another word of caution, steel wool pads with or without soap, or scrubbies should not be used because they could scratch the finish.

To clean the tin covers, I usually use fine, dry steel wool. After cleaning, I spray with an aerosol furniture wax and polish it.

It is not advisable to use a cleaner that contains lye for cleaning the inside of tea kettles or other items to remove lime deposits. If it gets on the finish, it will destroy the shine. Usually vinegar will soften the lime deposits if left to soak overnight or longer.

The last step is to spray the piece with a wax polish. This usually gives it a good shine and protects it from rusting. *Caution:* Do not spray pieces that you intend to use with wax.

Granite Ware's Future

If only manufacturers, jobbers, and retailers could have foreseen what has happened to granite ware today, I feel they would have stockpiled their warehouses and waited for our generation to come along. The 15¢ and 20¢ specials of yesteryear would bring dollars today.

Collectors like myself have caused granite ware to stray from its intended, versatile, everyday use, and instead become a highly sought-after collectable. Oh yes, there are times when I find a piece in "mint condition" and the first thought that enters my mind is "Gee, I can use this piece." Then it automatically finds a spot in the collection. Use that beauty? Never! How many times have you said exactly that? Eventually, I do break down and use some of my treasured granite ware with great care. I do enjoy cooking in it, especially over the wood-burning stove. I also have fun showing off those beautiful colors and shapes.

I feel granite ware is a good investment because granite ware's future is just beginning. Granite ware has everything going for it. It is a very durable collectable with a wonderful range of colors, shapes, and uses. It was produced in quantity, and there is a wide selection today to choose from. Someone in almost everyone's family has at one time or another used granite ware; therefore, there is a general familiarity with it. Not only is it treasured by collectors like myself, it is also sought after by decorators to add that special touch of color and shape. Because of our care and research, future generations will be able to continue to enjoy this great collecting experience.

Granite ware has become so popular that it has been featured in many leading antique and decorating magazines, and newspapers. Granite ware collector clubs continue to organize. The National Graniteware Society, mentioned earlier, is growing each year. The annual convention of this group has become an eagerly awaited "happening" where granite ware collectors from all over the country get together to talk granite ware, show off their treasures, and buy and sell. Besides the national organization, exciting local and regional granite ware clubs are springing up all over the nation.

For further information on your area, contact:

The National Graniteware Society
4818 Reamer Road
Center Point, IA 52213
Phone # (319)842-2514

For further information in New York state, contact the author.

Section 1

Teapots, Coffee Pots, Coffee Biggins, Coffee Boilers, and Coffee Roasters

All items in this section are favorites among collectors because they come in so many colors, shapes, and sizes. They can be either American or foreign made.

Teapots and Coffee Pots

Rarely are there two identical coffee or teapots; even the covers tend to vary. I have heard collectors say that a particular cover is not correct because it is tin rather than granite ware. It is interesting to note that most of the time when a coffee or teapot was purchased, it came with a tin cover unless a granite ware cover was specified. If one chose a granite ware cover, it would cost an additional 10¢, depending on the manufacturer's policy.

Unusual handles such as cast iron, strap handles, or weld-shaped handles that are bulged on the inside to give a better grip tended to give each coffee or teapot its own individual look.

The shape of the spout helps to determine whether it's a coffee pot or teapot. Goose-neck shape spouts are usually called teapots by today's collectors, whereas short, triangular-shaped spouts are called coffee pots. There can be exceptions to the rule. Early advertisements (e.g. Lisk Mfg. Co. of Canandaigua, NY) showed goose-neck "pots" advertised as percolators. Most often, percolators have a glass insert in the cover and a removable coffee basket.

Coffee and teapots had to be made for different size stove openings. For example, the 7" to 9" stove openings seemed to be the most popular size. The 1917 Sears Roebuck Catalog advertised their "Flat Bottom Ware" would fit any size lid opening. It was advertised in blue and white enameled ware and Peerless gray enameled ware.

Capacity size of various coffee pots, teapots, coffee boilers, and coffee biggins seem to vary greatly in the old catalogs and advertisements. With this in mind, I have chosen not to specify the exact capacity size (e.g. 1¾ cup size instead of 2 cups size).

The different metal trims for covers, spouts, bands and bottoms, whether fancy or plain, were sometimes made by a company other than the granite ware manufacturer. These companies often did not have the facilities to stamp out the metal parts. Instead, the metal parts were shipped to the granite ware manufacturer where they were applied to the coffee or teapot bodies. The 1892 Manning Bowman Catalog advertised decorated "pearl agateware" with white metal mountings and protection bands. These items could be ordered with special inscriptions commemorating birthdays, anniversaries, Christmas, a person's name, or a place, at an extra cost ranging from $1.00 to $1.50 depending on how much lettering and decorations were ordered. An example would be "To Mother, Christmas 1892." These were patented June 5, 1883, registered July 13, 1885. Only highly skilled, trained workers were able to do this type of decorating. All pewter trimmed teapots and coffee pots are rare. Some are rarer than others because of their color, size, unusual shape, or trim.

Coffee Biggins

The coffee biggin is a coffee pot with an additional top insert called a "biggin." Each biggin may contain additional parts. The biggin can be granite or metal. It can have one of several types of bottoms - perforated, screened, or an open bottom that holds a cloth bag. Some biggins contain one or two spreaders which have perforated bottoms to spread the water evenly through the coffee. Most coffee biggins have goose-neck spouts, contrary to the early way of thinking - that "pots" with a goose-neck spout were teapots. In fact, some of the old trade catalogs from the 1800's advertised teapots with goose-neck spouts, as well as coffee biggins with goose-neck spouts. I believe that these items had more than one function - that goose-neck coffee pots or biggins also were used as teapots by removing the biggin part.

Coffee Boilers

Coffee boilers, or camp coffee pots, as they were known, got their name from their large capacity.

They were used in the home for large family gatherings and on the farm at harvest time. The cowboys and pioneers also used them along the trail. Can't you just imagine those thirsty pioneers or cowboys, after a long day's work or journey, finally reaching that long-awaited cup of coffee brewing on the campfire in a granite coffee boiler?

Coffee Roasters

Coffee roasters were used on the stove top. A quantity of coffee beans were placed in the drum and the handle was then turned slowly until the beans were roasted to perfection.

Overview

Many of the items in this section are rapidly becoming endangered species. Coffee pots, coffee biggins, and coffee boilers are being replaced by the instant coffee craze and the electric coffee makers which both reflect an easier way of life. The teapot's future also was threatened by the invention of the tea bag, and pre-roasted ground coffee has all but eliminated the need for individual coffee roasters. In times to come, future generations will only be able to imagine a coffee pot sitting on the back burner of a wood-burning stove, pouring forth the aroma of fresh brewed coffee, inviting "all who enter." For these reasons, it is important for authors and collectors like myself to help preserve this part of our American heritage for generations to come.

Plate 1, Row 1:

1. Teapot, pewter trimmed, white decorated with a castle scene.
2. Teapot, pewter trimmed, white decorated with heron and rushes.
3. Teapot, pewter trimmed, white decorated with fuchsias. Handle is unique combination of decorated granite ware and pewter. Note: Rare footed base.
4. Teapot, pewter trimmed, white decorated with morning glorys.
5. Teapot, pewter trimmed, white decorated with pink roses.

Plate 1, Row 2:

1. Teapot, pewter trimmed, white decorated with blackberries.
2. Teapot, pewter trimmed, white decorated with calla lilies.
3. Teapot, pewter trimmed, large squatty shape, white decorated with band of violets.
4. Teapot, pewter trimmed, squatty shape, white decorated with band of violets, inscribed on front and back, "Oakland."

Plate 1, Row 3:

1. Teapot, pewter trimmed, creme color, decorated with wildflowers. Bottom section, brown and white relish pattern.
2. Teapot, pewter trimmed, light green, decorated with daisies and leaves.
3. Teapot, pewter trimmed, pink, decorated with apple blossoms.
4. Teapot, pewter trimmed, white, decorated with heron and rushes scene. Handle is unique combination of decorated granite ware and pewter.

Plate 2, Row 1:

1. Coffee pot, fancy pewter trimmed, solid robin egg blue, marked "Ideal New England Enamel Co., Middletown, Conn.," in an oval.*Note:* LaLance and Grosjean Co. also made robin egg blue. I have a coffee boiler labeled Robin Egg Blue.
2. Teapot, pewter trimmed, blue and white fine mottled. The cover is not hinged. Marked "Manning Bowman & Co."
3. Coffee pot, pewter trimmed, blue and white fine mottled.
4. Teapot, pewter trimmed, blue and white fine mottled, marked "Manning Bowman & Co."

Plate 2, Row 2:

1. Teapot, pewter trimmed, gray mottled, scalloped top edge.
2. Teapot with metal holder and alcohol burner, pewter trimmed, gray medium mottled. *Note:* This type was used at the table because it could be tilted for serving.
3. Teapot, pewter trimmed, gray large mottled, "Belle" shaped. Can also hold a biggin top because the cover is not hinged.

Plate 2, Row 3:

1. Teapot, pewter trimmed, white, squatty shape, copper trimmed bottom.
2. Coffee pot, lower section light brown and white relish pattern.
3. Coffee pot, pewter trimmed, covered hinged spout, metal bottom, fine mottled reddish brown and white, marked "Manning Bowman & Co."

Plate 3, Row 1:

1. Coffee pot, pewter trimmed, large mottled gray, hinged covered spout, copper bottom.
2. Coffee pot, pewter trimmed, hinged covered spout, white decorated with bachelor buttons.

Plate 3, Row 2:

1. Coffee pot, pewter trimmed, white decorated with blackberries, hinged covered spout, copper bottom.
2. Coffee pot, pewter trimmed, white decorated with heron and rushes scene, hinged covered spout, copper bottom.
3. Teapot, pewter trimmed, white decorated with lilies of the valley and fern, copper bottom.

Plate 3, Row 3:

1. Teapot, pewter trimmed, mottled gray, squatty shape, metal bottom.
2. Teapot, pewter trimmed, fancy embossed metal body, lower section is mottled gray granite ware.
3. Coffee pot, pewter trimmed, mottled gray, hinged covered spout, copper bottom.
4. Teapot, pewter trimmed, mottled gray, squatty shape, copper bottom.

Plate 4, Row 1:

1. Teapot, reddish brown and white fine mottled, pewter spout, brass-plated cover with wooden handle and knob, marked "Germany." Emblem is a lion standing on a teapot with his two front paws.
2. Coffee pot, reddish brown and white fine mottled, brass-plated ribbed cover, brass-plated hinged covered spout, metal bottom and wooden handle.
3. Coffee pot, reddish brown fine mottled, brass-plated hinged cover and knob, wide brass-plated band covering the top of the pot, wooden handle and metal bottom.

Plate 4, Row 2:

1. Coffee pot, medium mottled cobalt blue and white, wooden handle and knob.
2. Coffee pot, white deocrated with forget-me-nots and a wild rose, trimmed with gold bands, fancy embossed brass-plated cover, wooden handle and knob, copper bottom, marked "Patent-Pending."
3. Teapot, cobalt blue and white large swirl, wooden handle and matching granite ribbed cover.

Plate 4, Row 3:

1. Teapot, fine mottled blue and white, brass-plated ribbed cover, wooden handle and knob, brass-plated bottom, marked "Patent-Pending."
2. Teapot, white decorated with blue birds and dahlias, trimmed in brown, nickel-plated cover, wooden handle and knob.
3. Coffee pot, green relish, covered hinged spout, wooden handle and knob.
4. Coffee pot, medium mottled brown and white, brass-plated cover and body band, wooden handle and knob.

Note: Wood-handled teapots and coffee pots are harder to find.

Plate 5, Row 1:

1. Coffee biggin, squatty shape, black biggin, cream bottom with black trim, four pieces, chrome-plated copper cover.
2. Coffee biggin, pewter trimmed, light green decorated with daisies and leaves, five pieces.
3. Coffee biggin, squatty shape, fine mottled blue and white, three pieces.
4. Coffee biggin, solid yellow with black trim, five pieces, Bakelite knob, handled biggin.

Plate 5, Row 2:

1. Coffee biggin, red and white medium swirl with red trim. *Note:* This is known as "Snow on the Mountain." It has a lumpy effect to the white enamel. Usually the predominant color is white. Most of the time this is foreign made. Four pieces.
2. Coffee biggin, blue and white large swirl, four pieces. The spreader is perforated aluminum. The biggin part has a perforated metal bottom.
3. Coffee biggin, shaded gray and decorated, three pieces.
4. Coffee biggin, red and white medium mottled with red trim, "Snow on the Mountain," four pieces.

Plate 5, Row 3:

1. Coffee biggin, blue and white medium mottled, four pieces, tin biggin and spreader, weld handle.
2. Coffee biggin, solid light blue decorated with gold bands, three pieces, unusual glass cover.
3. Coffee biggin, blue decorated with apple blossoms, pewter biggin and trim, five pieces.
4. Coffee biggin, medium mottled gray, four pieces, tin biggin and spreader, weld handle.

Note: **This photo is a breakdown of Plate 5 showing selected biggin parts.**

Plate 6, Row 1:

1. Coffee biggin, squatty shape, blue and white fine mottled, three pieces. Consists of cover, squatty pot, and handled coffee biggin with fancy perforated bottom. Note hook on top of pot - this is to keep the biggin secure when pouring.
2. Coffee biggin, pewter trimmed, blue decorated with apple blossoms. Consists of five pieces including pot and cover, pewter biggin with screened bottom, and two piece stemmed spreader.

Plate 6, Row 2:

1. Coffee biggin, five pieces, pewter trimmed, light green decorated with daisies and leaves, fancy ribbed pewter cover, pewter strap-handled waste container for passing around at the table to hold the coffee waste. A coffee biggin part which has no perforation in the bottom and is used to hold the cloth coffee bag after use.

Plate 6, Row 3:

1. Coffee biggin, five pieces, solid yellow with black trim. Consists of cover with Bakelite knob, pot, two perforated spreaders, and a handled perforated biggin. *Note:* In a 1968 magazine ad, it shows a coffee biggin like this one advertising French-style coffee.
2. Coffee biggin, squatty shape, four pieces including pot, perforated black biggin, perforated spreader, and a chrome-plated copper cover.

Plate 7, Row 1:

1. Coffee biggin, red and white medium mottled, four pieces.
2. Coffee biggin, red and white with red trim, medium swirl, "Snow on the Mountain," four pieces.
3. Coffee biggin, red and white with red trim, checkered pattern. *Note:* This is a square type pattern, four pieces.

Plate 7, Row 2:

1. Coffee biggin, blue and white medium mottled, "Snow on the Mountain," four pieces.
2. Coffee biggin, gray medium mottled, four pieces, tin biggin, perforated spreader, and weld handle.
3. Coffee biggin, blue and white fine mottled with red trim, four pieces.
4. Coffee biggin, gray medium mottled, four pieces, tin biggin with cover, spreader, and pot with weld handle. *Note:* The pot has a coffee pot spout which is unusual because most coffee biggins have a goose-neck spout.
5. Coffee biggin, light blue and white large swirl with black trim and handle, triple coated, three pieces.

Plate 7, Row 3:

1. Coffee biggin, white with black trim, four pieces.
2. Coffee biggin, white with blue trim, squatty shape, four pieces including handled biggin.
3. Coffee biggin, white with blue trim, four pieces.
4. Coffee biggin, white decorated with gold bands, four pieces including handled biggin.

Section 1, Plate 7

31

Plate 8, Row 1:

1. Coffee biggin, tall style, unusual color, green and white medium mottled, four pieces including handled biggin.
2. Coffee biggin, tall style, shaded light blue and white, four pieces including handled biggin.
3. Coffee biggin, tall style, blue and white large swirl, four pieces including handled biggin.
4. Coffee biggin, red and white large mottled, "Snow on the Mountain," three pieces.

Plate 8, Row 2:

1. Coffee biggin, white and light blue medium mottled with dark blue trim, four pieces.
2. Coffee biggin, tall style, cobalt blue and white medium mottled, four pieces including handled biggin.
3. Coffee biggin, tall style, shaded dark blue to lighter blue, four pieces including handled biggin.
4. Coffee biggin, tall style, light blue and white checkered pattern with red trim, light blue handles and spout, four pieces including handled biggin. *Note:* Tin cover not original.

Plate 8, Row 3:

1. Coffee biggin, cobalt blue and white checkered pattern with red trim, cobalt blue handle and spout, three pieces.
2. Coffee Biggin, tall style, fine mottled pink and white with red trim, four pieces including handled biggin.
3. Coffee biggin, tall style, large mottled blue and white, "Snow on the Mountain," four pieces.
4. Coffee biggin, red and white large mottled with red trim, four pieces.

Plate 9, Row 1:

1. Mugs, four, cobalt blue and white large swirl.
2. Coffee boiler, cobalt blue and white large swirl, shallow pit bottom. *Note:* Pit bottom refers to the shape of the bottom. It is made to fit into the exact lid opening on wood-burning stoves.

Plate 9, Row 2:

1. Mug, cobalt blue and white large swirl, two cup size.
2. Mug, cobalt blue and white large swirl, two cup size.
3. Mug, cobalt blue and white large swirl, one cup child's size.
4. Coffee roaster, black and white medium mottled, small size, solid metal drum.

Plate 9, Row 3:

1. Coffee roaster, black and white medium mottled, large size, screen style drum.
2. Coffee roaster, black and white medium mottled, medium size, solid metal drum.

35

Plate 10, Row 1:

1. Coffee boiler, cobalt blue and white large swirl.
2. Coffee boiler, old red and white large swirl trimmed in dark blue.
3. Coffee boiler, blue and white large swirl.

Plate 10, Row 2:

1. Coffee boiler, shaded blue known as "Bluebelle Ware." Distributed by Norvell Shapleigh Hardware Co., St. Louis.
2. Coffee boiler, green and white large swirl, "Emerald Ware." Strong Mfg. Co., Siebring, Ohio
3. Coffee boiler, reddish brown and white medium mottled, Cream City "Garnet Ware" manufactured by Geuder, Paeschke & Frey Co., Milwaukee, Wis.

Plate 10, Row 3:

1. Coffee boiler, lavender blue and white large swirl.
2. Coffee boiler, brown and white relish pattern.
3. Coffee boiler, blue and white large swirl.

Plate 11, Row 1:

1. Coffee boiler, blue and white large swirl.
2. Coffee boiler, black and white fine mottled, goose-neck spout. *Note:* It is rare to find a goose-neck spout on a coffee boiler.
3. Coffee boiler, cobalt blue and white medium mottled.

Plate 11, Row 2:

1. Coffee boiler, dark green adh white larege swirl trimmed with dark blue, known as "Chrysolite."
2. Coffee boiler, dark blue and white relish pattern.
3. Coffee boiler, brown and bluish gray large swirl.

Plate 11, Row 3:

1. Coffee boiler, brown and white large swirl.
2. Coffee boiler, blue and white large swirl.
3. Coffee boiler, green and white large swirl, "Emerald Ware," Strong Mfg. Co., Siebring, Ohio.

Plate 12, Row 1:

1. Coffee boiler, brown and white fine mottled, inside and outside, known as "Onyx Ware."
2. Coffee boiler, solid dark gray labeled "Sterling Gray," Central Stamping Co.
3. Coffee boiler, white with black trim, labeled "Belmont Stamping and Enameling Co."

Plate 12, Row 2:

1. Teapot, dark blue and white medium mottled.
2. Coffee pot, light blue and white medium mottled, nickel-plated cover with brass thumb rest and bottom, marked "L & G Mfg. Co." in an oval.
3. Coffee pot, dark green and white large swirl, "Chrysolite," distributed by Hibbard Spencer Bartlett and Co., Chicago.
4. Coffee pot, cobalt blue and white fine mottled, marked "Elite–Austria," Chicken Wire pattern.

Plate 12, Row 3:

1. Coffee pot, white with green veining, medium mottled, marked "Elite."
2. Coffee pot, dark green and white fine mottled, marked "Elite–Austria–4."
3. Teapot, brown and white large swirl.
4. Coffee pot, green and white large swirl, "Emerald Ware," Strong Mfg. Co., Siebring, Ohio. *Note:* Popularly known by collectors as "Apple Green and White" or "Kelly Green and White."

Plate 13, Row 1:

1. Teapot, squatty shape, small size with metal pedestal, blue and white fine mottled. *Note:* Teapot bottom fits smaller section of three-part wood-burning stove lid. Aluminum cover has fitted glass insert, three piece stemmed aluminum coffee basket marked "Universal Percolator; Landers, Trary & Clark; New Britain, Conn., U.S.A. N01104 D.R.G.M. N027-1098-PAT'D MAY 22, 94; MAY 11, 97; JULY 12, 98; MAY 22, 06; JULY 16, 07." Pot marked "ELITE."
2. Teapot, tall squatty shape with metal pedestal, blue and white fine mottled, aluminum coffee basket and cover with glass insert. Pot marked "ELITE." Model is No. 1210.
3. Teapot, squatty shape with metal pedestal, medium size, blue and white fine mottled, aluminum coffee basket and cover with glass insert, marked "ELITE," model No. 1109. *Note:* See Introduction to this section for explanation of teapot, coffee pot or percolator terminology.

Plate 13, Row 2:

1. Coffee pot, light green with fine cobalt blue mottling, cover with glass insert, not hinged to pot.
2. Teapot or percolator, blue and white fine mottled, nickel-plated copper cover with glass insert, aluminum coffee basket, with corrugated stem base, advertised as "Lisk Percolator" made by the Lisk Mfg. Co. Ltd., Canandaigua, New York.
3. Teapot, large squatty shape with metal pedestal, cobalt blue decorated with lighter blue decorations and trimmed in gold, aluminum coffee basket, marked "Universal 1108" and dated the same as pots in Row 1.
4. Teapot, blue and white fine mottled, matching granite cover with glass insert.

Plate 13, Row 3:

1. Teapot, red and white medium swirl, circa 1960's.
2. Coffee pot, reverse cobalt blue and white large swirl, triple coated. *Note:* I refer to this color as Reverse cobalt blue and white because it appears the cobalt blue was applied first with white over it.
3. Teapot, cobalt blue and white medium mottled.
4. Teapot, brown and white medium mottled.

Section 1, Plate 13

43

Plate 14, Row 1:

1. Teapot, gray large mottled. Note unusual straight spout, spout and seams riveted, iron handle, tin cover with wood and pewter finial. Marked "GRANITE IRONWARE –PATENTED MAY 30, 1876.
2. Teapot, dark green and white large swirl, "Chrysolite."
3. Coffee pot, dark green and white large swirl, "Chrysolite."
4. Coffee pot, gray medium mottled, nickel plated, brass cover and spout cover, pewter finial and handle.

Plate 14, Row 2:

1. Coffee pot, dark green and white medium swirl, "Chrysolite."
2. Coffee pot, solid cobalt, white inside.
3. Coffee pot, brown and white large swirl.
4. Coffee pot, blue and white large swirl.

Plate 14, Row 3:

1. Coffee pot, lavender cobalt blue and white large swirl.
2. Coffee pot, aqua green and white large swirl.
3. Coffee pot, light blue and white fine mottled.
4. Coffee pot, blue and white large swirl.

Plate 15, Row 1:

1. Teapot, dark green and white large mottled, "Chrysolite."
2. Teapot, white with green veins, medium swirl, "Snow on the Mountain," marked "Elite–Austria."
3. Teapot, green and white large swirl, "Emerald Ware."
4. Teapot, white and blue medium mottled.

Plate 15, Row 2:

1. Teapot, brown and white large swirl.
2. Teapot, green and white large swirl, "Emerald Ware."
3. Teapot, seamless, "old" red and white large swirl with black trim and handle, white inside.
4. Teapot, dark lavender blue with lighter blue large swirl.

Plate 15, Row 3:

1. Teapot, blue and white large swirl with black trim and knob, weld handle. *Note:* Not often seen with this type handle. "Columbian Ware," Bellaire Stamping Co., Bellaire, Ohio.
2. Teapot, white and light blue large swirl.
3. Teapot, blue and white large swirl.
4. Teapot, cobalt blue and white large swirl.

Plate 16, Row 1:

1. Coffee pot, blue and white large swirl.
2. Coffee pot, cobalt blue and white large swirl.
3. Coffee pot, green and white large swirl, "Emerald Ware."
4. Coffee pot, white with light blue medium swirl.
5. Teapot, lavender blue and white large swirl.

Plate 16, Row 2:

1. Coffee pot, green and white large swirl, "Emerald Ware."
2. Coffee pot, light lavender blue and light gray medium swirl.
3. Coffee pot, aqua green and white medium mottled. *Note:* Pot is seamless with round tapered-shaped bottom.
4. Coffee pot, green and white large swirl, "Emerald Ware."
5. Teapot, blue and white fine mottled.

Plate 16, Row 3:

1. Coffee pot, blue and white large swirl.
2. Teapot, dark green and lighter green large swirl. *Note:* Pot has been redipped at the factory over an original color of cobalt blue and white swirl.
3. Coffee pot, blue and white large swirl.
4. Coffee pot, unusual green and white large swirl.
5. Teapot, "old" red and white medium mottled.

Plate 17, Row 1:

1. Teapot, large squatty shape, footed, electric, solid blue gray, ribbed body, glass cover insert, advertised as Lisk Percolator. Marked "Pat'd. August 12, 1924, Better Lisk Quality, Lisk Mfg. Co. Ltd., Canandaigua, New York.
2. Teapot, large squatty pedestal shape, solid green, ribbed body, glass cover insert.
3. Coffee pot, straight sided, yellow and white large swirl with black trim, glass knob insert, circa 1930's.
4. Coffee pot, red and white large swirl with black trim, glass knob insert, circa 1930's.

Plate 17, Row 2:

1. Teapot, brown and white large swirl, redipped at the factory over cobalt blue and white swirl.
2. Teapot, pink, white, blue, green and dark blue, "End of Day" large swirl.
3. Coffee pot, blue and white large swirl with ribbon effect, "Azure Ware."
4. Teapot, small squatty shape, dark green with veins of white, pink, yellow, and maroon, "End of Day," marked "Elite"–Austria, Chicken Wire pattern.

Plate 17, Row 3:

1. Coffee pot, shaded blue, "Bluebelle Ware," distributed by Norvell Shapleigh Hardware Co., St. Louis.
2. Coffee pot, blue shading to lighter blue, unusual shading.
3. Coffee pot, deep sea green shading to a moss green, advertised as "Shamrock Ware." Norvell Shapleigh Hardware Co., St. Louis was sole distributor.
4. Teapot, small squatty shape, deep violet shading to a lighter violet, shaded. "Thistle Ware."

Plate 18, Row 1:

1. Coffee pot, blue and white large swirl.
2. Coffee pot, lavender and white medium swirl, marked in a circle, "PURITY WARE B.G.B. REG'D." *Note:* Only piece I have seen in this color.
3. Coffee pot, blue and white large mottled.

Plate 18, Row 2:

1. Coffee pot, white with blue veins, chicken wire pattern.
2. Coffee pot, blue and white large swirl, "Azure."
3. Coffee pot, cobalt blue and white large swirl, "Dresden Ware," triple coated on heavy steel base, seamless, riveted hollow handle, black edged, Banner Stamping Works, advertised in the Butler Brothers Catalog, Spring 1912.
4. Teapot, blue and white large swirl.

Plate 18, Row 3:

1. Teapot, brilliant green shaded to a lighter green.
2. Coffee pot, known as shaded, blended, or banded. Ad states "triple coated pure white lining guaranteed acid proof. Outside is shading of green and ivory, rich luster finish, black edges. All covers heavily enameled. Sizes larger than ordinary. Tea and coffee pots and teakettles drawn from one piece. "Old Ivory," Genuine Triple Coated Blended Enameled Ware. Banner Stamping Works U.S.A."
3. Teapot, shading of green and ivory, same as #2.
4. Coffee pot, Brown shading to gold, labeled "Enamel Art Ware," Norvell Shapleigh Hardware Co., St. Louis.

Plate 19, Row 1:

1. Coffee pot, white with green veins large mottled, "Elite"–Austria.
2. Coffee pot, blue and white large swirl.
3. Coffee pot, solid cobalt blue with unusual shaped granite handle.
4. Coffee pot, cobalt blue and white large swirl.

Plate 19, Row 2:

1. Teapot, blue and white large swirl.
2. Coffee pot, cobalt blue and white large swirl.
3. Coffee pot, dark cobalt blue and white large swirl. *Note:* I believe this to be "Azurelite" from the Enterprise Enamel Company, Bellaire, Ohio. It's the darkest of all the cobalt blue and white. I have a marked salesman's sample wash basin that is the same color. The cobalt blue is almost a black.
4. Coffee pot, blue and white large swirl.

Plate 19, Row 3:

1. Teapot, "Belle" shape, blue and white fine mottled, seamless.
2. Coffee pot, aqua green and white large swirl.
3. Coffee pot, "Belle" shape, cobalt blue and white large swirl, seamless.
4. Teapot, light blue and white medium mottled, weld handle.

Plate 20, Row 1:

1. Teapot, blue and white large swirl.
2. Teapot, gray large mottled, labeled "Cream City Gray Ware," 101 Acid Resisting, "Cleans like China." Geuder, Paeschke and Frey Co. Manufacturers, Milwaukee, U.S.A.
3. Teapot, solid light mauve rose with dark brown trim, labeled "L. & G. Mfg. Co., Woodhaven, N.Y."
4. Coffee pot, white with green veining medium mottled, "Elite" Austria.

Plate 20, Row 2:

1. Coffee pot, blue and white medium mottled.
2. Teapot, yellow and white large swirl with black trim, circa 1960's, lightweight.
3. Teapot, blue and white large swirl.
4. Teapot, shaded with blue trim, decorated with fruit, circa 1970's, lightweight, one of the distributors was J.M. Fields.
5. Teapot, light blue and white medium mottled, brass-plated ribbed cover with metal thumb rest and copper bottom, marked "L. & G. Mfg. Co."

Plate 20, Row 3:

1. Teapot, cobalt blue and white with black trim, large swirl.
2. Teapot, blue and white with black trim, large swirl.
3. Coffee pot, dark green and white large swirl, "Chrysolite."
4. Coffee pot, white with light blue veining, large mottling.
5. Coffee pot, cobalt blue and white large swirl.

Section 1, Plate 20

Plate 21, Row 1:

1. Coffee pot, light blue and white large swirl, unusual shaped seamed bottom.
2. Coffee pot, blue and white large swirl.
3. Coffee pot, blue and white large swirl.
4. Teapot, blue and white large swirl, weld handle.

Plate 21, Row 2:

1. Coffee pot, light green and white, relish pattern.
2. Coffee pot, cobalt blue and white large swirl.
3. Teapot, gray large mottled, iron handle, marked "Granite Iron Ware," Nov. 20, 1876.
4. Coffee pot, lavender blue and white large swirl.

Plate 21, Row 3:

1. Teapot, dark blue and white, relish pattern, copper-plated ribbed cover, metal trimmed bottom, marked "L. & G. Mfg. Co."
2. Teapot, blue, cobalt blue, and white, medium mottled, "End of Day," cobalt blue trim and handle, "Royal Granite Steel Ware," Crown Industries, Binghamton, N.Y.
3. Teapot, light green and white, relish pattern, copper-plated cover and thumb rest, copper trimmed bottom, marked "L. & G. Mfg. Co."
4. Coffee pot, cobalt blue and white fine mottled, marked "Elite."

Plate 22, Row 1:

1. Coffee pot, blue and white large mottled.
2. Coffee pot, dark blue and white relish pattern.
3. Coffee pot, cobalt blue and white large swirl.

Plate 22, Row 2:

1. Teapot, dark brown shading to lighter brown, shaded.
2. Coffee pot, deep voilet shading to a lighter violet, shaded, "Thistleware." Distributed by Norvell Shapleigh Hardware Co., St. Louis.
3. Teapot, solid cobalt blue, unusual shaped tubular granite handle.
4. Coffee pot, deep sea green shading to a moss green, shaded, advertised as "Shamrock Ware." Norvell Shapleigh Hardware Co., St. Louis was the sole distributor.
5. Teapot, brilliant blue shading to lighter blue, shaded.

Plate 22, Row 3:

1. Teapot, green and white large swirl, "Emerald Ware."
2. Coffee pot, blue and white large swirl.
3. Coffee pot, brown and white large swirl.
4. Teapot, blue and white large swirl. This color is referred to by collectors as "Iris."
   Note: I could not find any information on this as proof.

Plate 23, Row 1:

1. Coffee pot, dark solid gray, brass oblong insert on top of handle that is dated and patented 2, 25-13.
2. Coffee pot, light gray medium mottled, straight sided, cover has glass insert, includes gray coffee basket.
3. Teapot, gray medium mottled. *Note:* Universal shaped tubular handle has diamond shaped cutouts.
4. Teapot, gray medium mottled.

Plate 23, Row 2:

1. Teapot, gray medium mottled, weld handle. Note the size of the goose-neck spout.
2. Teapot, gray medium mottled, weld handle. *Note:* The spout and handle look like they were meant to go on a smaller pot.
3. Coffee pot, gray large mottled, weld handle.
4. Teapot, gray large mottled, weld handle.

Plate 23, Row 3:

1. Coffee pot, gray medium mottled.
2. Teapot, gray trimmed in cobalt blue, medium mottled.
3. Coffee pot, gray trimmed in cobalt blue, large mottled.
4. Teapot, gray medium mottled, nickel-plated rim on top of pot, and nickel-plated cover marked "Extra Agate Nickel Steel Ware," L. & G. Mfg. Co.

Plate 24, Row 1:

1. Teapot, squatty shape, black, orange, yellow, red, and dark blue large swirl, black handle, spout and trim, "End of Day."
2. Teapot, red with veins of white, dark blue, and yellow, "End of Day," marked "Elite."
3. Teapot, squatty shape, dark cobalt blue shading to lighter cobalt, black handle, spout and trim.

Plate 24, Row 2:

1. Teapot, squatty shape, cobalt blue shaded to red, decorated with silver overlay Oriental scene, marked "Elite."
2. Teapot, squatty shape, white decorated with gray and cobalt ship scene.
3. Teapot, red with decorated grapes and bands of white beads, six-sided, marked "Elite."

Plate 24, Row 3:

1. Teapot, decorated with blue, green, and orange sponge effect, six-sided (hexagon), marked "Elite."
2. Teapot, large squatty shape, solid orange decorated with flowers and leaves, numbered 637.
3. Teapot, decorated with red, orange, and yellow sponge effect, six-sided (hexagon), black trimmed spout and handle, marked "Elite."

Plate 24, Row 4:

1. Teapot, small squatty shape, solid blue, marked "Scepter Germany 39," decorated.
2. Teapot, white decorated with pansies trimmed in gold.
3. Teapot, cobalt blue trimmed with white beads and bunches of light pink grapes, marked "Elite," decorated.

Plate 25, Row 1:

1. Teapot, white trimmed in brown, decorated with pink roses, brass-plated thumb rest.
2. Teapot, blue and white fine mottled, decorated in gold.
3. Teapot, tall squatty shape, white with light blue decorations trimmed in gold and light blue bands.

Plate 25, Row 2:

1. Teapot, decorated with a floral and leaf design, marked "Elite."
2. Teapot, six-sided (hexagon), decorated with a floral and leaf design trimmed in gold, marked "Elite."
3. Teapot, six-sided (hexagon), decorated with floral and leaf design, marked "Elite."
4. Teapot, decorated with a floral and leaf design, marked "Elite."

Plate 25, Row 3:

1. Teapot, shaded light blue and white, decorated with yellow and pink flowers, black trim, marked "Stewart Ware," Moundsville, West Virginia. *Note:* I believe this to be a product of United States Stamping Co. as they were located in Moundsville, West Virginia.
2. Teapot, white decorated with a windmill design trimmed with gold bands.
3. Coffee pot, shaded light blue and white, decorated with yellow and pink flowers, "Stewart Ware."

Plate 26, Row 1:

1. Teapot, white, decorated with a Blue Willow-type pattern.
2. Teapot, small squatty shape, brown shaded, decorated with trailing vine and flowers outlined in black, numbered 105.
3. Teapot, shaded green, deocrated with lilies.
4. Teapot, six-sided, white, decorated with a blue checkered pattern, marked "Elite."

Plate 26, Row 2:

1. Teapot, cobalt blue shaded, deocrated with trailing vine and flowers outlined in gold.
2. Teapot, blue and white decorated marked "Bonnie Blue," made in U.S.A. by Nesco Pat. 5-13-1926.
3. Teapot, small squatty shape, cobalt blue decorated with a single flower, circa 1940's.
4. Teapot, small squatty shape, solid light blue decorated with pink flowers, trimmed in gold.

Plate 26, Row 3:

1. Teapot, small squatty shape, shaded background of green, blue, red and white with blue and white stripes.
2. Teapot, green, decorated with bird and leaves, trimmed in gold, marked "Elite."
3. Teapot, eight-sided (octagonal), shaded green and cream, decorated with checkered bands of green and gold, marked "G.M.T. Co., Inc., Germany."
4. Teapot, small squatty shape, white, decorated with gold scallops and bands of blue dots.

Plate 26, Row 4:

1. Coffee pot, small with impressed panels, white with blue decorations.
2. Teapot, small squatty shape, cobalt blue with white and light blue daisy pattern, marked "Made in Yugoslavia. No. 12," mark shows two lions standing on a coffee pot.
3. Teapot, small squatty shape, light cream color, decorated with blue and pink forget-me-nots, No. 614.
4. Teapot, small squatty shape, cobalt blue, decorated with white and yellow flowers.
5. Teapot, small squatty shape, red, decorated with white and black dots, straight spout, marked "Made in Czechoslovakia."

Plate 27, Row 1:

1. Teapot, squatty shape, blue and white medium swirl.
2. Teapot, small squatty shape, original cobalt blue cover, pink and white large swirl.
3. Teapot, large squatty shape, blue and white large mottled.
4. Teapot, small squatty shape, white with green veins, large mottled, marked "Elite" Austria.
5. Teapot, squatty shape, blue and white, medium mottled trimmed with bands of gold.

Plate 27, Row 2:

1. Coffee pot, three pieces, dark blue with black coffee basket insert and black handle, glass insert on cover. *Note:* Part of label on pot reads "Cup Percolator. Covered Sauce Pan Holds 1⅛ pints for General Cooking. Full Porcelain Enamel, Easy to Clean."
2. Teapot, squatty shape, Apple Green outside, Tangerine inside, advertised as harmonizing colors, "Vollrath Ware," Sheboygan, Wis.
3. Coffee pot, glass cover insert marked "Even Spray," gray granite coffee basket, label reads "Vollrath Ware. Apple Green. Harmonizing Color Tangerine. The Vollrath Co., Sheboygan, Wis., U.S.A. 5 Reg. U.S. Pat. Off. Copyrighted 1929 by T.V. Co."
4. Coffee pot, straight sided, white with black trim.
5. Teapot, white with black trim.

Plate 27, Row 3:

1. Teapot, gray large mottled, weld handle.
2. Coffee pot, blue, cobalt blue, and white large mottled, cobalt blue trim and handle, "End of Day," "Royal Granite Steel Ware," Crown Industries, Binghamton, N.Y.
3. Teapot, white with black trim, "Belmont Enameled Ware," The Belmont Stamping and Enamel Co., New Philadelphia, Ohio, U.S.A.
4. Teapot, blue and white large swirl.
5. Teapot, solid gray, extra large weld handle.

Plate 27, Row 4:

1. Coffee pot, mauve pink and white, relish pattern.
2. Coffee pot, white with pale blue veins, marked "Elite," chicken wire pattern.
3. Coffee pot, dark cobalt blue with very small mottling.
4. Teapot, aqua green and white large swirl.
5. Teapot, cobalt blue and white with very fine mottling.

Plate 28, Row 1:

1. Teapot, blue and white large mottled.
2. Teapot, black with white flecks, speckled.
3. Coffee pot, white with blue trim, weld handle.
4. Teapot, gray large mottled, weld handle.
5. Coffee pot, light blue and white fine mottled.

Plate 28, Row 2:

1. Coffee pot, gray medium mottled.
2. Coffee pot, solid light blue.
3. Teapot, gray medium mottled.
4. Coffee pot, blue and white fine mottled, black trim.
5. Coffee pot, cobalt blue and white with very fine mottling.

Plate 28, Row 3:

1. Coffe pot, solid yellow with black trim, advertising "Gincy's Favorite Drink. Boat House Coffee." Advertising cross-collectible.
2. Teapot, solid blue, marked "Quadruple Coated, Heavy Steel, Acid Proof. For Hospital Use. Meinecke & Co., N.Y."
3. Teapot, white with red trim.
4. Teapot, gray large mottled, weld handle.
5. Coffee pot, solid dark brown.
6. Coffee pot, white with blue trim.

Plate 28, Row 4:

1. Coffee pot, blue and white relish pattern, wooden handle, brass lid and copper bottom, marked "Patent Pending."
2. Teapot, blue and white fine mottled, nickel-plated copper cover and bottom, wooden handle, marked "Manning Bowman Quality, Meriden, Conn. 05550."
3. Teapot, light pink and white, relish pattern, wooden handle.
4. Teapot, blue and white, relish pattern, wooden handle.
5. Coffee pot, brown and white fine mottled, wooden handle, nickel-plated copper cover and bottom, marked "Pat'd. May 21, 1889 Manning Bowman and Co."

Section 1, Plate 28

73

Plate 29, Row 1:

1. Coffee pot, blue and white fine mottled, trimmed in dark blue, unusual metal thumb rest.
2. Coffee pot, light green and white, relish pattern.
3. Coffee pot, solid cobalt blue.
4. Teapot, blue and white fine mottled.

Plate 29, Row 2:

1. Teapot, solid cobalt blue, unusual shaped thumb rest.
2. Teapot, white trimmed in dark green, marked "Savory Ware," made by Lisk-Savory Corp., Canandaigua, N.Y.
3. Teapot, gray and light gray, like a relish pattern (not old), made in Romania.
4. Teapot, squatty shape, yellow trimmed in black.

Plate 29, Row 3:

1. Coffee pot, blue and white large mottled.
2. Coffee pot, gray large mottled, unusual iron handle, marked "Granite Iron Ware, Pat. May 30, '76, July 3, '77."
3. Teapot, blue and white, relish pattern, pewter trimmed.
4. Coffee pot, gray medium mottled.
5. Teapot, dark cobalt blue and white large swirl, "Azurelite," Enterprise Enamel Co., Bellaire, Ohio.

Plate 29, Row 4:

1. Coffee pot, dark gray medium mottled.
2. Coffee pot, gray medium mottled.
3. Teapot, small squatty shape, white trimmed with dark blue.
4. Coffee pot, gray large mottled.
5. Teapot, dark gray medium mottled.

Section 2

Table Related Serving Items

Plate 1, Row 1:

1. Sugar bowl, white, decorated with fuchsias, handles are a combination of decorated granite ware and pewter, pewter trimmed, footed.
2. Coffee urn, white, decorated with floral and fern pattern, pewter trimmed, alcohol burner.
3. Creamer, white, decorated with fuchsias, pewter trimmed, handles are a combination of decorated granite ware and pewter, footed.

Plate 1, Row 2:

1. Cereal bowl, blue and white, relish pattern, pewter trimmed.
2. Waste bowl, white, decorated with fuchsias, pewter trimmed, ring handles and footed. *Note:* These were used to pass around at the table to empty the left-over coffee from the cups.
3. Waste bowl, squatty shape, brown and white, relish pattern, pewter trimmed, ring handles.

Plate 1, Row 3:

1. Sugar bowl, white, decorated with calla lilies, pewter trimmed.
2. Creamer, white, decorated with calla lilies, pewter trimmed.
3. Sugar bowl, white, decorated with a castle scene, pewter trimmed.

Plate 2, Row 1:

1. Syrup, squatty shape, gray large mottled, with hinged cover, pewter trimmed.
2. Sugar bowl, squatty shape, gray large mottled, pewter trimmed.
3. Castor set, gray large mottled, pewter trimmed, five glass castors. *Note:* I have seen variations of castor sets where the granite ware is on the lower part of the pedestal only. The metal trim can also vary in decoration.
4. Sugar bowl, gray large mottled, pewter trimmed.
5. Creamer, gray large mottled, pewter trimmed.

Plate 2, Row 2:

1. Sugar bowl, squatty shape, white, decorated with rose and fuchsias, pewter trimmed.
2. Double egg cup, white, decorated with wild rose pattern, trimmed in dark brown, center handle.
3. Sugar bowl, blue, decorated with apple blossoms, pewter trimmed.
4. Condiment, three sections, white.
5. Sugar bowl, white, decorated with mountain home, pewter trimmed.

Plate 2, Row 3:

1. Sugar bowl, white, decorated with morning glories, pewter trimmed.
2. Pickle castor, three pieces, blue, decorated with apple blossoms, pewter trimmed castor with cover and pewter frame. *Note:* Only one of these I have seen.
3. Creamer, white, decorated with morning glories, pewter trimmed.

Plate 3, Row 1:

1. Syrup, white, nickel over brass cover and thumb rest.
2. Creamer, squatty shape, black, orange, yellow, red, and dark blue with black trim and handle, large swirl, "End of Day."
3. Molasses pitcher, orange, decorated with black checkered design, black trim, marked "Made in Germany."
4. Oval platter, gray large mottled, marked "Granite Iron Ware, Pat, May 30, '76 and July 3, '77."
5. Spooner, brown and white large swirl, black trim.
6. Molasses pitcher, white with dark blue trim.

Plate 3, Row 2:

1. Syrup, squatty shape, cobalt blue and white large swirl, pewter top with dolphin. *Note:* Cover is not original.
2. Honey pot, squatty shape, cobalt blue and white large swirl. *Note:* I believe this to be a honey pot.
3. Oval platter, cobalt blue and white large swirl.
4. Creamer, squatty shape, cobalt blue and white large swirl, black trim.
5. Sugar bowl, squatty shape, cobalt blue and white large swirl, black trim and handle, cover missing.

Plate 3, Row 3:

1. Creamer, squatty shape, cream and green.
2. Mustard or horseradish pot with ladle, white, decorated with brown, white, and black bands.
3. Oval platter, red, cobalt blue, white, yellow, green, large swirl, "End of Day," color is on both sides.
4. Mustard or horseradish pot with ladle, white, decorated with blue bands.
5. Creamer, squatty shape, solid cobalt blue.
6. Sugar, squatty shape, solid cobalt blue.

Plate 3, Row 4:

1. Syrup, gray medium mottled, pewter trimmed, pewter cover has figure of a lady's head.
2. Molasses pitcher, gray large mottled, thumb lift on cover.
3. Oval platter, blue and white large swirl, white inside.
4. Molasses pitcher, blue and white large swirl, triple coated. This is advertised in Norvell Shapleigh's 1910 catalog as "Blue Diamond Ware," made in the United States, Distributed by Norvell Shapleigh Hardware Co., St. Louis. Has seamless body, enamel cover with spun knob, round handle and covered lip.

Plate 4, Row 1:

1. Butter dish, large size, white decorated with blue design.
2. Creamer, white, decorated with blue design.
3. Butter dish, white, decorated with blue and pink flowers, pewter trimmed, has butter knife rest.
4. Salt or pepper shaker, light blue and white large swirl, seamless body, screw-on metal top, 1½" x 2½". *Note:* I have seen these in two sizes, this is the shorter one. Both had the screw-on metal top, the other one was a darker blue and white swirl.
5. Butter dish, blue and white large mottled, seamless body and spun knob.

Plate 4, Row 2:

1. Sugar bowl, gray medium mottled.
2. Salt and pepper shakers, dark gray medium mottled, 1¾" x 3", strap handle, nickel-plated copper covers. These covers do not screw on, they are made to fit tightly over the top, marked "Extra Agate Nickel Steel Ware," L. & G. Mfg. Co.
3. Butter dish, gray medium mottled, seamless body, spun knob, small size, marked "L. & G. Mfg. Co."
4. Creamer, squatty shape, gray large mottled, seamless body and rolled handle.

Plate 4, Row 3:

1. Butterdish, white, blue, and brown large mottled, spun cover knob, "End of Day."
2. Salt or pepper shaker, white with cobalt blue strap handle, nickel-plated cover does not screw on, fits tightly over the top, 1¾" x 3½", marked "L. & G. Mfg. Co."
3. Butter dish, large, white and light blue medium mottled, marked "B. Frer 15" with a shield and leaves.
4. Egg cup, white with black trim, labeled "Polar Ware Company, Sheboygan, Wisconsin, Reg. U.S. Pat. Office."
5. Mustard or horseradish pot, white, decorated with gold bands, marked "G.B.N.," man standing with a shield in his hand and a lion standing beside him.
6. Butterdish, solid dark olive green, decorated with gold bands.

Plate 4, Row 4:

1. Creamer, squatty shape, white with blue veining, chicken wire pattern, mark shows a lion standing on a coffee pot.
2. Sugar bowl, red and white large mottled, circa 1960's, marked "Japan."
3. Butter dish, white with cobalt blue trim.
4. Creamer, squatty shape, cobalt blue and white large swirl, black trim and handle.
5. Sugar bowl, cobalt blue and white large swirl, cover missing.

Section 2, Plate 4

83

Plate 5, Row 1:

1. Creamer, squatty shape, blue and white large mottled, blue strap handle.
2. Sugar bowl, squatty shape, white with cobalt blue trim.
3. Creamer, squatty shape, white with cobalt blue trim.
4. Platter, white, decorated with a black swan and black trim.
5. Sugar bowl, squatty shape, blue and white large mottled, light gray inside with blue flecks, blue strap handles.

Plate 5, Row 2:

1. Creamer, blue and white large swirl, black trim, triple coated, "Blue Diamond Ware."
2. Gravy or sauce boat, blue and white large swirl, black trim and handle, seamless body, triple coated, "Blue Diamond Ware," distributed by Norvell Shapleigh Hardware Co., St. Louis.
3. Sugar bowl, blue and white large swirl, seamless body, enameled cover with spun knob, beaded handles, triple coated, made in United States, "Blue Diamond Ware."
4. Creamer, squatty shape, white with cobalt blue trim, rim of tin cover has perforated strainer portion to line up with spout on creamer for pouring. Marked "Pyrolite Ware," Germany, mark shows face of a lion.

Plate 5, Row 3:

1. Sugar bowl, green shading to a lighter green.
2. Sugar bown, squatty shape, light blue and white large swirl, cover is missing.
3. Creamer, squatty shape, white with aqua blue shading.
4. Sugar bowl, squatty shape, greenish gray, shaded.

Plate 5, Row 4:

1. Sugar bowl, squatty shape, light blue and white medium mottled, mottled inside also, black trim and handles.
2. Creamer, squatty shape, white, decorated with blue oriental pattern.
3. Fruit bowl, solid blue, fancy cutouts, 9" diameter.
4. Sugar bowl, squatty shape, white with dark blue mottling inside and outside, large mottled, black trim and handles.

Plate 6, Row 1:

1. Creamer, squatty shape, blue, gray, and white large swirl, black trim and handle, "End of Day."
2. Footed gravy or sauce boat, light blue and white fine mottled, cobalt blue trim and handle.
3. Creamer, green and white large swirl, trimmed in coblat blue, "Emerald Ware."
4. Footed gravy of sauce boat, white with cobalt blue trim and handle, marked "L. & G. Mfg. Co."

Plate 6, Row 2:

1. Creamer, squatty shape, dark brown and white very fine mottled, "Onyx Ware," made by Columbian Enameling and Stamping Co., Terre Haute, Indiana.
2. Molasses pitcher, deep violet shaded, enamel cover with spun knob, covered spout and thumb rest.
3. Gravy or sauce boat, white and light blue large mottling, trimmed in cobalt blue.
4. Molasses pitcher, white decorated with blue checkered pattern, marked "Elite."

Plate 6, Row 3:

1. Molasses pitcher, solid light blue.
2. Sugar bowl, squatty shape, greenish gray, shaded.
3. Egg cup, white with black trim.
4. Sugar bowl, squatty shape, white with cobalt blue trim, marked L. & G. Mfg. Co.
5. Creamer or measure, white with cobalt blue trim, marked L. & G. Mfg. Co.
6. Sugar bowl, squatty shape, gray medium mottled.
7. Creamer, white with cobalt blue trim, cover has molded spout cover and knob that is recessed into top of cover, "Vollrath Ware," Sheboygan, Wisconsin.

Plate 6, Row 4:

1. Creamer, squatty shape, charcoal gray and white inside and out, medium mottled.
2. Sugar bowl, squatty shape, red and white large mottled inside and out, black trim, circa 1970's.
3. Syrup, gray medium mottled, nickel plated copper top with thumb lift.
4. Creamer, squatty shape, red and white large mottled inside and out, black trim, circa 1970's.
5. Creamer, squatty shape, blue and white, relish pattern.

Plate 7, Row 1:

1. Syrup, gray and white large mottled.
2. Honey pot, light gray outside, white inside, insulated tin top, white porcelain knob.
3. Creamer, squatty shape, blue and white large mottled, black trim, white inside.
4. Syrup, dark green and white large swirl, "Emerald Ware," nickel plated copper cover with thumb lift.
5. Creamer, squatty shape, aqua green and white large swirl, dark blue trim.
6. Sugar bowl, gray and white fine mottled inside and out.

Plate 7, Row 2:

1. Creamer, squatty shape, light blue with black decoration trimmed in gold, marked "Germany."
2. Sugar bowl, squatty shape, light blue with black decoration trimmed in gold, marked "Germany."
3. Syrup, white and light blue, medium mottling.
4. Syrup, white and light blue, medium mottling.
5. Open sugar, squatty shape, solid blue, decorated, marked "Scepter Germany."
6. Creamer, solid blue, decorated, marked "Scepter Germany."

Plate 7, Row 3:

1. Creamer, solid blue, decorated with white bands, trimmed in black.
2. Creamer, squatty shape, dark green with veins of white, pink, yellow, and maroon, marked "Elite. Austria," "End of Day."
3. Sugar bowl, squatty shape, solid light blue outside, white inside, marked "Quadruple Coated. Heavy Steel Acid Proof. MEINECKE & CO. N.Y. FOR HOSPITAL USE. CZECHO-'SLOVAKEA. L."
4. Sauce or gravy boat with attached drip tray, white, decorated with floral leaf design.
5. Creamer, squatty shape, solid light blue outside, white inside.
6. Creamer, squatty shape, white, decorated with gray and cobalt blue scene.
7. Sugar bowl, shaded cobalt blue with decorated panels, eight sided.

Plate 7, Row 4:

1. Syrup, squatty shape, unusual shaded green, nickel plated copper cover with thumb rest.
2. Creamer, dark green, shaded, white inside, "Shamrock Ware."
3. Molasses pitcher, dark green shaded, white inside, enamel cover, spun knob, covered spout and thumb lift, "Shamrock Ware."
4. Fruit bowl, white, decorated with pears, trimmed in dark brown.
5. Molasses pitcher, brown shaded, white inside.
6. Creamer, squatty shape, brown shaded, white inside.

Plate 8, Row 1:

1. Oblong pudding or vegetable dish, red and white inside and out, black trim, large swirl, circa 1950's.
2. Oval footed soup tureen, gray medium mottled, black wooden handle inserts.
3. Oblong pudding or vegetable dish, cobalt blue and white, large swirl, white inside.

Plate 8, Row 2:

1. Oblong pudding or vegetable dish, white and bluish gray, mottled inside and out, large mottled.
2. Oval pudding or vegetable dish, white and bluish gray inside and out, large mottled.
3. Soup tureen, white shading to light blue, trimmed with gold bands, decorated, shaded, marked "TORSEINE REGISTERED MADE IN AUSTRIA."

Plate 8, Row 3:

1. Footed round soup tureen with ladle, solid brilliant cobalt blue outside, white inside, trimmed in black, solid color.
2. Oblong pudding or vegetable dish, yellow and white with black trim, large swirl, circa 1920's.

Plate 8, Row 4:

1. Oval pudding or vegetable dish, dark solid cobalt blue outside, white inside.
2. Oblong pudding or vegetable dish, extremely dark green with tiny white flecks, fine mottled.
3. Footed round soup tureen, white with black trim, cover not original, marked "L. & G. Mfg. Co."

Plate 9, Row 1:

1. Chafing dish with metal stand and cover, deep mauve pink and white relish, metal part on handle marked "M.B. & Co. Pat. Jan. 3, 1893.
2. Oval soup tureen, gray medium mottled, black wooden handle inserts.

Plate 9, Row 2:

1. Footed round soup tureen, light blue and white large mottled.
2. Oval pudding or vegetable dish, brown and white large swirl outside, white inside, trimmed in black.
3. Chafing dish with granite ware stand, gray large mottled, wooden handle and knob, circa 1890 with alcohol burner.

Plate 9, Row 3:

1. Oblong pudding or vegetable dish, bluish gray fine mottled.
2. Oval pudding or vegetable dish, blue, gray and white large swirl, white inside, trimmed in black, "End of Day."
3. Oblong pudding or vegetable dish, blue and white, white inside, black trim.

Plate 9, Row 4:

1. Chafing dish, white with metal cover, stand and alcohol burner, metal band on chafing dish is dated Pat. May 23, 1899. Alcohol burner marked with a large "S. & Co. Reg. U.S. Pat. Off. Sternau & Co. Pat. Feb. 17, 1908, other Pat. Pending No. 865."
2. Footed round soup tureen, white with blue veining, Chicken Wire pattern.

Section 3

Coffee Urn, Mugs, Cups, Saucers, Plates, Soup Plates, Tumblers, and Coasters

Plate 1, Row 1:

1. Large mug, green and white, black trim, large swirl, "Emerald Ware" Strong Mfg. Co., Sebring, Ohio.
2. Cup, light blue, cobalt blue, and white, cobalt blue trim and handle, medium mottled, "End of Day," "Granite Steel Ware," Crown Industries, Binghamton, N.Y.
3. Coffee urn, gray medium mottled, rivited handles, brass spigot.
4. Cup, open handle, gray medium mottled, dark blue trim. *Note:* This type of cup was made to stack into each other e.g. used in picnic sets.
5. Mug, dark blue, decorated with a floral design.

Plate 1, Row 2:

1. Cup, brown and white with black trim, fine mottled, "Onyx Ware."
2. Saucer, brown and white with black trim, fine mottled, "Onyx Ware." Labeled "Columbian Enameling and Stamping Co., Terre Haute, Ind."
3. Mug, gray medium mottled, labeled "Enamel Warewell Second."
4. Cup, gray medium mottled, large 5¼" diameter by 2⅜". Labeled "New England Quality Ware," Pat'd. July 20, 1909, December 3, 1912. Made in U.S.A., Nesco. No. 11.
5. Mug, gray medium mottled.

Plate 1, Row 3:

1. Mug, blue and white fine mottled, black trim.
2. Mug, gray mottled.
3. Saucer, gray large mottled, 6⅞" diameter.
4. Mug, gray medium mottled.
5. Mug, dark green and white large swirl, blue trim, "Chrysolite."

Plate 2, Row 1:

1. Plate, red and white inside and out, black trim, large swirl, circa 1960's, lightweight.
2. Mug, red and white, black trim, large swirl, circa 1960's, lightweight.
3. Mug, "old" red and white, dark blue trim, white inside, large swirl, triple coated, heavyweight.
4. Dinner plate, three sections, orange and yellow inside and out, black trim, large swirl, circa 1970's, lightweight.
5. Mug, red and white with black trim, large swirl, circa 1960's, lightweight.
6. Mug, white with yellow checkered design, circa 1970's.
7. Plate, yellow and white inside and out, black trim, large swirl, circa 1960's, lightweight.
8. Mug, yellow and white, white inside, dark blue trim, large swirl, circa 1960's.
9. Mug, yellow and white, black trim, large swirl, circa 1960's, lightweight.

Plate 2, Row 2:

1. Cup, brown and white, black trim, large swirl.
2. Plate, brown and white, black trim, white inside, 9" diameter, large swirl.
3. Cup, brown and white, black trim, large swirl.
4. Cup, brown and white, black trim, large swirl. *Note:* All these cups are different sizes and shapes.
5. Saucer, brown and white outside, white inside, black trim, large swirl.
6. Luncheon plate, brown and white outside, white inside, black trim, 6" diameter, large swirl.
7. Cup, brown and white, black trim, large swirl.

Plate 2, Row 3:

1. Mug, blue and white, black trim, large swirl.
2. Saucer, white, black trim, labeled "Belmont Ware," The Belmont Stamping and Enameling Company, New Philadelphia, Ohio.
3. Mug, gray medium mottled, rivited handle.
4. Saucer, green and white inside and outside, black trim, fine mottled.
5. Cup, Azure Marble Enamel, pure white with azure blue marbelized finish, rich black handles and edges. Illustrated in Lee Manufacturing Co. Catalog (1915), Chicago, Illnois.
6. Saucer, white, dark green trim, labeled "Savory Ware," No. 9 porcelain enamel on Ingot Iron, Armco. Also marked and fired "Savory Ware" in the enamel.
7. Cup and saucer, blue and white inside and outside, black trim, fine mottled.
8. Saucer, dark blue and white, white inside, black trim, large mottled.
9. Cup, light blue and white swirl inside and outside, black trim.

Plate 2, Row 4:

1. Mug, cobalt blue and white, black trim, large swirl.
2. Plate, cobalt blue and white, white inside, black ttrim, large swirl.
3. Mug, brown and bluish gray inside and outside, brown trim, large swirl.
4. Luncheon plate, yellow and white inside and outside, black trim, large swirl, 7¼" diameter, circa 1960's, lightweight.
5. Cup and saucer, yellow and white, black trim, large swirl, circa 1960's, lightweight.
6. Mug, brown and bluish gray inside and outside, brown trim, large swirl.
7. Three-piece table setting – Plate, saucer, and cup, cobalt blue and white, black trim, large swirl.

Plate 3, Row 1:

1. Saucer, blue and white, white inside, blue trim, medium mottled.
2. Plate, blue and white, white inside, blue trim, medium mottled, 9" diameter.
3. Mug, barrel shape, blue and white, black trim, large mottled, Coonley Mfg. Co., Cicero, Illinois.
4. Four-piece table setting - dinner plate, luncheon plate, saucer, and cup. White with gold bands, handle is wrapped in a woven, cane-type material to keep fingers cool.
5. Three-piece table setting - plate, cup, and saucer. Blue and white outside, white inside trimmed in black, large mottled.

Plate 3, Row 2:

1. Mug, blue and white, black trim, large swirl.
2. Cup, blue and white large swirl.
3. Three-piece table setting - plate, saucer, and cup. Blue and white outside, white inside, black trim, large swirl.

Plate 3, Row 3:

1. Cup and saucer, dark green and white outside, white inside, black trim, large swirl, "Chrysolite."
2. Saucer, gray medium mottled.
3. Mug, cream with green trim, open handle, known as cream and green. These were meant to stack inside each other and belonged in a picnic set. Similar to a tumbler with a handle.
4. Cup and suacer, cream with green trim, cup labeled "Golden Rule. Enameled Steel Metal Ware." Cream and green.
5. Cup and saucer, blue and white, black trim, large swirl.

Plate 3, Row 4:

1. Plate, twelve-sided, reddish brown and white, whtie inside, fine mottled.
2. Cup and saucer, white with a blue border, gold trim, border is like a blue spongeware effect.
3. Plate, blue and white inside and outside, dark blue trim, fine mottled.
4. Cup and saucer, child's size, white with cobalt blue trim.
5. Saucer, gray, large mottled, labeled "Old Hampshire Gray," Certified Made in America, The Republic S. & E. Co., Canton, Ohio, U.S.A.

Plate 4, Row 1:

1. Soup plate, red and white inside and outside, trimmed in dark blue, large swirl, circa 1960's, lightweight.
2. Soup plate, gray medium mottled, labeled "Iron City." Durable, Absolutely Pure. Easy to Clean as China. Federal Enameling and Stamping Company, Pittsburgh, Pa.
3. Soup plate, yellow and ;white, black trim, large swirl, circa 1960's.
4. Coasters, set of 6, solid color inserts on both sides, rims marked TOWLE STER-LING 101.

Plate 4, Row 2:

1. Coaster, green and white outside, white inside, black trim, large swirl, "Emerald Ware."
2. Soup plate, light blue and white inside and outside, large mottled.
3. Double shot glass, cobalt blue with very fine veins of white, white inside.
4. Tumbler, blue and white inside and outside, black trim, fine mottled, only 2¾" diam., 2¾" high, child's size.
5. Tumbler-shaped medicine cup, white with black trim, marked inside "1 tea. - 2 oz."
6. Soup plate, mauve pink and white outside, w;hite inside, large mottled.
7. Coaster, blue and white, white inside, black trim, large swirl, "Blue Diamond Ware."

Plate 4, Row 3:

1. Plate, dessert size, 6½" diam., aqua green and white, white inside, cobalt blue trim, large swirl.
2. Cup, flared shape, aqua green and white, cobalt blue tirm, large swirl.
3. Baby's mug, cobalt blue and white with black trim, large swirl. Note the way the bottom is made larger, making it harder to tip over.
4. Cup, child's size, "old" red and white with red trim, white inside, triple coated, large swirl.
5. Child's set or 3-piece starter set. Plate, cup and saucer, blue and white outside, white inside, black trim, large swirl.
6. Mug, gray with black trim, decorated with a black and green silhouette of a boy and girl playing with a dog, marked "Germany."
7. Plate, dessert, orange and white inside and outside, black trim, large swirl, circa 1960's.
8. Mug, white with light green, green trim, medium mottled, marked "Elite."

Plate 4, Row 4:

1. Tumbler, cobalt blue and white outside, black trim, large swirl.
2. Soup plate, cobalt blue and white outside, white inside, black trim, large swirl.
3. Tumbler, green and white inside and outside, black trim, large mottled. *Note:* Not sure of age of this piece.
4. Plate, light green and white, white inside, black trim, large swirl.
5. Tumbler, brown and white, black trim, large swirl.
6. Plate, blue, white, and gray outside, white inside, black trim, large swirl, "End of Day."
7. Tumbler, blue and white inside and outside, black trim, large mottled. *Note:* Not sure of age of this piece.

Plate 5, Row 1:

1. Cup and saucer, light blue and white, black trim, large mottled.
2. Farmer's cup, deep violet shaded, black trim, shaded, "Thistle Ware."
3. Saucer, deep violet shaded, black trim and handle, "Thistle Ware."
4. Mug, tumbler-shaped, blue and white outside, blue trim, fine mottled.
5. Cup and saucer, blue, light blue, and white, black trim, medium mottled, "End of Day."

Plate 5, Row 2:

1. Mug, dark green and white, black trim, large swirl, "Emerald Ware."
2. Mug, blue and white, black trim, medium swirl, seamed body and bottom. Note unusual shape because most mugs are seamless.
3. Saucer, blue and white inside and outside, black trim, fine mottled.
4. Mug, white, decorated with Indians, brown trim.
5. Cup, child's size, gray large mottled.
6. Mug, tumbler-shaped, blue and white trimmed in cobalt blue, fine mottled.

Plate 5, Row 3:

1. Tumbler, dark solid blue trimmed in black, labeled "Ski Blu." Steel Base. Standard Qualtiy, Sanitary, Vitreous Enamel. Quartz Rock Surface, Columbian Enameling and Stamping Co., Terre Haute, Indiana U.S.A.
2. Mug, blue and white with black trim, fine mottled.
3. Tumbler, steel blue gray shaded, black trim.
4. Mug, shaded blue with black trim, labeled "Bluebelle Ware." Enameled No. 30 BB, Norvell Shapleigh Hardware Co., St. Louis, Made in the U.S.A., Trademark Registered U.S. Pat Off.
5. Covered soup mug, cobalt blue and white, white inside, black trim, large swirl, circa 1960's, lightweight.
6. Child's mug, blue and white, fine mottled.
7. Saucer, white with black trim, labeled "Republic," made by Republic S. & E. Co., Canton, Ohio, U.S.A.

Plate 5, Row 4:

1. Mug, dark green and white with black trim, "Chrysolite."
2. Mug, dark brown and white inside and outside, black trim, medium mottled, seamed, "Onyx Ware."
3. Mug, blue and white with black trim, large swirl.
4. Plate, gray large mottled.
5. Mug, gray medium mottled.
6. Tumbler, gray medium mottled.
7. Mug, dark green and white with black trim, large swirl, "Chrysolite."
8. Mug, dark green and white with black trim, large swirl, "Chrysolite."

Section 3, Plate 5

103

Section 4

Trays, Beer Stein, Coffee Flasks, Camp Mugs, Poached Egg Cup, Chopper, Oyster Patty

Plate 1, Row 1:

1. Oblong tray, white trimmed in black, black outside, decorated with covered wagon scene. Marked ING-RICH SIGNUM PERFECTIONIS PORCELIRON. BEAVER FALLS, PA.

Plate 1, Row 2:

1. Corrugated tray or table mat, brown and white outside, white inside, black trim, large swirl. *Note:* This style is shown in the 1892 Manning Bowman Co. Catalog with narrow nickel bands and they are advertised as corrugated table mats.
2. Beer stein, cobalt blue and white with cobalt blue trim, white inside, large swirl, fancy pewter embossed cover and thumb lift. Man's name embossed on cover - P. Pollot. Cross collectible. The only one the author has ever seen.
3. Advertising beer tray, white inside, green outside with green trim. Advertises "Dawes Brewery Black Horse Ale and Porter, The National Breweries Limited, Lachine, P.O. Box 80, St. Maurices, Montreal." Advertising cross collectible.

Plate 1, Row 3:

1. Round tray, red and white inside and outside, dark blue trim, circa 1960's, lightweight.
2. Round tray, light blue and white outside, white inside, large swirl.
3. Round tray, dark blue and white inside and outside, black trim, large swirl, circa 1960's, lightweight.

Section 4, Plate 1

105

Plate 2, Row 1:

1. Coffee flask. *Note:* Often mistakenly referred to as canning jars by today's collectors. Round, seamless, dark gray medium mottled, 4½" high, 3½" diameter, nickel-plated, cork-lined screw-on top, "Royal Granite Enameled Steel Ware."
2. Coffee flask, round, seamless, gray medium mottled, 5" high, 4¾" diameter, "Royal Granite Enameled Steel Ware," distributed by the Lockwood-Luethemeyer Henry Co.
3. Oblong tray with handles, white with fine green veins, white inside, medium mottled, marked "Elite."

Plate 2, Row 2:

1. Tray, blue and white, white inside, medium mottled.
2. Coffee flask, solid blue. The metal band that holds the screw-type metal cover is secured to the top of the coffee flask body by a cork lining. 4½" high, 3½" diameter.
3. Coffee flask, solid blue, screw on metal top, 5" high, 4¾" diameter.
4. Oblong tray, solid blue with black trim, black outside, decorated with mountain scene. Marked "Ing-Rich 1901-1951 Fifty Years of Service in Porcelain Enameling." Advertising 50th anniversary, cross collectible.

Plate 2, Row 3:

1. Oval tray, gray medium mottled.
2. Coffee flask, brown and white fine mottled, metal screw-top, "Onyx Ware."
3. Tray, blue and white, white inside, black trim, "Columbian Ware."

Plate 3, Row 1:

1. Mug, blue and white with black trim, large swirl, called camp or mush mug. 4⅞" high, 5½" diameter.
2. Oblong tray, white with solid light blue border, black trim and back, decorated, marked "Ing-Rich Signum Perfectionis Porceliron, Beaver Falls, Pa."
3. Coffee flask, blue and white, white inside, metal screw-on top, large swirl. Labeled "Mosaic Triple Coated Ware," D with a C and J superimposed in a triangle mark. *Note:* Originally sold for 29¢.

Plate 3, Row 2:

1. Mug, light blue and white with light blue trim, large mottled, camp or mush mug, 6" high, 6" diameter. *Note:* These mugs were also used for cooking mush over campfires, thus, the name camp or mush mug.
2. Egg poacher insert, blue and white large mottled. *Note:* There should be 5 of these that fit into a graniteware or tin egg poacher bottom. Poacher should also have a graniteware or tin cover.
3. Mug, cobalt blue and white large swirl, camp or mush mug, 4½" high, 6" diameter.
4. Chopper, solid light blue handle, cross collectible, marked "Chopette Stainless Steel Blade." Wooden chopping block marked "Chopette Pat. applied for Rochester, N.Y."
5. Oblong tray, cobalt blue and white, white inside, black trim, large swirl.
6. Oyster patty, gray medium mottled, 3 shell-shaped feet. *Note:* These were used for baking oysters.

Plate 3, Row 3:

1. Oblong tray, aqua green and white, white inside, large mottling, brass eyelet for hanging.
2. Coffee flask, gray and white fine mottled, metal screw-on top. 4½" high, 3½" diameter.
3. Coffee flask, dark blue and white medium mottled, metal screw-on top. 5" high, 4" diameter.
4. Square tray, gray medium mottled.

Section 5

Bread Boxes, Cake or Pie Carriers, Salt Boxes, Sugar Shakers, Cannisters, Cup Holders, Onion Holder, Seife, Soda, and Sand Holders, Tooth Brush Holders

Plate 1, Row 1:

1. Round bread box, white with black trim and lettering, top of cover is vented.
2. Oblong bread box, solid red, brass handle, hinges, and latch, back side of cover is vented.

Plate 1, Row 2:

1. Round bread box, white with light blue veins, Chicken Wire pattern.
2. Salt box, white with dark blue trim, wooden cover, marked "Germany."
3. Salt box, white with dark blue trim and back.

Plate 1, Row 3:

1. Salt box, white with light blue veins, chicken wire pattern.
2. Salt box, pink and white with red trim, medium mottled, marked "SEL," French for salt.
3. Round bread box, gray and light gray, medium mottled, brass hinge handle, and latch.

Plate 2, Row 1:

1. Salt box, "old" red and white with red trim, large mottled, "Snow on the Mountain."
2. Salt box, gray large mottled.
3. Salt box, blue and white with red trim, fine mottled.

Plate 2, Row 2:

1. Salt box, solid green with embossed white lettering, fancy back, marked "Germany."
2. Salt box, "old" red and white with red trim, decorated with Feather pattern trimmed in gold, matching cover.
3. Salt box with "SALT" embossed on front, gray medium mottled, marked "L. & G. Mfg. Co."

Plate 2, Row 3:

1. Salt box, solid red with black back and trim.
2. Sugar shaker, gray and light gray fine mottled. *Note:* The cover does not screw on. Instead, a metal inner band on the bottom inside edge of the cover acts as a spring holding the cover secure while shaking. These were used to sprinkle powdered sugar, flour, and a combination of spices and sugar over food.
3. Sugar shaker, gray medium mottled. The tin cover does not screw on, but fits over the top of the shaker. The strap handle is applied by rivets. The body and bottom are seamed.
4. Salt box, white with fancy back.
5. Sugar shaker, reddish brown and white, white inside, medium mottled, seamed. *Note:* Cover fits same as cover on No. 2 in this row.
6. Sugar shaker, white with green trim, seamless body, seamed bottom, has large cork plug in center of the bottom for filling.

Plate 2, Row 4:

1. Salt box, white decorated with a blue windmill scene, much like a Blue Delph scene.
2. Salt box, solid red, labeled "Genuine Swedish K.E.R. Enameled Ware. Guaranteed Pure and of Higher Quality." marked on bottom, "KOCKUMS K.E.R. SWEDEN 15 CM."
3. Salt box shape, solid blue, decorated with pink and white flowers, marked "Mehl."

Plate 3, Row 1:

1. Sugar cannister, white with dark blue trim. The cover has a recessed strap handle.
2. Flour cannister, blue and white with blue trim, fine mottled.
3. Flour cannister, cream trimmed in green with black embossed lettering. *Note:* Collecotrs refer to this color as "Cream and Green." The Lisk 50th Anniversary Catalog refers to this color as "Flintstone Ivory Enameled Ware Green trim."

Plate 3, Row 2:

1. Meal cannister, solid blue outside, white inside.
2. Pepper cannister, white with dark blue trim.
3. Tea cannister, light gray and black with black trim, white inside, large swirl, triple coated, marked "Elite" Austria.
4. Coffee cannister, white with dark blue trim. The cover has a recessed strap handle.

Plate 3, Rows 3 and 4:

1. Ten-piece cannister set. Red and white shaded, decorated in gold. Covers and bodies are ribbed. The flour cannister, the largest in the set, is marked "B. & W. 16. TORSEINE REGISTERED. MADE IN AUSTRIA." This is the only one in the set that is marked "B. & W." The rest are all marked "TORSEINE REGISTERED. MADE IN AUSTRIA." They are all marked with a different number. The pepper, the smallest in the set, is marked "7," next larger one marked "8," and so on.

Plate 4, Row 1:

1. Three-piece partial cannister set, "old" red and white with red trim, white inside with tiny blue specks, large swirl outside, fine mottled inside.
2. Three-piece partial cannister set, gray and white trimmed in gray, relish pattern. *Note:* All these are the same size. The covers fit over the top of the cannisters.

Plate 4, Row 2:

1. Five-piece partial cannister set, white and light blue, dark blue trim, large mottled, "Snow on the Mountain."

Plate 4, Row 3:

1. Four-piece partial cannister set, "old" red and white trimmed in red, large mottled, "Snow on the Mountain."
2. Spice cannisters, 4 pieces, solid light blue background, trimmed in gold, decorated with a Dutch boy and girl, marked "GES. GESCHUTZT."

Plate 4, Row 4:

1. Four spice cannisters plus tea cannister, solid dusty orange, black knob and trim, marked "Elite–Czeclo–Slovokia–Registered." All numbered "12."

Section 5, Plate 4

Plate 5, Row 1:

1. Holder, white, decorated with blue windmill scene, brass hook for hanging a cup or washcloth, bottom part of holder is shell-shaped. This possibly held the soap or could have been used as a drip tray when the wet washcloth was hung on the hook.
2. Utility rack, gray and light gray medium mottled, holds seife, soda, and sand cups. Rack has fancy, scalloped edges. *Note:* When the soda and sand were mixed together, they formed a cleaning mixture for scouring pots and pans (such as cast iron).
3. Holder, white with light blue veins, Chicken Wire pattern, scalloped bottom edge, metal hook holds cup or washcloth.

Plate 5, Row 2:

1. Utility rack, seife, soda, and sand, white with light blue veining trimmed in dark blue, Chicken Wire pattern.
2. Toothbrush holder, wall type, solid white, holds three toothbrushes.

Plate 5, Row 3:

1. Utility rack, triangle shape, solid white, has a handle on the rack for carrying from one place to another. Holds seife, soda, and sand cups.
2. Holder for scouring powder (SKUREPULVER), solid red.
3. Holder for soap, solid red, "SABE" is "soap." Note: These never seemed to have covers like the salt boxes.

Plate 5, Row 4:

1. Utility rack, seife, soda, and sand, perforated back, gray and white large mottled.
2. Mug, dark blue and white fine mottled, strap handle. This mug has a tin lid that is pierced for sprinkling the cleansing powder. Labeled "Wrigleys Established 1876. Crystalline. Cleans everything bright--Glassware, Agate Ware, Porcelain Enamel-ed Bathtubs, Wash Bowls and much more. This cup alone is worth fully the price after powder is used. Fill cup with water and lid will pry off easily. Crystalline cannot scratch. Made by The Wrigley Mfg. Co., Philadelphia."
3. Holder for onions, marked "SWIEBELN," white trimmed with dark blue, perforated front, fancy back.

Section 6

Utensil Racks and Utensils, Skimmers, Cocoa Dippers, Spoons, Spatulas, Ladles

Plate 1, Row 1:

1. Utensil rack, blue and white large mottled, two original utensils, handled perforated skimmer and soup ladle.
2. Handled, perforated skimmer, cobalt blue and white with green veins, medium mottled inside and out, black handle, "End of Day."
3. Utensil rack, dark green with heavy white mottling, large mottled, triple coated, "Snow on the Mountain." Utensils not original.

Plate 1, Row 2:

1. Hand skimmer, charcoal gray and white inside and outside. This one is very unusual because it has no holes perforated in the center for skimming.
2. Soup ladle, "old" red and white inside and outside, dark blue trim and handle.
3. Soup ladle, "old" red and white inside and outside, black handle.
4. Utensil rack with three original utensils, cream with red decoration, perforated handled skimmer, side snipe ladle with pouring lip and soup ladle.
5. Cocoa dipper, gray medium mottled, black turned wooden handle, smaller size - 3⅜" top opening. The lower granite part of the handle is applied to the granite cocoa dipper body by rivets, the wooden handle is applied down into the inside granite part of the handle with nails.
6. Hand skimmer, gray medium mottled, diamond perforated center. *Note:* These were used for skimming milk and other liquids.
7. Cocoa dipper, gray medium mottled, black trim, wooden handle. This is the larger size - 3⅝" top opening.

Plate 1, Row 3:

1. Cocoa dipper, white with tubular hollow handle. *Note:* A hook for hanging is on the top part of the handle.
2. Hand skimmer, white, perforated diamond-shaped center.
3. Hand skimmer, white, perforated with finger ring.
4. Skimmer, white with tubular handle, fancy perforated center.
5. Skimmer, solid blue, handled, perforated center.
6. Cocoa dipper, brown shaded, metal part on lower section of handle fastens to cocoa dipper body, black turned wooden handle fits inside of metal section.
7. Cocoa dipper, shaded blue, white inside and black trim, tubular handle, "Bluebelle Ware. Norvell Shapleigh Hardware Co., St. Louis."

Plate 2, Row 1:

1. Utensil rack, light gray medium mottled. *Note:* Utensils not original, three utensils, dark gray medium mottled, large handled, perforated flat skimmer, tasting spoon with applied side handle, and small handled perforated skimmer.
2. Soup ladle, large, unusual green and white, white inside, dark blue handle, large swirl. *Note:* Not Emerald Ware.
3. Basting or mixing spoon, blue and white inside and outside, black handle, large swirl, 15" long, "Columbian Ware."
4. Spoon and spice rack, solid blue, back row has six round holes for spice containers. Front row has six oblong holes for spoons.
5. Spoon, white with light blue handle.
6. Spoon, dark green and white outside, white inside, large swirl, "Chrysolite."
7. Spoon, white with red trim, marked "Elite" Austria.

Plate 2, Row 2:

1. Utensil rack, solid black, three matching utensils are gray inside, black outside with black handles, side snipe ladle, soup ladle, and tasting spoon.
2. Utensil rack, "old" red and white with red trim, large mottled. Note: White utensils are not original.
3. Spatula, perforated, cobalt blue outside, white inside.
4. Spatula, perforated, gray medium mottled inside and outside with brick red handle.

Plate 2, Row 3:

1. Spoon, cream and green.
2. Soup ladle, cream and green.
3. Fish tool, perforated, white with black hollow handle.
4. Cake turner, perforated, white with black handle.
5. Handled skimmer, perforated, flat, black and white medium mottled inside and outside.

123

Plate 3, Row 1:

1. Handled skimmer, perforated, gray medium mottled.
2. Handled skimmer, perforated, gray medium mottled.
3. Utensil rack with original utensils, white, decorated with light blue violets, trimmed in gold. Utensil set includes: Soup ladle; handled, perforated skimmer, and tasting spoon with handle applied on the side.
4. Handled skimmer, perforated, flat, blue and white inside and outside, black handle, large swirl.
5. Handled skimmer, perforated, blue and white inside and outside, black handle, large swirl.

Plate 3, Row 2:

1. Dipper, flared shape, dark blue and white inside and outside, fine mottled, black turned wooden handle.
2. Soup ladle, brown and white outside, white inside, black handle and trim, large swirl.
3. Soup ladle, blue and white outside, white inside, black handle, fine mottled.
4. Soup ladle, red outside, decorated with black and red squares on the handle, white inside.
5. Soup ladle, brown and white inside and outside, black handle and trim, "Onyx Ware."

Plate 3, Row 3:

1. Spatula, gray large mottled. *Note:* The top of the spatula is tapered.
2. Spatula, gray medium mottled.
3. Spatula, perforated center, gray large mottled, unusual shape. When spatula is held in right hand, the bottom left side is turned down and the right side is turned up so that whatever is being picked up will not slide off the right side of spatula.
4. Spatula, small size, gray medium mottled.

Plate 4, Row 1:

1. Spoon, basting or mixing, blue and white outside, white inside, black handle, large mottled.
2. Spoon, blue and white outside and inside, black handle, large mottled.
3. Spoon, blue and white outside, white inside, solid blue handle, medium mottled.
4. Spoon, blue and white inside and outside, medium mottled.
5. Spoon, dark green and white, white inside, large swirl, 17¼" long, "Chrysolite."
6. Spoon, blue and white inside and outside, large swirl.
7. Spoon, dark lavender blue and gray outside, gray inside, large swirl, black handle.
8. Spoon, dark blue and white inside and outside, medium mottled, black handle.

Plate 4, Row 2:

1. Spoon, cobalt blue with white and green veins, white inside, large mottled, black handle, "End of Day."
2. Spoons - set of 3. Solid white, basting or mixing, large - 15½" long, medium - 13½" long, small - 10½" long.
3. Spoon, white with green Relish pattern handle, 19⅜" long. *Note:* These were used when making and stirring apple butter in large kettles.
4. Spoon, white with green Relish pattern handle.
5. Spoon, gray medium mottled, 17¼" long.
6. Spoon, gray large mottled.
7. Spoon, gray large mottled.

Plate 4, Row 3:

1. Ice cream spoon, gray and white inside and out, fine mottled, cast iron base. Wooden handle was applied with a metal part, then riveted onto the wooden handle. *Note:* This spoon was used for scooping ice cream from the old ice cream makers.
2. Slotted cake spoon, brown and white inside and outside, medium mottled, black turned wooden handle, "Onyx Ware." *Note:* This type of spoon was used for stirring cake batter.
3. Skimmer, perforated, applied wooden handle, marked "Agate, L. & G. Mfg. Co."
4. Spoon, blue and white inside and out, large swirl.
5. Pickle dipper, solid yellow with green handle and trim. *Note:* This was used for dipping pickles out of the old wooden pickle barrels at the country store. The hole in the center was for draining off the juice.
6. Handled skimmer, blue and white, white inside with black handle, large mottled. The author has never seen another one of these and is not sure what it is meant to be. It is not perforated, and it is almost flat except for the entire outside edge turns up slightly. If anyone has proof of what this might be, the author would love to hear from them.
7. Spoon, perforated, white with black handle.
8. Soup ladle, gray medium mottled, black wooden turned handle.

Plate 5, Row 1:

1. Spoon, blue and white outside, white inside, large swirl, black handle.
2. Spoon, white with blue and white handle, large swirl.
3. Spoon, blue and white inside and outside, large swirl.
4. Spoon, cobalt blue and white, white inside, large mottled, black handle.
5. Spoon, cobalt blue and white, white inside, large swirl.
6. Spoon, blue and white inside and outside, black handle, large swirl.
7. Spoon, light blue and white outside, white inside, large mottled.

Plate 5, Row 2:

1. Skimmer ladle, perforated, cobalt blue and white inside and outside, large swirl, black handle.
2. Side snipe ladle, gray medium mottled.
3. Oyster ladle, perforated bottom, gray mottled.
4. Skimmer ladle, perforated, blue and white outside, white inside, black handle, fine mottled.
5. Oyster ladle, perforated bottom, gray medium mottled.
6. Ladle, flat bottom, white inside and outside, black handle. Note: This was used to scrape food out of the bottom of the pan.
7. Skimmer ladle, fancy perforated, light blue and white outside, white inside, fine mottled, marked "Elite."

Plate 5, Row 3:

1. Spoon, brown and white inside and outside, black handle, medium mottled.
2. Spoon, blue and white outside, white inside, black handle, large swirl.
3. Spoon, gray medium mottled. *Note:* This spoon is unique because the handle and spoon part were made separately. The handle was riveted with one rivet to the spoon part. The author believes the spoon part was made from the same mold as the small thumb scoop body because they are identical in shape and size. It would have been less expensive for the company to just make the handle and apply it to the scoop body.
4. Side snipe ladle, gray large mottled. These are used to make pouring easier. *Note:* Side snipe ladles are called this because they have a side pouring lip. Ladles can be oval or round. They are used for pouring gravies, sauces and other liquids.
5. Side snipe oval ladle, white.
6. Spoon, blue and white inside and outside, large swirl.
7. Tasting spoon, side handle, white with fine blue veins inside and outside, large mottled. *Note:* This is called a tasting spoon because it has a spoon shape, whereas the side snipe ladles have a pouring lip.

Plate 6, Row 1:

1. Ladle, cobalt blue and gray outside, white inside, large mottled.
2. Soup ladle, light blue and white, black handle and trim, medium mottled.
3. Soup ladle, blue and white outside, black handle and trim, large swirl.
4. Soup ladle, green and white outside, large swirl, dark blue trim and handle, "Emerald Ware."
5. Soup ladle, light blue and white outside, black trim and handle, medium mottled.
6. Soup ladle, light blue and white outside, white inside, black handle and trim, fine mottled.
7. Soup ladle, blue and white outside, white inside, medium swirl.

Plate 6, Row 2:

1. Handled skimmer, flat perforated, light blue and white outside, white inside, black handle, fine mottled.
2. Spatula, blue and white inside and outside, black handle, fine mottled.
3. Spatula or turner, perforated, gray inside and outside, medium mottled.
4. Spatula or turner, fancy perforated, blue and white inside and outside, medium mottled.
5. Spatula or turner, fancy perforated, white with fine light blue veins inside and outside, Chicken Wire pattern.
6. Spatula or turner, perforated, white with brick red handle.
7. Handled skimmer, flat perforated, gray medium mottled.

Plate 6, Row 3:

1. Handled skimmer, flat perforated, cobalt blue and gray inside and outside, large mottled.
2. Handled skimmer, flat perforated, white inside and outside, light blue handle.
3. Handled skimmer, flat perforated, shaded brown outside, white inside, brown handle.
4. Handled skimmer, flat perforated, blue and white outside, white inside, fine mottled.
5. Handled skimmer, perforated, white with fine blue veins inside and outside.

Section 7

Biscuit Sheet, Rolling Pin, Biscuit Cutters, Pudding Pans, Custard Cups, Egg Separators, Butter Melting Set, Oblong and Round Cake Pans, Pie Plates, Jelly Roll Pans, Bread Pans, Lady Finger Pans, Cake Molds, Tart Pans, Muffin Pans, Bread Raisers

Plate 1, Row 1:

1. Biscuit sheet, blue and white outside, white inside, large swirl, black trim, holds twelve biscuits. Biscuit size only ¹⁄₁₆" deep x 2¼" diameter; sheet size 11" x 8½".
2. Rolling pin, white with gray screw-on handles, cast iron base.
3. Biscuit cutter, gray medium mottled, 3⅜" diameter, hollow spun knob, seamless, top has two air holes.
4. Biscuit cutter, brown and white with black strap handle, 2¼" diameter, "Onyx Ware." *Note:* Handle was applied through slits on top of biscuit cutter. Cutter has one large air hole on top.

Plate 1, Row 2:

1. Pudding pan, brown and white outside, white inside, black trim, large swirl.
2. Custard cup, light blue and white, white inside, black trim, large swirl.
3. Custard cup, gray large mottled.
4. Custard cup, white with green trim, marked "Savory Ware," made by Lisk Savory Corporation.
5. Pudding pan, white decorated with blue, marked "Nesco Made in U.S.A."

Plate 1, Row 3:

1. Pudding pan, white shading to blue, black trim, decorated with pink and yellow flowers, marked "Stewart, Moundsville, W. Va."
2. Egg separator, cobalt blue with very fine white veining, white inside, perforated around outside edge, slotted in center. *Note:* Used to separate the yoke from the white of the egg.
3. 3-piece butter melting set, light blue decorated with dark blue florets, dark blue trim, white inside, pouring spout on each side. *Note:* Drip tray is not attached.
4. Oblong cake pan, dark green, white and black, white inside, triple coated, "End of Day."

Plate 1, Row 4:

1. Custard cup, Apple Green outside, Tangerine inside, advertised as "Harmonizing Colors," "Vollrath Ware," Sheboygan, Wis.
2. Jelly roll pan, cobalt blue and white outside, white inside, black trim, 1" deep, large mottled.
3. Custard cup, blue and white, white inside, fine mottled, black trim.
4. Egg separator, solid blue inside and outside.
5. Bread pan, solid blue, rounded, ribbed bottom, ring for hanging. *Note:* There sould also be a top part. They were held together with a metal strap that fits into the groove on the sides and bottom of the bread pans. This type pan was said to have made a more uniform loaf of bread and a better crust making it more digestable.
6. Custard cup, cobalt blue and white, black trim, large swirl.

133

Plate 2, Row 1:

1. Lady finger pan, cobalt blue and white outside, white inside, large swirl. These were used to bake the delicate little Lady Finger cakes.
2. Lady Finger pan, mottled gray, marked "Agate Nickel Steel Ware," L. & G. Mfg. Co.
3. Lady Finger pan, smaller size, cobalt blue and white outside, white inside, large swirl.

Plate 2, Row 2:

1. Bread pan with envelope ends, light blue, cobalt blue and white, cobalt blue trim, large mottled, "End of Day." "Granite Steel Ware," Crown Industries, Binghamton, N.Y. *Note:* Envelope ends refer to the seam shape on each end of the bread pan because it is shaped like an envelope flap.
2. Bread pan, black and white, medium fine mottled, seamed ends. *Note:* Seamed ends refer to the rolled-over edge seams on each end of the bread pan.
3. Bread pan, blue and white with black trim, large mottled, seamed ends.
4. Bread pan, gray large mottled, seamed ends.

Plate 2, Row 3:

1. Tube cake mold, 8-sided, blue and white with black trim, large swirl. *Note:* The difference between a tube cake mold and a tube cake pan is that the tube cake mold molds the sides of the cake in different shapes whereas the tube cake pan has a rounded shape.
2. Tube cake pan, round, cobalt blue and white outside, white inside, black trim, large swirl.
3. Tube cake mold, blue and white with black trim, fine mottled.

Plate 2, Row 4:

1. Pie plate, coblat blue and white outside, white inside, black trim, large swirl.
2. Lady Finger pan, gray large mottled.
3. Pie plate, green and white, white inside, black trim, large swirl, "Chrysolite."

Plate 3, Row 1:

1. Handled cast iron biscuit sheet, solid blue outside, white inside, biscuit size ⅝" deep x 3" diameter, pan size 7¾" x 11¼" high. Marked "18" with a star between 18 and 70, "PILSEN" 6.
2. 2-handled pudding pan, light blue and white, large swirl.
3. Jelly roll pan, light blue and white outside, white inside, large swirl. *Note:* Jelly roll pans are called this because they have straight sides rather than angled sides like a pie plate. They are used for making jelly roll cakes.
4. Custard cup, cobalt blue and white with black trim, large swirl.

Plate 3, Row 2:

1. Grooved tray, gray medium mottled, grooved bottom.
2. Individual muffin cup, gray medium mottled, marked "Agate Nickel Steel Ware, L. & G. Mfg. Co.
3. Lady Finger pan, light and dark gray fine mottled.
4. Individual muffin cup, white with green veining, marked "Elite."
5. Jelly roll pan, light blue and white, white inside, large swirl.

Plate 3, Row 3:

1. 2-handled pudding pan, cobalt blue and white, large swirl. *Note:* The handled pudding pans are harder to find than ones without handles.
2. Tart or individual muffin cup, gray mottled.
3. Pudding pan, white with black trim, labeled "Flintstone Porcelain Enameled Ware," Lisk Mfg. Co. Ltd., Reed Mfg. Co., Canandaigua, N.Y.
4. Oval bread pan, blue and white with black trim, fine mottled.

Plate 3, Row 4:

1. Jelly roll pan, dark blue and white with black trim, white inside, Relish pattern.
2. Individual muffin cup, dark blue and white with black trim, Relish pattern. *Note:* These were used to bake a sample of a cake mixture.
3. Pudding pan, blue and white with black trim, large swirl.
4. Shallow tube pan, cobalt blue and white with black trim, white inside, fine mottled.

Plate 4, Row 1:

1. Deep pie plate, cobalt blue and white, large swirl, black trim, white inside.
2. Large pudding pan, green and white large swirl with black trim, "Emerald Ware."
3. Pie plate, blue and white, white inside, large swirl, "Lava Ware," Cleveland Stamping and Tool Co., Cleveland, Ohio.
4. Large pudding pan, brown and white with black trim, large swirl.
5. Pie plate, green and white with black trim, white inside, large swirl, "Emerald Ware."

Plate 4, Row 2:

1. Tube cake mold, 8-sided, aqua green and white, large mottled, white inside, black trim.
2. Tart pan, gray large mottled.
3. Tube cake pan, round, gray mottled, marked "Agate Nickel Steel Ware," L. & G. Mfg. Co.
4. Deep tube cake pan, round, cobalt blue and white, white insdide, black trim, medium mottled.
5. Tart pan, blue and white, white inside, blue trim, fine mottled.

Plate 4, Row 3:

1. Large pudding pan, cobalt blue and white with black trim, large swirl.
2. Pie plate, white with green trim, labeled "Savory Ware."
3. Custard cup, white trimmed in black, "Belmont Ware."
4. Shallow tube cake mold, aqua green and white, white inside, black trim, large swirl.

Plate 4, Row 4:

1. Oblong bread pan, solid blue outside, ring for hanging.
2. Pie plate, blue and white, white inside, blue trim, large mottled.
3. Oval bread pan, gray large mottled.

Plate 5, Row 1:

1. Pie plate, cobalt blue and gray outside, solid gray inside, large mottled.
2. Pie plate, brown and white, white inside, black trim, large swirl.
3. Tube cake pan, round, blue and white outside, white inside, black trim, large mottled.
4. Pie plate, solid cobalt blue outside, white inside.
5. Pie plate, brown and bluish gray inside and outside, large swirl.

Plate 5, Row 2:

1. Tart pan, gray mottled.
2. Tube cake pan, round, blue and white, large swirl, "Lava Ware," Cleveland Stamping and Tool Co., Cleveland, Ohio.
3. Pie plate, brown and gray inside and outside, large mottled.
4. Pie plate, blue, gray, and cobalt blue, gray inside, large swirl, "End of Day."

Plate 5, Row 3:

1. Eight-cup muffin pan, cobalt blue and white inside and outside, large swirl. *Note:* These are harder to find swirled inside and outside.
2. Pudding pan, black and white with black trim, large swirl.

Plate 5, Row 4:

1. Six-cup muffin pan, light blue and white outside, white inside, large swirl. *Note:* Six-cup muffin pans in swirl or mottled colors seem to be harder to find than the eight-cup muffin pans.
2. 12-cup muffin pan, light gray, almost white with very tiny blue flecks inside and outside, speckled pattern.
3. Six-cup muffin pan, gray large motled.

141

Plate 6, Row 1:

1. Eight-cup muffin pan, light blue and white inside and outside, large swirl.
2. Eight-cup wire framed muffin pan, gray large mottled. *Note:* Each cup is riveted and crimped over the wire frame to hold cups in position.
3. Eight-cup wire framed muffin pan, gray large mottled. Note the difference in the cup shape on the two gray pans shown.
4. Eight-cup muffin pan, blue and white outside, white inside, large mottled.

Plate 6, Row 2:

1. Nine-cup muffin pan, gray large mottled.
2. Nine-cup muffin pan, dark gray large mottled.

Plate 6, Row 3:

1. Nine-cup muffin pan, gray large mottled. Note the different size of cups and depths of cups on these three muffin pans.

Plate 6, Row 4:

1. Eight-cup muffin pan, cobalt blue and white outside, white inside, black trim, large swirl.
2. Eight-cup Turk's head turban-style muffin pan, gray large mottled. *Note:* Turk's head turban-style refers to the swirl, ribbed shape in the muffin cup.

143

Plate 7, Row 1:

1. Six-cup muffin pan, blue and white outside, white inside, large swirl.
2. Eight-cup muffin pan, wire framed, mottled gray. Note thumb rest at each end of the wire frame.
3. Six-cup muffin pan, shallow, aqua green and white, white inside, cobalt blue trim, large swirl.

Plate 7, Row 2:

1. Eight-cup muffin pan, strapped, gray mottled. The original manufacturer's mark has been blotted out and "OPAL" marked above it. *Note:* Strapped refers to the strapped piece that is applied to the edges of the muffin cup on the underside only, whereas the inside is seamed together.
2. Six-cup muffin pan, cobalt blue and white inside and outside, large mottled.
3. Eight-cup muffin pan, deep, gray mottled, marked "Extra Agate Nickel Steel Ware."

Plate 7, Row 3:

1. 12-cup Turk's head turban-style muffin pan, gray large mottled. Note: The 12-cup size in these are hard to find.
2. 12-cup muffin pan, deep, gray large mottled.

Plate 8, Row 1:

1. Eight-cup muffin pan, shallow, cobalt blue and white, white inside, large swirl.
2. 12-cup muffin pan, shallow, strapped, gray medium mottled, inside view. Note the rounded outside corners.
3. Eight-cup muffin pan, deep, cobalt blue and white inside and outside, large swirl.

Plate 8, Row 2:

1. 12-cup muffin pan, deep, gray large mottled.
2. Eight-cup muffin pan, shallow, strapped, gray large mottled. Note the inside view showing the seams.
3. 12-cup muffin pan, deep, strapped, gray large mottled, marked "Agate Seconds." *Note:* Factory marked seconds are rare and highly sought after by collectors.

Plate 8, Row 3:

1. Eight-cup muffin pan, deep, gray large mottled.
2. Eight-cup muffin pan, cobalt blue and white inside and outside, large swirl.
3. Eight-cup muffin pan, redipped, brown and white inside and outside, large mottled. *Note:* This color was applied at the factory over an existing color of cobalt blue and white. When a piece is redipped at the factory with the new color, the existing color can be seen slightly through the new color. Therefore, one can tell what type of swirl, mottling, or color it was originally.

Plate 9, Row 1:

1. 6-cup muffin pan, shallow, seamed, gray medium mottled. Note: The six cups are assembled with a rolled seam effect. Where the seams come together, it is offset. Unusual large shallow shaped cups.
2. 9-cup muffin pan, cobalt blue and white, white inside, black trim, large swirl.
3. 6-cup muffin pan, light blue and white outside, white inside, large swirl.

Plate 9, Row 2:

1. 8-cup Turk's head turban-style muffin pan, gray medium mottled, marked "Agate Nickel Steel Ware," L. & G. Mfg. Co.
2. 12-cup muffin pan, light blue and white outside, white inside, cobalt blue trim, medium mottled.
3. 8-cup muffin pan, shallow, strapped, gray mottled, marked "Agate Ware," L. & G. Mfg. Co.

Plate 9, Row 3:

1. 12-cup muffin pan, deep, wire framed with strap handles, gray large mottled.
2. 8-cup Turk's head muffin pan, deep, strapped, gray medium mottled, inside view, unusually large cups. _Note:_ This is very unusual for a Turk's head muffin pan because it is strapped.
3. 12-cup muffin pan, riveted wire frame, strap handles, gray mottled.

Plate 10, Row 1:

1. Nine-cup Turk's head turban-style muffin pan, shallow, gray large mottled.
2. Nine-cup muffin pan, deep, white inside and outside with cobalt blue trim, marked "L. & G. Mfg. Co."
3. Six-cup Turk's head turban-style muffin pan, light gray medium mottled.

Plate 10, Row 2:

1. Nine-cup muffin pan, deep, "End of Day." The color on the inside and outside is a dark plum color with gray and white large mottling.
2. Nine-cup Turk's head turban-style muffin pan, deep, gray large mottled.

Plate 10, Row 3:

1. Eight-cup muffin pan, shallow, light brown and white inside and outside with black trim, large mottled, "Onyx Ware."
2. Cornstick pan, solid red outside, solid cream color inside, cast iron base marked "NO. 273 Griswold Crispy Cornstick Pan. Erie Pa. U.S.A. 930."
3. Eight-cup muffin pan, deep, dark solid coblat blue outside, white inside.

Plate 10, Row 4:

1. Six-cup muffin pan, deep strapped, gray medium mottled. *Note:* The "Agate Ware" stamp is almost blotted out by the manufacutrer and in very faint lettering on the other cup it is marked "PEERLESS."
2. 11-cup rounded muffin pan, light gray motled, cast iron base. *Note:* The cups and strap-type handles seem to be welded together very crudely. Marked on handle "3. W. & L. Mfg. Co."
3. Six-cup muffin pan, deep, strapped, gray medium mottled, inside view.

Plate 11, Row 1:

1. Oblong bread pan, seamed ends, cobalt blue and white outside, white inside, medium swirl.
2. Footed bread raiser, blue and white outside, white inside, black trim and handles, medium mottled, large size, vented tin domed cover with strap handle.
3. Oblong bread pan, seamed ends, brown and white inside and outside, medium mottled.

Plate 11, Row 2:

1. Footed bread raiser, cobalt blue and white, white inside, black trim, medium mottled, granite handles, vented tin domed cover with strap handle, small size.
2. Footed bread raiser, gray mottled, matching gray granite vented domed cover with strap handle, small size.

Plate 11, Row 3:

1. Footed bread raiser, gray medium mottled, matching gray, granite vented domed cover with strap handle, medium size.
2. Oblong bread pan, envelope ends, gray large mottled.
3. Oblong bread pan, envelope ends, gray medium mottled. Note ring for hanging.

153

Section 8

Bowls and More Shapes in Molds

Plate 1, Row 1:

1. Cereal bowl, white, decorated with orange and gold bands, trimmed in cobalt blue. Rabbit and bird in center seem to be beside a potting shed, three sprays of flowers decorate the sides of the bowl. Marked "NEWCO, Made in Nigeria 7CM." Age unknown.
2. Dough or salad bowl, blue and white outside, white inside with black trim, fine mottled.
3. Cereal bowl, white decorated with orange and gold bands, trimmed in cobalt blue. Rabbit in center eating a carrot, bird is perched on a shovel handle. A Nigerian woman with some sort of feather in her hand adorns the side of the bowl - looks like she might be trying to chase the rabbit away. Marked "NEWCO Made in Nigeria 7CM." Age unknown.

Plate 1, Row 2:

1. Nest of 4 mixing bowls, solid red, solid green, solid yellow, and cobalt blue with black trim. Vollrath Company, Sheboygan, Wisconsin, circa 1920's. *Note:* These all stack into each other. That's why they are called a nest of bowls.

Plate 1, Row 3:

1. Mixing or serving bowl, yellow and white with black trim, large mottled, lightweight, circa 1960's.
2. Mixing bowl, greenish blue and white with black trim, large mottled.
3. Rimmed mixing bowl, black and cream with black trim, large swirl, hole in the rim for hanging.

Plate 1, Row 4:

1. Serving bowl, blue and white with black trim, medium swirl.
2. Three red and white bowls, circa 1960's. The three are shown together to compare the different variations in color.
3. Rimmed bowl, blue and white large swirl, "Columbian Ware."

Plate 2, Row 1:

1. Salad or mixing bowl, cobalt blue and white with black trim, large swirl.
2. Serving bowl, brown and white with black trim, large swirl.
3. Salad or mixing bowl, green and white with cobalt blue trim, large swirl, "Emerald Ware."

Plate 2, Row 2:

1. Nest of three bowls, yellow and white with black trim, circa 1960's.
2. Bowl, green and white with black trim, lightweight, large mottled, circa 1970's.

Plate 2, Row 3:

1. Dessert bowl, gray large mottled.
2. Bowl, white, decorated with lavender iris, trimmed in cobalt blue, marked "Bumper Harvest," made in China, age unknown.
3. Bowl, white, decorated with roses, trimmed in cobalt blue, marked "Bumper Harvest," made in China.
4. Salad or mixing bowl, brown and white with black trim, large swirl.

Plate 2, Row 4:

1. Dough or salad bowl, red and white with cobalt blue trim, large swirl, lightweight, circa 1960's.
2. Soup bowl, cobalt blue and white with black trim, medium swirl.
3. Mixing bowl, side handle, gray medium mottled. *Note:* The handle was used for holding the bowl while mixing and pouring.
4. Soup bowl, blue and white with black trim, large swirl.

Plate 3, Row 1:

1. Scalloped mold, gray large mottled. *Note:* The author believes molds were made and used for numerous purposes, e.g. to mold gelatins, pudding, ice cream, etc.
2. Oval rabbit mold, fluted with rabbit imprint, gray medium mottled. *Note:* This could have been used to mold candy or an individual serving of gelatin with the rabbit imprint.
3. Scalloped tube mold, gray medium mottled.
4. Oval rabbit mold, fluted with rabbit imprint, solid white.
5. Scalloped mold, gray large mottled. *Note:* This mold has impressed rings on the bottom whereas No. 1 on this row has a plain bottom.

Plate 3, Row 2:

1. Fish mold, solid white, large size, note ring for hanging.
2. Footed mold, gray medium mottled, rolled-top edge and four little riveted feet on the rounded bottom to keep mold from tipping, melon shaped, medium size. Marked "Agate Nickel Steel Ware," L. & G. Mfg. Co. *Note:* This type is not meant to have a cover because of the rolled-top edge.
3. Fish mold, solid cobalt blue outside, white inside, medium size, note ring for hanging.

Plate 3, Row 3:

1. Melon mold, white with tin cover and handle. *Note:* Most of the tin covers are numbered, denoting the size of the mold. The larger the number, the bigger the mold. This one is No. 40.
2. Melon mold, gray medium mottled, marked "Agate Nickel Steel Ware," L. & G. Mfg. NO. 50. *Note:* The molds that are meant to have a tin cover have a ¾" recessed ridge around the top edge for the cover to fit over.
3. Melon mold, white, marked "Saxony," NO. 50.
4. Melon mold, solid blue outside, white inside, NO. 40.
5. Melon mold, gray mottled, NO. 30, small size.

Plate 3, Row 4:

1. Turk's head turban-style mold, gray large mottled, 6½" diameter. *Note:* Turk's head molds have straight style ribbing whereas Turk's head turban-style molds have swirled ribbing.
2. Fluted ice cream mold, white, ring for hanging. *Note:* Ice cream molds are usually deeper.
3. Turk's head tube-style turban mold, blue and white medium swirl outside, gray inside.
4. Scalloped ice cream mold, white with ring for hanging.
5. Turk's head turban-style mold, light blue, cobalt blue, and white with white inside, cobalt blue trim, large mottled, "End of Day." "Granite Steel Ware," Crown Industries, Binghamton, N.Y.

Plate 4, Row 1:

1. Turk's head tube-style turban mold, solid brown outside, white inside, ring for hanging.
2. Turk's head scalloped turban mold, reddish brown with fine white specks outside, white inside, fine mottled, marked "Elite."
3. Ring-shaped mold, blue and white inside and outside, cobalt blue trim, fine mottled, Note solid rounded tubed center with outside collar edge.
4. Scalloped mold with flower imprint, solid light blue outside, white inside.
5. Turk's head tube-style turban mold, light blue and white with dark blue trim, white inside, medium mottled.

Plate 4, Row 2:

1. Oval mold, solid blue, white inside with black trim, marked "Cream City Ware," Milwaukee, with a star in the middle of a circle.
2. Turk's head turban-style mold, white with light blue trim, ring for hanging.
3. Oblong shell-shaped mold, white.
4. Ring mold, solid red outside, cream inside, black trim, marked "Cream City Ware," Milwaukee, with a star in the middle of a circle.

Plate 4, Row 3:

1. Ribbed tube-style mold, gray large mottled.
2. Ribbed oval mold, white with cobalt blue trim.
3. Turk's head tube-style turban mold, white with black trim.
4. Shell mold, brown shading to tan, white inside, ring for hanging.
5. Turk's head tube-style turban mold, solid cobalt blue, white inside.

Plate 4, Row 4:

1. Round tube mold, blue and white inside and outside, fine mottled.
2. Oval fluted shallow mold, white.
3. Melon mold, green and white, tin cover with handle, NO. 80, Relish pattern.
4. Oval fluted mold with strawberry imprint, blue and white inside and outside, fine mottled.
5. Turk's head tube-style turban mold, light green and white inside and outside, mottled.

Plate 5, Row 1:

1. Turk's head turban-style ice cream mold, dark blue and white inside and outside, ring for hanging, medium mottled.
2. Turk's head turban-style ice cream mold, light and dark gray fine mottled.
3. Ribbed-style tube mold, cobalt blue and white, white inside, black trim, medium mottled.
4. Turk's head tube-style turban mold, gray medium mottled, marked "Agate Nickel-Steel Ware," L. & G. Mfg. Co."

Plate 5, Row 2:

1. Turk's head tube-style turban mold, blue, cobalt blue, and white, large mottled, cobalt blue trim, "End of Day" pattern. "Granite Steel Ware," Crown Industries, Binghamton, N.Y.
2. Oval fluted mold with strawberry imprint, gray medium mottled.
3. Oval fluted mold with rabbit imprint, blue and white outside, white inside, triple coated, large swirl.
4. Turk's head turban mold, blue and white outside medium mottled, light gray with blue specks inside, medium mottled.
5. Turk's head turban-style mold or muffin cup, gray medium mottled.

Plate 5, Row 3:

1. Tube mold, 8-sided, aqua green and white outside, white inside, black trim, large mottled.
2. Turk's head turban-style mold or muffin cup, blue and white outside, white inside, dark blue trim, fine mottled.
3. Oval ribbed mold, white.
4. Round fluted mold, light blue, white inside, ring for hanging.
5. Round fluted mold with flower imprint, blue and white, white inside, fine mottled, ring for hanging, marked "Elite."

Plate 5, Row 4:

1. Oval fluted mold with grape imprint, white, ring for hanging.
2. Shell mold, blue, white inside, ring for hanging.
3. Oval fluted mold with corn imprint, gray medium mottled.
4. Turk's head tube-style turban mold, reddish brown outside.
5. Round fluted mold with flower imprint, white and light blue, fine mottled, ring for hanging.
6. Oval fluted mold with wheat imprint, gray medium mottled.
7. Oblong shell mold, white, ring for hanging.

Section 9

Graters, Grinders, Noodle Maker,
Batter Jugs, Scoops

Plate 1, Row 1:

1. Flat Ideal grater, gray medium mottled. *Note:* The word "IDEAL" is embossed on the bottom part of the grater.
2. Clamp-on food grinder, green and dark green, medium mottled, labeled NO. E. 5 SPONG LONDON. MADE IN ENGLAND.
3. Grater, blue and white medium mottled.
4. Grater, gray medium mottled.

Plate 1, Row 2:

1. Grater, flat handle, solid blue.
2. Revolving grater, white with fine light blue veins, Chicken Wire pattern, round neck, round wooden pusher, perforated metal drum, imprinted on the metal part, "J.D.A. Original."
3. Revolving grater, gray and white medium mottled, square wooden pusher, imprinted on the metal part, "G.M.T. Co. Inc., Germany."
4. Revolving grater, white decorated with a blue windmill pattern, imprinted on the metal part, "ALICE DUPLEX."
5. Flat grater with handle, solid blue.

Plate 1, Row 3:

1. Large grater, solid cobalt blue.
2. Clamp-on noodle cutter, blue outside, white inside, has five cutting blades, cuts four noodles at a time.
3. Small revolving grater, gray with tiny gray specks, fine mottled, square wooden pusher, imprinted on metal "PARIS. BOB. PARIS."
4. Grater, solid reddish brown.

Plate 1, Row 4:

1. Grater, solid blue.
2. Grater, white with coblat blue trim, marked "Germany."
3. Grater, small size, solid blue. Note the different shape and size variations on all the graters.

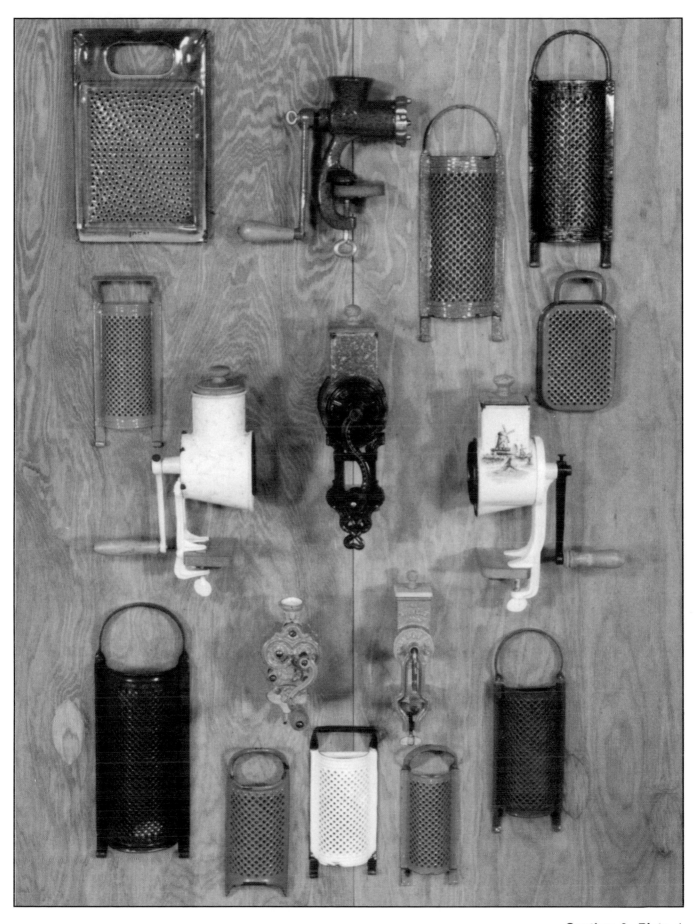

Plate 2, Row 1:

1. Batter jug, matching granite cover, gray medium mottled, wooden bail handle, seamed body and spout with tin spout cover, riveted ears and bottom strap tipping handle. Marked "Extra Agate Nickel Steel Ware," L. & G. Mfg. Co. *Note:* Batter jugs were used for storing batter in a warm place such as warming ovens on top of woodburning stoves. The batter would then always be ready for cooking. The tin spout cover was used to keep dirt and insects out of the batter.
2. Batter jug, dark blue and white, white inside, Relish pattern, tin cover, wooden bail handle, tin spout cover, seamed body and spout, riveted ears and bottom strap tipping handle.

Plate 2, Row 2:

1. Large spouted batter jug, gray large mottled, riveted ears, wire-shaped bottom tipping handle, bail handle, tin spout cover, seamed spout and body, tin cover with cat's eye knob. *Note:* Imprinted wheel emblem on each side of spout. This is the emblem of the Central Stamping Co., N.Y. Labeled "Primo Aluminum Enamel Ware," Extra Coated. Guaranteed Absolutely Pure, Patented Sept. 2, 1902, April 25, 1904, Nov. 8, 1904.
2. Batter jug, gray large mottled, riveted ears, spout and wire-shaped bottom tipping handle, seamed body, tin spout cover and wooden bail handle.

Plate 2, Row 3:

1. Short style batter jug, gray medium mottled, tin cover, wooden bail handle, tin spout cover, riveted ears and large strap handle, seamed body and spout. Unusual because the large strap handle is near the top part of the batter jug.
2. Small batter jug, gray medium mottled, riveted ears, spout, bottom strap tipping handle, seamed body, wooden bail and tin cover.
3. Batter jug, gray large mottled, riveted ears, spout, and bottom strap tipping handle, tin cover and spout cover, seamed body. Unusual because this one has a seam on each side. Most have one seam down the back.

Plate 3, Row 1:

1. Spice scoop, gray medium mottled, pieced back, riveted strap handle and body, advertised in Butler Bros. Catalog, Spring 1912, as a spice scoop.
2. Spice scoop, gray large mottled.

Plate 3, Row 2:

1. Grocer's scoop, gray large mottled, seamless body, tubular open-end seamed handle applied to body by three rivets, rolled edge.
2. Grocer's scoop, gray medium mottled, seamless body, tubular open-end seamed handle applied to body by 4 rivets, rolled edge.
3. Large grocer's scoop, gray mottled, seamless body, tubular closed-end seamed handle applied to body by 4 rivets, rolled edge.
4. Grocer's scoop, gray large mottled, strap handle with slightly rolled edge, riveted to body with 2 rivets.
5. Grocer's scoop, gray medium mottled, semi-covered top, seamed to bottom part of body, strap handle rolled up on the sides, 3 rivets hold handle to body.

Plate 3, Row 3:

1. Thumb scoop, white with cobalt blue handle.
2. Thumb scoop, blue and white outside medium mottled, white with tiny blue specks inside, fine mottled.
3. Wooden-handled candy scoop, gray medium mottled, seamless, rolled edge, marked "Agate," L. & G. Mfg. Co.
4. Scoop, solid blue outside with white inside.
5. Agate seamless scoop, gray large mottled, tubular seamed handle, closed end, riveted to body with 4 rivets.
6. Scoop, solid white, seamed top section, handle riveted.
7. Scoop, gray and charcoal gray medium mottled. *Note:* Scoop was made without a handle.
8. Scoop, solid blue outside, white inside, marked "Germany."

Plate 3, Row 4:

1. Scoop, gray medium mottled.
2. Small thumb scoop, gray mottled. *Note:* The author believes this is the smallest size thumb scoop made, only 5⅜" from handle to bottom of scoop.
3. Scoop, gray large mottled.
4. Druggist's scoop, gray mottled. *Note:* The body of the druggist's scoop and the handle are molded all in one piece.
5. Large scoop, solid cobalt blue, white inside.
6. Candy scoop, gray medium mottled.
7. Candy scoop, solid white. *Note:* These were used in stores where they kept candy in the long, glass, tube-type containers.
8. Tea scoop, "Greystone Enameled Ware," shown in Matthai-Ingram Co. Catalog, Baltimore, Md., U.S.A.

Plate 3, Row 5:

1. Thumb scoop, gray large mottled.
2. Thumb scoop, gray large mottled.
3. Thumb scoop, dark gray medium mottled.
4. Thumb scoop, gray medium mottled, marked "Agate Nickel Steel Ware," L. & G. Mfg. Co.
5. Thumb scoop, dark gray medium mottled.
6. Thumb scoop, gray medium mottled, marked "L. & G. Mfg. Co."
7. Flat bottom thumb scoop, gray medium mottled.

Section 10

Churns, Milk Pan, Hand Skimmer, Milk Pitcher, Scales, Butter Carriers, Chocolate Pots

Plate 1, Row 1:

1. Butter churn, rotating barrel style, solid blue, wooden holding frame. *Note:* This type rotates around when turned by the side crank that is held in place by two metal straps on the body of the churn. Cover is also held in place with a metal strap that can be tightened.
2. Milk pan, brown and white, large swirl, white inside. *Note:* Fresh milk is poured into these to be skimmed clean.
3. Hand skimmer, perforated, gray medium mottled, used for skimming milk or other liquids.

Plate 1, Row 2:

1. Milk pticher, light blue, orange, black, gray, and white, large swirl, "End of Day."
2. Butter churn, floor model crank style, gray medium mottled, side crank, wooden frame and cover, butterfly paddles. *Note:* The churned butter was placed on the wooden cover and cut to size needed.

171

Plate 2, Row 1:

1. Buttermilk churn, floor model dasher type, white with cobalt blue trim and lettering. *Note:* The churn inside is separate from the outer part. The section between the churn and outer wall holds ice for chilling the buttermilk. Two brass spigots, one for pouring the buttermilk, the other for letting the water out from the melted ice. Advertising cross collectible.
2. Brass scale, used for showing item weighed on the graniteware scale trays on Row 2.
3. Butter churn, top geared crank-style paddle, lavender blue and white large swirl, side water or ice compartment riveted to the churn. The water compartment has a spigot for letting the water out. Footed bottom, 2-piece wooden cover with a small round hole with a wooden cover and knob, one solid paddle on a rod rotates when cranked to churn the butter. Part of label reads, "Usman and Agertor. Manufacturers of 20th Century Buttermaker, Dairy Supplies etc. Pat'd. February 6, 1900."

Plate 2, Row 2:

1. Butter churn, floor model, dasher type, blue and white large swirl, seamed body, black riveted handles, wooden dasher and cover. This type also comes with a granite cover for storing after the butter is churned. *Note:* The author has seen them in three different sizes. This one, 17¾" high x 8¼" diameter, is the smallest of the three seen.
2. Scale tray with strap metal holder, blue and white large swirl, black trim, white inside.
3. Scale tray with round rod metal holder, dark green and white large swirl, white inside, black trim, "Chrysolite." *Note:* The two side metal holders are grooved to hold the ½" deep by 10" diameter tray.
4. Butter churn, floor model dasher type, unusual shade of green shading to off white, seamed body, black riveted handles, wooden dasher and cover.

Plate 3, Row 1:

1. Chocolate or coffee pot, light blue and white specks, fine mottled, hinged cover, seamless body with black wooden side handle.
2. Oval butter kettle or carrier, gray medium mottled, seamed body, small size, riveted ears, black wooden bail handle with acorn knob on cover, Marked "Granite Iron Ware. Pat. May 30, '86, July 3, '77."
3. Chocolate or coffee pot, blue with fine dark specks, cobalt blue trim, fine mottled, hinged cover, seamed body, riveted black wooden side handle.

Plate 3, Row 2:

1. Oval butter kettle or carrier, aqua green and white, cobalt blue trim, large swirl. Note wide metal strap carrying handle with extra support piece welded in the center of the handle, rolled oval granite cover handle.
2. Oval butter kettle or carrier, aqua green and white, cobalt blue trim, large swirl. note narrow metal strap carrying handle. Fancy metal handle on cover. Even though these are alike in color, note the different type handles.

Plate 3, Row 3:

1. Oval butter kettle or carrier, gray medium mottled, medium size, metal strap handle, wooden cover knob. This one is 1½" longer in diameter than the one in Row 1.
2. Steam coffee pot, brown and white Relish pattern, advertised in Manning Bowman & Co. 1892 catalog as "The International Pot." Pearl agate reservoir. The bag or pack holds the ground coffee and thus keeps the liquid extract or beverage perfectly clear and pure. Marked "Manning 844 Patent."
3. Steam coffee pot holder, nickel plate goes with item No. 2 in Row 3. Holds the hot water to keep beverage hot while serving or for a period of time.

Section 11

Milk Cans, Cream Cans, Coffee Carriers

Plate 1, Row 1:

1. Milk can, matching cover, green and white, white inside, blue trim, large swirl, wire-shaped ears, wooden bail handle, seamless body, "Emerald Ware."
2. Milk can, matching cover, cobalt blue and white, white inside, large swirl, wire-shaped ears, wooden bail handle, seamless body.
3. Milk can, matching cover, blue and white, white inside, large swirl, flat sided ears, seamless body, wooden bail handle. Note the different lengths of the bail handles on the three milk cans.

Plate 1, Row 2:

1. Cream can, tin cover, lavender blue and white, white inside, large swirl. *Note:* The black flat riveted ears are on the body instead of the neck, wire bail, four-piece seamed body.
2. Milk can, matching cover, blue and white with black trim, large mottled, wooden bail handle, flat ears and seamless body.
3. Milk can, matching cover, green and white with blue trim, white inside, large swirl, flat ears, seamless body, wooden bail handle, "Emerald Ware."
4. Cream can, tin cover, flared top, blue and white with dark blue trim, fine mottled, flat ears on body with black wooden bail handle.

Plate 1, Row 3:

1. Coffee carrier, matching cover, blue and white medium mottled, wire ears, bail handle used for carrying coffee. In the Agate 1890 cookbook, it advertises this as a utility kettle for milk, beer or oysters. *Note:* These all seem to have the same tapered shape to avoid tipping over easily.
2. Coffee carrier, tin cover, pink and white with black trim, large swirl, wire ears and bail, seamed body.
3. Milk can, flared top, blue and white with dark blue trim, fine mottled, flat ears on body and black wooden bail handle.
4. Coffee carrier, orange and white with red trim, wire bail, checkered pattern. *Note:* These have been termed "coffee carriers" by today's collectors even though they were advertised as "utility kettles."

Plate 1, Row 4:

1. Boston milk can, matching cover, reddish brown with white specks, fine mottled, four-piece seamed body and side strap handle. *Note:* These are called Boston milk cans because of the side handle.
2. Milk can, tin cover, blue and white large swirl, flat ears, black wooden bail and seamed body.
3. Boston milk can, matching cover, white with dark blue trim, side strap handle and wooden bail.

Plate 2, Row 1:

1. Coffee carrier, tin cover, blue and white with red trim, wire ears, checkered pattern.
2. Coffee carrier, matching cover, dark blue and white with light blue trim, large mottled, wire bail, and seamess body, "Snow on the Mountain."
3. Coffee carrier, matching cover, white with light blue mottling, large mottled, wire bail.
4. Coffee carrier, light blue and white with light blue trim, large mottled, wire ears and bail. _Note:_ The lumpy effect is referred to as "Snow on the Mountain." It's called this when heavy coats of white enamel are applied over a contrasting color.
5. Coffee carrier, "old" red and white with red trim, large mottled, wire ears and bail, seamless body.

Plate 2, Row 2:

1. Cream can, tin cover, gray medium mottled, seamed, flat ears and wire bail.
2. Cream can, matching cover, brown shading to a lighter brown, wooden bail handle, flat ears, seamless body.
3. Cream can, matching cover, dark blue and white with black trim, large swirl, wire ears, wooden bail handle, seamless body. _Note:_ This color is popularly known by today's collectors as "Iris."
4. Cream can, deep violet shading to a lighter violet, "Thistle Ware" distributed by Norvell Shapleigh Hardware Co.
5. Cream can, green and white, white inside with blue trim, large swirl, wooden bail and seamless body, "Emerald Ware."
6. Cream can, tin cover with wire ring, gray medium mottled, wire bail and seamed body.

Plate 2, Row 3:

1. Boston cream can, tin cover, gray medium mottled, side strap riveted handle and seamed body.
2. Boston cream can, tin cover, cobalt blue and white, large swirl, strap handle and seamed body.
3. Boston cream can, gray medium mottled, side strap handle, seamed body.
4. Cream can, grayish blue and white inside and outside, black trim and handle, large mottled, side rolled handle, seamless body.
5. Boston cream can, tin cover, gray medium mottled, side rolled riveted handle.

Plate 2, Row 4:

1. Boston cream can, blue and white with light blue trim, medium mottled, side strap handle, wire bail and seamed body.
2. Boston milk can, dark blue and white with dark blue trim, side strap handle, Relish pattern.
3. Boston cream can, gray large mottled, side strap handle and seamed body, marked "Granite Iron Ware."
4. Boston milk can, cobalt blue and white with black trim, large mottled, rolled handle and seamed body.
5. Boston cream can, light green and white with dark blue trim, Relish pattern.

179

Plate 3, Row 1:

1. Boston milk can, blue and white with light blue tirm, large mottled, side strap handle, wire bail and seamed body.
2. Milk can, gray medium mottled, seamed body.
3. Milk can, blue and white with black trim, large swirl, flat ears, seamless body and wire bail, "Columbian Ware."

Plate 3, Row 2:

1. Milk can, matching cover, blue and white with black trim, large swirl, wire shaped ears, bail and seamless body.
2. Cream can, gray medium mottled, flat ears, seamed body and wire bail.
3. Cream can, matching cover, white with black trim, wooden bail and seamless body.
4. Milk can, solid blue with black trim, wire bail and seamless body.

Plate 3, Row 3:

1. Cream can, gray large mottled, flat ears, black wooden bail and seamed body.
2. Cream can, unusual shade of green, shading to an off-white, wire ears and bail, seamless body.
3. Cream can, matching cover, shaded blue, "Bluebelle Ware" distributed by Norvell Shapleigh Hardware Co., St. Louis.
4. Cream can, matching lock cover, deep sea green shading to a moss green, "Shamrock Ware," Norvell Shapleigh Hardware Co., St. Louis, sole distributor.
5. Cream can, gray large mottled, seamed body, wire bail.

Plate 3, Row 4:

1. Milk can, brown and white with black trim, large swirl, flat ears, wire bail and seamless body.
2. Milk can, unusual green and white with black trim, large swirl, flat ears, seamed body and black wooden bail.
3. Milk can, light blue and white with dark blue trim, large swirl, seamless body and wire bail.

Plate 4, Row 1:

1. Milk can, blue and white with dark blue trim, fine mottled, wire ears, heavy bail handle and seamless body.
2. Milk can, flared top, gray medium mottled, domed granite cover with wooden acorn knob, seamless body and wooden bail.
3. Milk can, blue and white matching cover, black ears, cover, handle and trim, large swirl, wire bail, and seamless body, "Columbian Ware," Bellaire Stamping Co.

Plate 4, Row 2:

1. Milk can, blue and white with light blue trim, medium mottled, seamed body and wire bail.
2. Coffee carrier, light blue and white with light blue trim, medium mottled.
3. Coffee carrier, pink, white, and green, large swirl, wire ears and bail, seamed body, "End of Day."
4. Coffee carrier, matching cover, blue and white medium mottled, wire bail.
5. Cream can, white with light blue veining, large swirl, wooden bail.

Plate 4, Row 3:

1. Boston cream can, reddish brown and white, side strap handle, seamed body, Relish pattern.
2. Cream can, blue and white with black trim, large swirl, wire ears and bail, seamless body.
3. Cream can, light blue and white with black trim and ears, wire bail and seamed body, fine mottled.
4. Cream can, dark green and white, dark blue trim, large swirl, seamed body, "Chrysolite."
5. Cream can, blue and white fine mottled, wire ears, wooden bail, seamless body, marked "Elite" Austria.

Plate 4, Row 4:

1. Milk can, gray large mottled, seamed body and wooden bail.
2. Boston milk can, gooseneck spout, gray medium mottled, strap handle and wire bail.
3. Milk can, matching cover, gray large mottled, seamed body, flat shaped ears. *Note:* The seam on lower section is in the front of milk can instead of on the sides.
4. Milk can, cobalt blue and white with black trim, large swirl, flat ears, wire bail and seamless body.

Plate 5, Row 1:

1. Milk can, blue and white with black trim, large swirl, wire bail and seamless body.
2. Milk can, deep sea green shading to a moss green, wire-shaped ears, seamless body, "Shamrock Ware."
3. Cream can, flared top, no cover, gray medium mottled, wire bail and seamless body.
4. Milk can, light blue and white with black trim, seamless body and wire bail. *Note:* Very unusual wavey-type mottling. The Lee Manufacturing Co. Premium House Catalog, Chicago 1915, advertises a product with very similar mottling, labeled Triple Coated Blue and White, pure white inside but no manufacturer's name.

Plate 5, Row 2:

1. Cream can, matching cover, blue and white with black trim, large swirl, wire bail and seamless body.
2. Milk can, gray medium mottled, wire bail and seamed body.
3. Milk can, dark green and white, large swirl, wire bail and seamless body, "Chrysolite."
4. Milk can, dark blue and white with dark blue trim, wooden bail and seamed body, Relish pattern.

Plate 5, Row 3:

1. Cream can, gray large mottled, labaled "Made in the U.S.A. by Savory Inc. No. 71."
2. Cream can, dark green and white, large swirl, "Chrysolite."
3. Cream can, matching cover, light blue and white, Chicken Wire pattern, riveted wire ears and wooden bail, marked with lion standing with front feet on coffee pot. "Paragon Quadruple Coated Steel Enamel Ware," imported by the New England Enameling Co., sole agents for U. S. and Canada.
4. Cream can, cobalt blue and white with black trim, large swirl, wooden bail and seamless body.
5. Cream can, blue and white, large swirl, wooden bail and seamed body.
6. Cream can, lavender blue and white, large swirl, wire bail and seamless body.

Plate 5, Row 4:

1. Cream can, blue and white, large swirl, wire bail and seamless body.
2. Milk can, matching lock cover, deep sea green shading to a moss green, "Shamrock Ware."
3. Milk can, matching cover that locks when turned, shaded tan to brown, black wooden bail and seamless body.
4. Cream can, blue and white, medium mottled, wooden bail and seamed body.

Section 12

Advertising and Cross Collectible Items

Advertising items come in many shapes and materials, and they are highly sought after whether advertising a product or company (e.g. Granite ware can even advertise granite ware). Some advertising items are considered cross collectibles because they belong in more than one collecting field (e.g. an advertising piece of granite ware belongs in the granite ware field as well as the advertising field.)

Plate 1, Row 1:

1. Counter top family scale with removable tray, white, decorated with a windmill and boat scene, the metal part that holds the tray has four heart cutouts. Marked "Eagle Trademark."
2. Wash basin, gray medium mottled, advertises "Royal Granite Steelware." *Note:* It is believed that these were given to the housewife or child by traveling salesmen who were promoting a particular company's ware. They were also used in store displays.
3. Ashtray, white with blue tea kettle, black lettering, seamless, non-leak, "Pyrolite Ware." Distributed by Leffler, Thiele & Co., 47 Murray Street, New York. The underside is marked "Pyrolite Ware" with the face of a lion. Germany.
4. Bean scoop, dark green, advertises a company and their products. *Note:* This particular piece is a good example of a cross collectible. It's not only collected for its scoop shape, but also for the company and product advertising.

Plate 1, Row 2:

1. Ashtray, yellow with black and red lettering. Advertises Ingram-Richardson Mfg. Co. Ing-Rich is their emblem, Signum Perfectionis Porceliron, Beaver Falls, Pa. Porcelain Enameling on sheet steel signs. Specialties, table tops and drain boards.
2. Ice cream scoop, white on a heavy metal base, cone shaped, fancy shaped metal ice cream release knob. Inside, brass ice cream release mechanism is dated "Pat. May 3, 1878," and is marked "NO. 5." The author doesn't consider this an advertising item but felt this was a very rare item and this was a good section to include it. *Note:* Some items are one-of-a-kind and it is difficult to find a section in which to place them.
3. Plate, cream and green on heavy metal base, advertises American Radiator Company Convention, Buffalo, N.Y., 1937.
4. Bowl, solid blue with black trim, advertises "Cream City Seamless Ware," made by Geuder Paeschke and Frey Company, Milwaukee, Wisconsin, showing items made for dairy use.
5. Mug, advertises the World's Fair, St. Louis 1904, Louisiana Purchase Exposition. Marked "Elite Austria," Norvell Shapleigh Hardware, St. Louis, Mo. Copyright 1903 by Rothschild, Meyers and Co.

Plate 1, Row 3:

1. Ashtray, red, advertises "Polar Ware" made by the Polar Ware Company, Sheboygan, Wisconsin, circa 1928.
2. Ashtray, advertises the 1937 Coronation of King George VI. Also advertises "Moffat."
3. Tray-type ashtray, brown shaded, advertises Samuel Stamping and Enameling Co. Suburban America's Finest Built-In Range.
4. Mug, blue shaded, advertises "Buy Enameled Ware of U.S. Shapleigh Hardware Co., St. Louis.
5. Ashtray, white with black trim, decorated with a polar bear, advertises "Polar Ware."

Plate 2, Row 1:

1. 50th Anniversary Catalog issued in 1939 by Lisk Manufacturing Co., Canandaigua, N.Y., advertising their "Flintstone Ivory Enameled Ware" with green trim. *Note:* This is popularly referred to by today's collectors as "Cream and Green."
2. Box of Mendets, three assorted sizes with wrench plus instruction sheet stating how 10¢ saves $10.00. Made by Collette Mfg. Co., Amsterdam, N.Y. Used to repair different size holes in all cooking utensils.
3. 1919 ad for the famous Lisk Roaster. The author knows of 4 different sizes including the salesman sample.

Plate 2, Row 2:

1. Card of Mendets, 5 pieces for the repair of holes in cooking utensils.
2. Pamphlet cookbook, advertises Lisk Products and a number of recipes. Back page shows a cut-away of a Lisk Percolator with aluminum percolating device held in place by the corrugated bottom of the pot. Front of book shows the Lisk three-piece roaster. Inside of book shows the roaster being used as a canner with a wire rack that could be bought separately. *Note:* There is a difference in describing a catlog cookbook from just a catalog or cookbook category (e.g. a catalog shows just the product to be sold, whereas the catalog cookbook shows the product to be sold along with recipes). Therefore, the author feels it should be classified as a catalog cookbook. A third catalog is a pamphlet cookbook advertising only several items along with a number of recipes.
3. Ad for Hibbard Spencer Bartlett & Co., Chicago, advertising "Chrysolite, Nu-Blu, and Revonoc."
4. Trade card advertising "Columbian Ware," shows the Eagle trademark. Distributor O.S. Levy, San Francisco, Cal.
5. New Perfection advertising pamphlet showing the New Perfection Broiler and how it was made to fit on the Perfection Oil Stove.

Plate 2, Row 3:

1. 1925 magazine ad for Nesco Oil Cook Stoves with blue chimneys. Also advertised cooking utensils in Nesco Royal Granite Ware - "Deep Blue and Gray and beautifully mottled." National Enameling and Stamping Co. Inc., Milwaukee, Wis.
2. Kalamazoo Stove ad for Kitchen Enamel Ranges in 5 colors, "As easy to clean as a china dish."
3. Magazine ad for "Vollrath Ware." This ad puts great emphasis on the wide range of subtle, pastel-like colors that go with any decorating schemes.

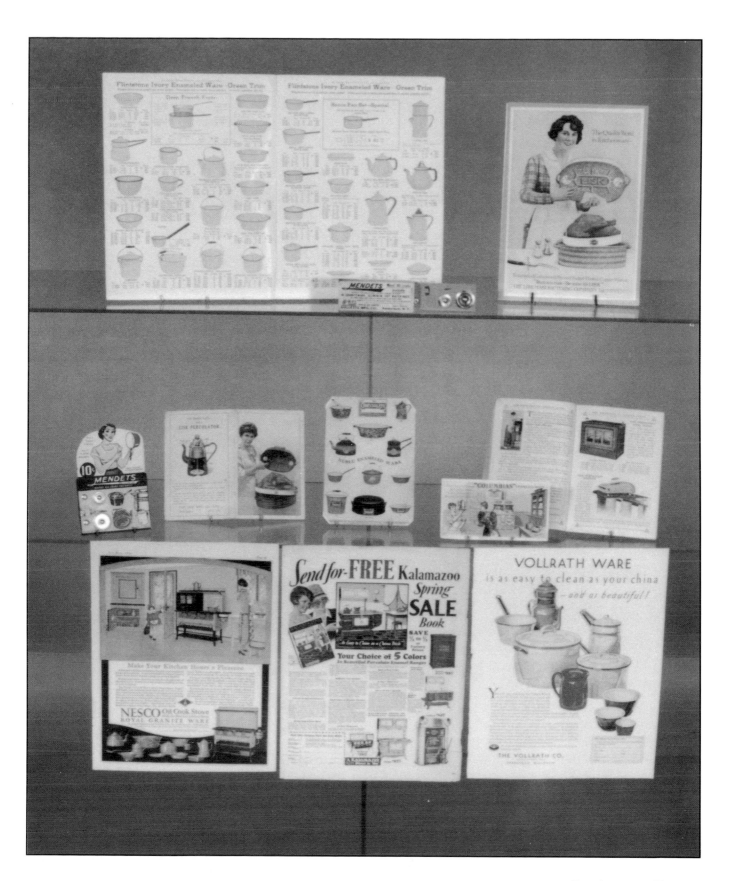

Plate 3, Row 1:

1. Oval advertising tray, gray with black lettering, two ears on each end of the back for hanging. It was hung on the wall in the store over a display of "Gray Agate" granite war to advertise the product and its name.

Plate 3, Row 2:

1. Oval sign, advertising on front and back. There are two holes on the outer rim so the sign can be hung and seen from both sides, either in the store or outside in front of the store.
2. Oval sign, advertising on front and back. It swings freely so advertising can be seen on both sides, either in the store or outside the store.

Section 13

Pitcher and Bowl Sets, Soap Dishes, Body Pitchers, Bed Pans, Chamber Pots, Toothbrush Holders, Water Pails, Water Carriers, Chamber Pails, Slop Buckets

Plate 1:

10-piece pticher and bowl set including covers, solid blue decorated with gold trim, only the small pitcher is marked No. 328. From left to right, Top row: mug, covered toothbrush holder with perforated top, large squatty-shaped pitcher, large wash bowl, small squattyt-shaped water pitcher which holds drinking water, covered soap dish. Bottom row: slop bucket with odorless cover. Valve center of the cover tapers down to a hole in the middle that has a flip-type valve. When the slop is poured in the large cover, it releases the center flip valve to open position. When all the slop is emptied, the valve flips closed again preventing odors to escape. The slop bucket should have a wooden handle that fits over the side ears and is wrapped with a cane material. *Note:* This is extremely rare as a set.

Plate 2, Row 1:

1. Squatty pitcher and bowl, blue and white with black trim and gold bands, medium mottled.

Plate 2, Row 2:

1. Squatty pitcher and bowl, red with black trim and handle.
2. Pitcher and bowl, white with black trim, labeled "Mi-Lady-Ware," "Enamelware For Health."

Plate 2, Row 3:

1. Pitcher and bowl, white with cobalt blue trim.
2. Squatty pitcher and bowl, white decorated with light lavender geometric design trimmed in gold. Note the different shaped handles on all the pitchers.

195

Plate 3, Row 1:

1. Hanging soap dish, solid blue, fluted bottom.
2. Body pitcher, pink, green and white with pink handle and trim, large swirl, "End of Day." *Note:* These are called Body Pitchers because of their unusually tall shape. They were usually used for bathing to pour rinse water over the body.
3. Body pitcher, white and orange checkered with orange trim and handle, checkered pattern.
4. Hanging soap dish, gray large mottled.

Plate 3, Row 2:

1. Water pail, small size, blue and white with black trim, large swirl, wooden bail.
2. Hanging soap dish, "old red and white," checkered pattern.
3. Pitcher and bowl, brown and white with black trim, large swirl.

Plate 3, Row 3:

1. Water pail, small size, deep violet shading to a lighter violet, "Thistle Ware."
2. Pitcher with ice lip, gray medium mottled. *Note:* Designed so that the curved top part of the lip holds back the ice while the liquid is being poured.
3. Water pail, blue and white with black trim, large swirl, wooden bail, "Columbian Ware."

Plate 4, Row 1:

1. Bed pan, white top, blue and white bottom with cobalt blue trim, fine mottled.
2. Chamber pot, cobalt blue with white lettering. *Note:* This could be a one-of-a-kind novelty. Perhaps someone at the factory made this for a joke.
3. Hanging soap dish, light blue and white with white insert, holds three toothbrushes, fine mottled.

Plate 4, Row 2:

1. Covered toothbrush holder, white with light blue veining, perforated top, large mottled.
2. Hanging soap dish, aqua green and white, large swirl.
3. Child's potty, cobalt blue and white with black trim and handle, large swirl.
4. Shell-shaped soap dish, gray large mottled.
5. Open toothbrush holder, blue and white with black trim, medium swirl. *Note:* On the bottom, there are two raised sections for the toothbrush to lay on, some have three raised sections. Marked "Made in Yugoslavia."

Plate 4, Row 3:

1. Hanging soap dish, light blue and white, large swirl.
2. Hanging soap dish, cobalt blue and white, medium swirl.
3. Covered toothbrush holder, old red and white, large swirl, perforated cover, marked "MINCHIN. MR. R," in a double circle, "MARMORE."
4. Chamber pot, blue and white with black trim, large swirl.

Plate 4, Row 4:

1. Hanging soap dish, brown and white, large mottled, "Onyx Ware."
2. Large covered chamber pot, cobalt blue and white with black trim, large swirl.
3. Bathtub-style soap dish, gray medium mottled, has a rolled-over back that fits over the top rim of the old bathtubs. Also has two shell-shaped feet that fit against the side of the tub.
4. Hanging soap dish, dark green and white, large swirl, "Chrysolite."

Section 13, Plate 4

199

Plate 5, Row 1:

1. Water pail, blue and white with black trim, large swirl, wooden bail.
2. Oval-shaped water carrier, blue and white, large mottled, 2-piece fancy embossed hinged cover. *Note:* This was used for carrying water. When carrying hot water, the cover helped to keep the water hot.

Plate 5, Row 2:

1. Water pail, dark green and white with black trim, large swirl, "Chrysolite."
2. Oval-shaped water carrier, white, 2-piece hinged cover. *Note:* This could be a child's size.
3. Water pail, light blue and white with black trim, large swirl, wooden bail.

Plate 5, Row 3:

1. Water pail, green and white with black trim, large swirl, wooden bail, "Emerald Ware."
2. Large water pail, cobalt blue and white with black trim, large swirl.

Plate 6, Row 1:

1. Large water carrier, dark green and white with black trim, seamed body, pouring lip, bottom tipping handle and wooden bail, large swirl, "Chrysolite." Shown in gray in the 1800's Matthai-Ingram Co. Catalogue.
2. Water pail, green and white with green trim, medium mottled, black bail, marked "Elite."

Plate 6, Row 2:

1. Water pail, brown shading to a lighter brown, black trim, wooden bail.
2. Small pail, light gray and white, fine mottled, wire bail and ears. *Note:* The author believes this was meant to be a child's sand pail.
3. Water pail, shaded blue, "Bluebelle Ware."

Plate 6, Row 3:

1. Small water pail, blue and white with black trim, large mottled, wooden bail.
2. Water carrier, gray medium mottled. Shown in Matthai-Ingram Co. 1800's Cat logue as part of a 3-piece toilet set. The other pieces are an oval-handled foot tub and a covered slop jar.

203

Plate 7, Row 1:

1. Chamber pail, white with blue mottling, wooden bail, matching cover fits over the top, large mottling. *Note:* Chamber pails were used for toilet purposes. The small pots were also emptied into them. They were then emptied and cleaned for everyday use.
2. Hanging tumbler holder, solid green.
3. Chamber pail, blue and white with black trim, large swirl, wooden bail.

Plate 7, Row 2:

1. Chamber pail, blue and white with black trim, large swirl, matching cover, "Columbian Ware."
2. Hanging toothbrush holder, white, holds 5 toothbrushes.
3. Hanging soap or sponge dish, solid white.
4. Chamber pail, dark lavender shaded, wooden bail.

Plate 7, Row 3:

1. Slop blucket, white with dark blue edges, decorated with grapes and leaves, odorless, tapered cover with flip-center insert, wooden wrapped handle.
2. Hanging soap dish, white, top section holds a toothbrush on each side, center top section holds a sponge or cloth and bottom section with insert holds soap.
3. Slop bucket, matching cover, pink, green, and white, large mottled, "End of Day," wooden bail. *Note:* Slop buckets were usually used for waste water and kitchen refuse.

Section 14

Dippers, Wash Basins, Pitchers, Water Coolers, Weather Vane, Water Heater

Plate 1, Row 1:

1. Windsor dipper, blue and white with black trim and hollow handle, large swirl.
2. Shaving basin, light gray and white with black trim, fine mottled. *Note:* Brush or soap holder attached inside. Has a ring applied on outer rim for hanging.
3. Windsor dipper, green and white with black trim and hollow handle, large swirl, "Emerald Ware."

Plate 1, Row 2:

1. Large wash basin with eyelet, green and white with black trim, large swirl, "Emerald Ware."
2. Windsor dipper, cobalt blue and white with black trim, medium swirl, hollow handle.
3. Large wash basin with eyelet, blue and white with black trim, large swirl.

Plate 1, Row 3:

1. Flared dipper, blue and white inside and outside, blue trim, large mottled.
2. Medium wash basin with eyelet, brown and white, Relish pattern.
3. Flat hook-handled dipper, cobalt blue and white with black trim, gray inside, large swirl.
4. Medium wash basin, dark plum color with gray and white mottling, medium swirl "End of Day."
5. Flat handled dipper with eyelet, blue and white with black trim and handle, large swirl.

Plate 2, Row 1:

1. Windsor dipper with eyelet, cobalt blue and white with black trim, large swirl, hollow handle.
2. Large wash basin with eyelet, cobalt blue and white with tiny green flecks, large mottled, "End of Day."
3. Flared dipper with eyelet, bluish gray and white inside and outside, large mottled, hollow handle.

Plate 2, Row 2:

1. Small wash basin with eyelet, light blue and white, medium swirl.
2. Wash basin with eyelet, white, decorated with gold bands inside and outside, black trim, very heavyweight. Labeled "Lisk's Four-Coated Enameled Steel Ware, Warranted No. 2," The Lisk Manufacturing Co. Limited.
3. Wash basin with eyelet, gray large mottled, labeled "Columbian Ware."

Plate 2, Row 3:

1. Deep wash basin with eyelet, dark green and white with black trim, large swirl, "Chrysolite."
2. Wash basin, light blue and white, large swirl.
3. Small wash basin with eyelet, brown and white with black trim, large swirl.

Plate 2, Row 4:

1. Windsor dipper with eyelet, blue and white with black trim, large swirl, hollow handle.
2. Windsor dipper, blue and white with black hollow handle, large swirl.

Plate 3, Row 1:

1. Flat hook-handled dipper, cobalt blue and white with black trim, large swirl.
2. Shallow wash basin with eyelet, cobalt blue and white with black trim, large swirl.
3. Dipper, gray medium mottled, hollow handle applied with a small lip-type bracket to dipper.
4. Wash basin with eyelet, blue and white with black trim, large swirl.
5. Dipper, cup shape, blue and white, large swirl, flat black handle with hook and eyelet, "Columbian Ware."

Plate 3, Row 2:

1. Large flared dipper, green and white with black trim, large swirl, "Emerald Ware."
2. Large wash basin with eyelet, "old red and white," white inside, black trim, large swirl.
3. Dipper, gray agate extra strong dipper, riveted hook handle. Advertised in the La Lance and Grosjean Mfg. Co. Catalog 1884.

Plate 3, Row 3:

1. Large wash basin with eyelet, gray large mottled.
2. Large wash basin, lavender blue and white, large swirl.

Plate 4, Row 1:

1. Wash basin with eyelet, dark blue and white, large swirl.
2. Flat hook-handled dipper, cobalt blue and white with black trim, medium mottled.
3. Wash basin with eyelet, dark green and white with black trim, large swirl, "Chrysolite."

Plate 4, Row 2:

1. Flared dipper, light green and white with dark brown hollow handle and trim, large mottled.
2. Large wash basin with eyelet, pink and white, white inside, pink trim, large swirl.
3. Flat hook-handled dipper, brown and white with black trim, white inside, large swirl.

Plate 4, Row 3:

1. Footed wash basin with eyelet, gray mottled. *Note:* Foot has been applied to wash basin with four rivets.
2. Flared dipper, cobalt blue and white, white inside, black hollow handle and trim, large swirl.
3. Wash basin with eyelet, lavender and white, white inside, large swirl.

213

Plate 5, Row 1:

1. Flared flat-handled dipper, cobalt blue and white, white inside. *Note:* Almost no mottling.
2. Flat-handled dipper, dark green and white with black trim, large mottled, "Chrysolite."
3. Wash basin with eyelet, cobalt blue and white with black trim, large swirl.
4. Flat hook-handled dipper, blue and white with flat black handle and trim, large swirl.
5. Flat handled dipper, rounded bottom, green and white with black handle and trim, large mottled.

Plate 5, Row 2:

1. Wash basin with eyelet, brown and white inside and outside, black trim, large mottled, "Onyx Ware."
2. Large wash basin with eyelet, blue and white with black trim, large swirl.
3. Child's wash basin with eyelet, light blue and white with light blue trim, white inside, large mottled, marked "Elite Austria 24."

Plate 5, Row 3:

1. Wash basin with eyelet, light blue and white, large swirl.
2. Wash basin with eyelet, blue and white with black trim, large mottled.
3. Wash basin with eyelet, blue and white with light blue trim, white inside, medium mottled. Lion standing on coffee pot with two front paws, Germany, 713, "Paragon Ware."

Plate 5, Row 4:

1. Flat hooked-handled dipper, deep, rounded bottom, blue and white inside and outside, black trim and handle, large swirl.
2. Flared dipper, green and white with brown hollow handle and trim, large swirl.

Plate 6, Row 1:

1. Water pitcher, seamless, blue and white wavey mottling, triple coated, black trim and handle.
2. Water pitcher, seamless, "old red and white" with dark blue trim, white inside, large swirl, triple coated, heavyweight.
3. Water pitcher, seamless, blue and white, white inside, black weld handle and trim, large swirl, "Columbian Ware."

Plate 6, Row 2:

1. Water pitcher, squatty shape, seamless, green and white with green trim, medium mottled, marked "Elite Austria."
2. Milk pitcher, seamless, green and white with black rolled handle and trim, large mottled.
3. Milk pitcher, cobalt blue and white with black handle and trim, medium mottled.
4. Water pitcher, seamless, dark green and white with dark blue trim, large swirl, "Chrysolite."

Plate 6, Row 3:

1. Convex water pitcher, blue and white, large swirl.
2. Milk pitcher, seamless, brown with tiny white specks, fine mottled, marked "Germany." *Note:* An unusually high lip.
3. Cloverleaf convex pitcher, green and white, Relish pattern. *Note:* This gets its name because of the cloverleaf-shaped top.

Plate 6, Row 4:

1. Water pitcher, blue and white inside and outside, black handle and trim, large swirl.
2. Water pitcher, seamless, dark green and white, large swirl, black trim. It is a darker green than the Emerald Ware.
3. Water pitcher, blue and white, large swirl, black handle and trim.

Plate 7, Row 1:

1. Water pitcher, brown and white with dark blue trim, Relish pattern.
2 Water pitcher, cobalt blue and white with cobalt blue trim, medium mottled, marked "Elite Austria."
3. Water pitcher, green and white with dark blue handle and trim, large swirl, "Emerald Ware."

Plate 7, Row 2:

1. Water pitcher, seamless, green and white with dark blue handle and trim, large swirl, "Emerald Ware."
2. Water pitcher, blue and white with black handle and trim, large swirl.
3. Water pitcher, dark green and white with black handle and trim, large swirl, "Chrysolite."
4. Water pitcher, seamless, blue and white with black handle and trim, large swirl, "Columbian Ware."

Plate 7, Row 3:

1. Water pitcher, cobalt blue and white with black trim, large swirl.
2. Pump or bellboy pitcher, cobalt blue. This type was also used at the water pump. *Note:* It has a top wooden bail to fit over the pump neck and also for carrying water plus a bottom tipping handle.
3. Cloverleaf convex pitcher, cobalt blue.
4. Water pitcher, cobalt blue and white with black handle and trim, large swirl.

Plate 7, Row 4:

1. Water pitcher, blue and white with blue trim, medium mottled.
2. Water pitcher, seamless, blue and white with light blue trim, fine mottled.
3. Water pitcher, blue and white with black trim, fine mottled.
4. Milk pitcher, blue and white with black handle and trim, fine mottled.

Plate 8, Row 1:

1. Body pitcher, seamed, reverse cobalt blue and white, heavy white enameling, cobalt blue handle and trim, large mottled, "Snow on the Mountain."
2. Body pitcher, seamed, blue and white with black trim, large swirl.

Plate 8, Row 2:

1. Water pitcher, seamless, brown, cobalt blue, and white with dark blue trim, gray with tiny blue flecks inside, large swirl, "End of Day."
2. Water pitcher, light green, white, and pink with black handlle and trim, medium swirl, "End of Day."
3. Water pitcher, blue, white, and light gray with black handle and trim, large swirl, "End of Day."

Plate 8, Row 3:

1. Water pitcher, deep sea green shading to a moss green. "Shamrock Ware" distributed by Norvell Shapleigh Hardware Co., St. Louis, sole distributor.
2. Milk pitcher, shaded blue with blue handle and trim. "Bluebelle Ware," made in U.S.A., distributed by Norvell Shapleigh Hardware Co.
3. Water pitcher, brown shaded with black handle and trim.

Plate 9, Row 1:

1. Water pitcher, seamless, brilliant lavender blue shading to a lighter lavender blue, black handle and trim.
2. Water pitcher, seamless, white, decorated with cobalt blue floral and leaf design trimmed in cobalt blue.
3. Water pitcher, cobalt blue and white with black handle and trim, large swirl.

Plate 9, Row 2:

1. Water pitcher, dark green and white with dark blue trim, large swirl.
2. Footed water pitcher, seamed, gray medium mottled, riveted rolled handle.
3. Water pitcher, aqua green and white with cobalt blue trim, large swirl.

Plate 3, Row 3:

1. Water pitcher, shaded blue with black handle and trim, "Bluebelle Ware," Norvell Shapleigh Hardware Co., St. Louis.
2. Water pitcher, green and white with green trim, medium mottled, marked "Elite Austria."
3. Water pitcher, green shaded with black handle and trim.

Plate 10, Row 1:

1. Water pitcher, seamless, "old red and white" with dark blue handle and trim, white inside, large swirl, heavyweight.
2. Water pitcher, green and white with blue handle and trim, large swirl, "Emerald Ware."
3. Water pitcher, brown and white with black trim, large swirl.
4. Water pitcher, lavender blue and white with black trim, large swirl.

Plate 10, Row 2:

1. Convex agate water pitcher, gray large mottled, fancy metal handle, rivets applied to inside of pitcher to hold the handle. Shown in La Lance and Grosjean Mfg. Co. Catalog 1884.
2. Milk pitcher, weld handle, brown and white with black handle and trim, medium mottled, "Onyx Ware."
3. Milk pitcher, weld handle, white, blue decorated, marked in a diamond "Made in U.S.A. Pat Nesco ?–13–26 (month unreadable) Bonny Blue Ware."
4. Convex agate water pitcher, gray medium mottled, fancy metal handle, larger than No. 1 on this row.
5. Milk pitcher, dark blue and white with black handle and trim, large swirl.

Plate 10, Row 3:

1. Water pitcher, blue and white with black handle and trim, large swirl.
2. Milk pitcher, light green and white with dark blue trim, Relish pattern.
3. Water pitcher, blue and white with black handle and trim, large swirl.
4. Milk pitcher, light blue and white with black handle and trim, medium mottled.
5. Water pitcher, blue and white with black handle and trim, large swirl.

Plate 10, Row 4:

1. Water pitcher, blue and white with black handle and trim, large swirl.
2. Water pitcher, seamless, no pouring lip, gray large mottled.
3. Water pitcher, blue with fine white specks, black handle and trim.
4. Water pitcher, weld handle, gray large mottled, "Nesco Ware."

Plate 11, Row 1:

1. Water pitcher, white, marked L. & G. Mfg. Co.
2. Collar base water pitcher, blue and white decorated with gold bands, trimmed in black, white inside, medium mottled.
3. Water pitcher, blue and white with black handle and trim, medium mottled. Note how high the handle is on the pitcher.

Plate 11, Row 2:

1. Water pitcher, cobalt blue and white with black handle and trim, medium swirl.
2. Water pitcher, dark green and white with blue handle and trim, large swirl, "Chrysolite."
3. Water pitcher, brown and white with black handle and trim, large swirl.

Plate 11, Row 3:

1. Water pitcher, blue and white with black handle and trim, large swirl.
2. Water pticher, solid blue with black handle and trim, marked with a teakettle emblem that has an "S" in the middle and three lines under the teakettle, made in Poland 15.
3. Water pitcher, blue and white with black handle and trim, large swirl.

Plate 12, Row 1:

1. Water cooler with matching granite cover, seamless, two sections, light blue and white, large swirl, wooden bail handle for lifting. *Note:* Top section lifts off and has a stone-type filter that fits on a collar around the bottom inside edge. The water is filtered through this into the bottom section supposedly purifying it for use. The bottom section has two side handles and a brass spigot for pouring. "Lava Ware," Cleveland Stamping and Tool Co., Cleveland, Ohio.
2. Water cooler with matching cover, seamless, two sections, blue, gray, and white, large swirl, wooden bail and brass spigot, "Lava Ware."

Plate 12, Row 2:

1. Rooster weather vane, solid gray, should have a directional base showing N.E.S.W.
2. Cylinder-shaped water cooler, seamed, cobalt blue and white, white inside and trim, large mottled, white full length insert that has a hole in the bottom where a charcoal filter fits, for supposedly purifying the water, cover knob marked "LUTECE 15 RUE DES IMMEUBLES INDUSTRIELS PARIS."
3. Cylinder-shaped gas water heater, light gray, Humphrey Tank Heater, Humphrey Co., Division of Kalamazoo. Pat. March 18, 1913.

229

Section 15

Lavabo and Basin Sets, Douche Set

In the 1884 La Lance & Grosjean Catalog, these were advertised as Toilet Fountains with Basins. Today's collectors call them lavabo sets but this could be the foreign name given to them. They also come in many colors and shapes. The tank part with the brass dolphin-shaped spigot held the water. The basin was used to hold water for washing. It serves the same purpose as our pitcher and bowl sets. All are considered rare. The douche set was also advertised with 7' of rubber tubing and three nozzles. The gray agate ones are American made whereas some of the colored ones are foreign made.

Plate 1:

Lavabo and basin, white, maroon, gray, blue, with black trim, large swirl, "End of Day, dolphin-shaped brass spigot.

Plate 2:

1. Lavabo and basin, blue and white with black trim, large swirl, dolphin-shaped brass spigot.
2. Lavabo and basin, blue and white with blue trim, large swirl, dolphin-shaped brass spigot.

Plate 3:

1. Lavabo and basin, green, gray, and white, large swirl, dolphin-shaped brass spigot, "End of Day."
2. Lavabo and basin, pink decorated with gold bands, rounded ribbed-shaped tank, brass spigot. Note how differently all the spigots are applied and their different shapes.

Plate 4:

1. Douche, white and blue medium mottled, brass dolphin-shaped spigot. It's interesting to note that in the La Lance & Grosjean 1884 Cookbook, the gray agate douche sets are the same size as the agate toilet fountain sets. Both sets were the same price - $5.75 each. *Note:* There is fancy scroll work on the front of the tank. The gray agate ones are embossed agate in the fancy scroll work. They each held eight quarts.
2. Lavabo and basin, white, red, and blue, with black trim, brass dolphin-shaped spigot, large swirl, "End of Day."

Section 15, Plate 1

Section 15, Plate 2

Section 15, Plate 3

Section 15, Plate 4

231

Section 16

Funnels, Fruit Jar Fillers, and Percolator Funnels

Plate 1, Row 1:

1. Funnel, "old red and white inside and outside," red tirm, large mottled, "Snow on the Mountain."
2. Funnel, dark cobalt blue and white, with black trim and handle, white inside, large swirl, Enterprise Enamel Co, "Azurelite," Bellaire, Ohio.
3. Large squatty-shaped funnel, cobalt blue and white, white inside with black trim, large swirl.
4. Funnel, white trimmed in light blue, marked "Sweden."
5. Funnel, light blue and white inside and outside, large mottled, "Snow on the Mountain."

Plate 1, Row 2:

1. Squatty-shaped funnel with pierced hanging ear, gray.
2. Squatty-shaped funnel, blue and white, white inside with black trim and handle, large swirl, "Columbian Ware."
3. Funnel, blue with white specks, white inside, fine mottled, marked "Elite Austria."
4. Funnel Elliptical, gray large mottled, rivited strap handle. *Note:* The author has seen at least 2 different shapes - in this one, only the spout part of the funnel is fluted.
5. Large squatty-shaped funnel, blue and white with black trim, fine mottled.
6. Squatty-shaped funnel, white, with black trim.

Plate 1, Row 3:

1. Large squatty-shaped funnel, blue and white with black trim and handle, large swirl. Note the short spout.
2. Funnel, gray, seamed body with riveted hanging ear.
3. Squatty-shaped funnel, gray, blue, and white inside and outside, black trim and handle, "Scotch Granite Acid Proof" made by U.S. Stamping Co., Moundsville, West Virginia.
4. Large squatty-shaped funnel, blue and white outside, white inside, black trim and handle, large swirl.

Section 16, Plate 1

233

Plate 2, Row 1:

1. Fruit jar filler, blue and white inside and outside, large mottled. *Note:* This was placed in the opening of the canning jar when filling the jar with food or liquids. It kept the food or liquids from spilling over the outside of the jar.
2. Fruit jar filler, gray large mottled.
3. Large fruit jar filler, cobalt blue and white inside and outside, black trim and handle, large swirl.
4. Fruit jar filler, gray large mottled.
5. Fruit jar filler, aqua green and white inside and outside, cobalt blue trim and handle, large mottled. *Note:* There is an uneven cobalt blue trim on the top edge.

Plate 2, Row 2:

1. Percolator funnel, solid light blue with white inside, perforated bottom section. *Note:* The bottom part of the cone-shaped tip is pierced and flat. The others come to a point. Marked "G.B.M."
2. Large percolator funnel, reverse cobalt blue and white large mottled, "Snow on the Mountain."
3. Percolator funnel, gray medium mottled, marked "L. & G. Mfg. Co."

Plate 2, Row 3:

1. Fruit jar filler, blue and white with cobalt blue trim, fine mottled.
2. Fruit jar filler, cobalt blue and white inside and outside, black trim and handle, medium mottled.
3. Fruit jar filler, blue and white medium mottled.
4. Fruit jar filler, blue, cobalt blue, and white, with cobalt blue trim, medium mottled, "End of Day," "Granite Steel Ware," Crown Industries, Binghamton, N.Y.

Plate 2, Row 4:

1. Fruit jar filler, gray large mottled, riveted strap handle.
2. Fruit jar filler, blue and white with black trim and handle, white inside, large swirl.
3. Fruit jar filler, white and green with green trim, large mottled, marked "Elite."
4. Fruit jar filler, gray large mottled.

Note the different lengths of all the necks.

Plate 3, Row 1:

1. Funnel, dark green and white, white inside, fine mottled, marked "Elite."
2. Funnel, cobalt blue and white, white inside, black trim, large swirl.
3. Squatty-shaped funnel, brown and white, white inside with black trim, large swirl.

Plate 3, Row 2:

1. Funnel, gray medium mottled, pierced ear for hanging, labeled "PRIMO Enameled Nickeled Steel Ware No. 02 Savory Incorporated, Newark, N.J., New York and Buffalo."
2. Funnel, "old red and white" inside and outside, black trim and handle, large swirl. Note the trace of black mixed in the red.
3. Elliptical funnel, gray large mottled. *Note:* This is the other elliptical-shaped funnel. The fluting goes higher up on the body of the funnel instead of fluting just on the spout.
4. Squatty-shaped funnel, green and white, white inside, dark blue trim, large mottled, "Emerald Ware." Note the short spout.

Plate 3, Row 3:

1. Small squatty-shaped funnel, cobalt blue and white, white inside, black trim and handle, large swirl.
2. Squatty-shaped funnel, brown shading to a lighter brown, white inside.
3. Large funnel, gray large mottled, weld handle, seamed. Labeled "Nesco Royal Granite Enameled Ware, National Enameling and Stamping Co. Inc." Nesco Ware is everywhere. Trademark Registered U.S. Patent Office, Made in U.S.A.
4. Squatty-shaped funnel, cobalt blue and white, white inside, black trim and handle, large swirl.
5. Small funnel, gray mottled, riveted ear for hanging, seamed. Marked with the same mark twice, "Extra Agate Nickel Steel Ware, L. & G. Mfg. Co."

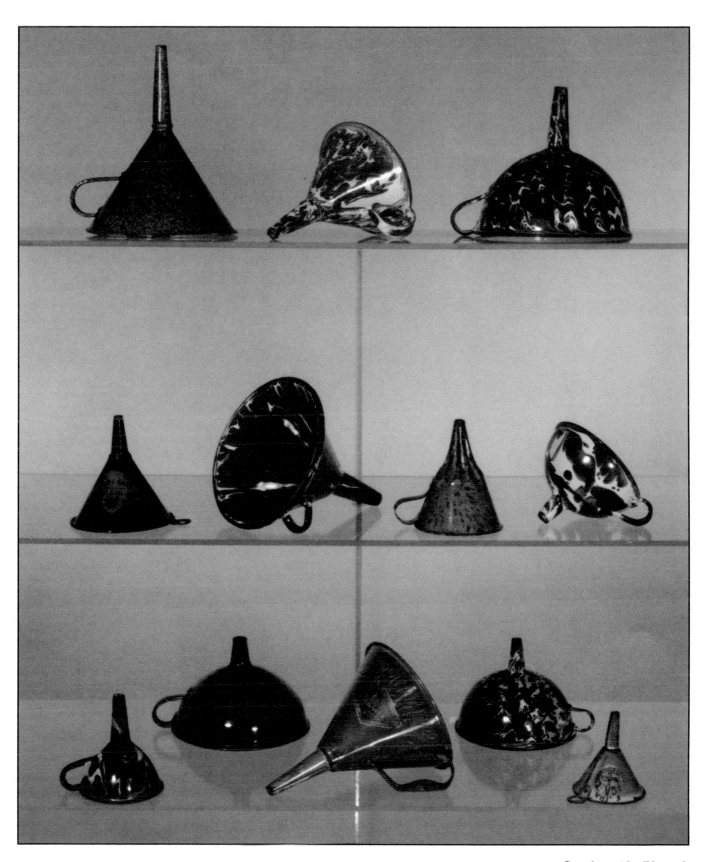

Section 17

Fry Pans, Two-Handled Egg Plates, Griddles and Stew Pans

Plate 1, Row 1:

1. Fry pan, unusual green and white, white inside, large swirl.
2. Fry pan, red and white inside and outside, black trim and handle, large swirl, handle is applied by a screw, circa 1970's, lightweight.
3. Fry pan, unusual green and white, white inside, black trim and handle, large swirl.

Plate 1, Row 2:

1. Fry pan, cast iron, heavy, lavender blue, gray, and white, white inside, large swirl, "End of Day." *Note:* The flat-shaped handle has been rolled back for more support and grip.
2. Fry pan, cast iron, heavy, dark grayish lavender and white, white inside, large swirl, "Lava Ware," Cleveland Stamping and Tool Company, Cleveland, Ohio.
3. Fry pan, cast iron, heavy, cobalt blue and white, white inside, large swirl.

Plate 1, Row 3:

1. Small fry pan, blue and white, white inside, black trim and handle, large swirl.
2. Fry pan, cast iron, heavy, green shadiing to cream, white inside, black handle.
3. Small fry pan, white with unusual blue color inside and outside, black trim and handle, medium swirl.

Plate 2, Row 1:

1. Fry pan, cast iron, heavy, grayish lavender and white, white inside, large swirl, "Lava Ware."
2. Fry pan, cast iron, cobalt blue and white, large swirl.
3. Fry pan, cast iron, light blue and white, white inside, large swirl, "Lava Ware."

Plate 2, Row 2:

1. Fry pan, white with cobalt blue trim, black handle, marked "KER SWEDEN 16CM." Distributed by Markt and Hammacher Company, N.Y., N.Y.
2. Fry pan, blue and white, white inside, black handle and trim, large swirl.
3. Fry pan, blue and white, white inside, black handle and trim, large mottled.
4. Fry pan, gray with tiny white flecks, "Speckled Ware." Advertises "Our 100th Year Granite City Steel 1878-1978." "39" is marked on the cold handle, advertising cross collect ible. *Note:* Cold handle is a handle usually constructed with an additional handle crimped over top of original handle making it cooler to grip.

Plate 2, Row 3:

1. Fry pan, dark green and white, white inside, black trim and handle, large swirl, "Chrysolite."
2. Fry pan, unusually large, light blue and white, white inside, black handle, large swirl.
3. Fry pan, lavender blue and white, white inside, black trim and handle, large swirl.

Plate 3, Row 1:

1. Fry pan, red and white inside and outside, large swirl, black trim and handle, handle is applied by screw, lightweight, circa 1970's. *Note:* These came in a set of three that stacked into each other.
2. Fry pan, blue and white, white inside, black trim and handle, large swirl.
3. Fry pan, cobalt blue and white, white, inside, medium mottled, marked "Elite Austria."

Plate 3, Row 2:

1. Fry pan, brown and white, white inside, black handle, large swirl.
2. Small fry pan, gray large mottled, rolled edge and handle, 5¾" diameter, 1¼" deep.
3. Fry pan, cobalt blue and white, white inside, black handle, large swirl.
4. Egg dish, back handle, blue and white, white inside, black handle and trim, large mottled, 4⅞" diameter, 1¼" deep. Advertised in Coonley Manufacturing Co. Catalog, April 9, 1915.
5. Fry pan, green and white, white inside, black trim and handle, large swirl, "Emerald Ware."

Plate 3, Row 3:

1. Fry pan, cobalt blue and white, white inside, black cold handle, large mottled.
2. Fry pan, light blue and white, white inside, black cold handle, large swirl. "National" embossed on handle, National Enameling and Stamping Company.
3. Fry pan, cobalt blue and white, white inside, black handle, large swirl.

Plate 4, Row 1:

1. Oval griddle, gray large mottled, riveted handle, L. & G. Mfg. Co.
2. Two-handled egg plate or pan, side-pouring spout, white with blue veins, white inside, Chicken Wire pattern.
3. Two-handled egg plate or pan, dark blue and white with dark blue trim, white inside. *Note:* The small ones generally don't have pouring spouts, Relish pattern.
4. Two-handled egg plate or pan, "old red and white," white inside, red trim, large mottled, "Snow on the Mountain." Marked Saint–Servias Belgique."

Plate 4, Row 2:

1. Oval-handled pan, gray mottled, agate. "Keystone" advertised in La Lance & Grosjean Mfg. Co. Catalogue, March 1, 1884.
2. Two-handled egg plate or pan, shallow, cobalt blue and white, white inside, black handle and trim, large swirl.
3. Two ear-type handled egg plate or pan, solid blue outside, white inside. Marked "Libertas Prussia Germany" showing the head of an eagle.
4. Oblong griddle, gray large mottled. "Agate" shown in the La Lance & Grosjean Mfg. Co. Catalogue March 1, 1884. The section that has the four round indentations can be flipped over onto the flat side with the handle that is riveted on the top end of the griddle. The food can be kept warm on this section of the griddle while more is being cooked.

Plate 4, Row 3:

1. Fry pan, solid red, cream inside, circa 1940's. Marked "Griswold–107 and 200."
2. Egg fry pan, gray medium mottled, four eyes, "Agate." Advertised in La Lance & Grosjean Mfg. Co. Catalogue March 1, 1884.
3. Two-handled egg plate or pan, blue and white, white inside, large swirl.

Plate 5, Row 1:

1. Shallow stew pan, cobalt blue and white, white inside, black trim and handle, large mottled. *Note:* Most fry pans have pouring lips, stew pans usually don't. Instead, they have a collar-top rim. They can be shallow or deep. The old Matthai-Ingram Co. Catalog shows a good example in their Graystone Ware.
2. Deep stew pan, blue and white, white inside, black trim and handle, large swirl, "Columbian Ware."
3. Shallow stew pan, blue and white, white inside, black trim and handle, large mottled.

Plate 5, Row 2:

1. Shallow stew pan, blue and white, white inside, blue trim, medium mottled, marked "Elite Austria."
2. Shallow stew pan, cobalt blue and white, white inside, medium mottled, marked "Elite Austria."

Plate 5, Row 3:

1. Deep stew pan, light blue and white, white inside, black trim and handle, very unusual mottling.
2. Deep stew pan, green and white, white inside, black trim and handle, large mottled.
3. Deep stew pan, cobalt blue and white, white inside, black trim and handle, large swirl.

Plate 5, Row 4:

1. Deep stew pan, blue and white, white inside, black trim and handle, large mottled.
2. Shallow stew pan, brown and white inside and outside, black handle and trim, medium mottled, "Garnet Ware."

Section 18

Tea Steepers or Baby Food Cups, Tea Strainers, Teakettles

Tea Steepers or Baby Food Cups

In old advertisements, these are called tea steepers or baby food cups. The Matthai-Ingram Co. Catalogue advertises them in their Graystone Ware as baby food cups with either tin or enameled covers, enameled covers costing more. This particular catalogue advertises them in three sizes, 4⅝" x 2¾", 5⅛" x 3½" and 4⅜" x 2¼". *Note:* Tea steepers or baby food cups were used to steep small amounts of tea or warm the baby's milk or food. Today's collectors refer to them as tea steepers.

Tea Strainers

Tea strainers come with various shaped bottoms. They can be screen or different types of fancy or plain perforations.

Teakettles

Teakettles come in many shapes and sizes including deep and shallow pit bottoms. *Note:* Pit bottoms were made to fit into the exact lid openings on wood-burning stoves. Other teakettles also were made for kerosene stoves with a larger bottom covering the burner so it could heat faster conserving fuel. The flat bottom teakettles were advertised to fit any size stove. Different handles, such as wire handles called Alaska handles, did not burn like the wooden ones did. Norvell-Shapleigh Hardware Co., St. Louis advertised them as coiled wire cold grip handles.

Plate 1, Row 1:

1. Tea steeper or baby food cup, blue and white, black trim and handle, large swirl, riveted strap handle and spout, tin cover.
2. Tea steeper, gray with matching Granite cover, black wooden Acorn knob, medium mottled.
3. Tea strainer, blue and white inside and outside, screen bottom, large swirl.
4. Tea steeper, green and white with matching granite cover, dark blue trim and handle, large swirl, riveted spout and handle, "Emerald Ware."
5. Tea steeper, tin cover, deep violet shaded, black trim and handle, "Thistle Ware."

Plate 1, Row 2:

1. Tea steeper, tin cover, brown and white, white inside, dark blue trim, Relish pattern.
2. Tea steeper, blue and white, white inside, medium blue trim, large mottled, wooden knob, riveted handle and spout. *Note:* This one has a matching hinged granite cover.
3. Tea strainer, aqua green and white inside and outside, large swirl, screen bottom.
4. Tea strainer, solid blue, fancy perforated bottom, marked "B.W. Germany."
5. Tea steeper, matching granite cover, dark green and white, large swirl, dark blue trim and handle, "Chrysolite."
6. Tea steeper, matching granite cover, blue and white outside and inside, light blue trim, fine mottled, riveted spout and handle.

Plate 1, Row 3:

1. Tea steeper, cobalt blue and white, black handle and trim, large swirl.
2. Tea steeper, gray mottled.
3. Tea strainer, white with very light green veining inside and outside, fancy perforated bottom, marked "Elite Austria."
4. Tea strainer, gray, perforated bottom.
5. Tea steeper, blue and white, white inside, black trim, large swirl.
6. Tea steeper, gray large mottled with matching cover, riveted spout and handle, unusually small.

Plate 1, Row 4:

1. Tea strainer, white, screen insert.
2. Tea steeper, dark blue and white, wide riveted strap handle and spout, large swirl.
3. Tea strainer, solid green, fancy perforated bottom.
4. Tea strainer, white, fancy perforated bottom.
5. Tea steeper, blue and white, white inside, fine mottled.
6. Tea strainer, white with cobalt blue trim, perforated bottom.

Plate 2, Row 1:

1. Teakettle, deep pit bottom on cast iron, cover swings to the side, wire bail, brown and white, Relish pattern. *Note:* Pit bottom refers to the shape of the bottom of the tea kettle. It has an extended section that fits down into the lid opening on a woodburning stove. This was believed to heat the kettle faster.
2. Teakettle, deep pit bottom, matching granite lid and handle, gray and white, Relish pattern. This size was made to fit into the top of a single burner, table top, kerosene stove.
3. Teakettle, shallow pit bottom, matching granite lid, cobalt blue and white, medium mottled.

Plate 2, Row 2:

1. Teakettle, bell shaped, solid dark cobalt blue, white inside, matching granite cover and handle.
2. Teakettle, solid yellow, black trim and handle.
3. Teakettle, elongated squatty shape, solid light green.
4. Teakettle, solid light blue, white inside. Marked "Made in Yugoslavia 14." Emblem of two lions with front paws standing on a teakettle.

Plate 2, Row 3:

1. Teakettle, gray mottled, riveted ears, marked "Extra Agate Nickel Steel Ware, L. & G. Mfg. Co." *Note:* Each ear has an added lip on opposite sides so the wooden bail handle does not rest on the teakettle. This keeps handle cool and also from burning hands.
2. Teakettle, "old red," white, dark blue, yellow, and green in the veins, Chicken Wire pattern, "End of Day."
3. Teakettle, squatty shaped, green and white, white inside, black trim, large swirl, wooden bail and knob.
4. Teakettle, cobalt blue and white, black trim, large swirl.

Plate 2, Row 4:

1. Teakettle, blue and white shaded, wooden bail, "Bluebelle Ware."
2. Teakettle, deep sea green shading to a moss green, wire bail with Alaska handle, semi-seamless body with flat bottom, "Shamrock Ware."

Plate 3, Row 1:

1. Teakettle, blue and white, white inside, black trim, large swirl.
2. Teakettle, nickel-plated trim, advertised in Manning Bowman and Company catalog as a "Kioto" Mottled Table Kettle. Patented June 5, 1883, registered January 13, 1885. This kettle could be purchased with the nickel-plated stand and spirit lamp or it could be purchased separately. Referred to as Relish pattern by today's collectors.
3. Teakettle, blue and white, white inside, black trim, large swirl.

Plate 3, Row 2:

1. Teakettle, gray medium mottled, wooden bail. The original mark has been blotted out and then marked "PEERLESS."
2. Teakettle with teakettle insert, gray medium mottled. *Note:* The unusual shape of the wire bail handle accommodates the insert. The riveted ears each have a center notch on top for locking the wooden bail handle upright. The handle has to be pulled up to be released. Both ears have an added lip on each side to keep the handle from resting on the teakettle. The insert's original blue mark has been blotted out, but can still make out "Extra Agate Nickel Steel Ware, L. & G. Mfg. Co."
3. Teakettle, gray large mottled, unusual side seam, wooden bail.
4. Teakettle, gray large mottled, unusual side handle and straight spout.

Plate 3, Row 3:

1. Oil stove teakettle with straight spout, black and white, medium mottled, "Snow on the Mountain" effect. Designed for the oil stove, its spread-out bottom helped to conserve fuel and prevent the flames from blackening the teakettle sides.
2. Teakettle, cobalt blue and white, white inside, black trim and wooden bail, large swirl.
3. Oil stove teakettle, gray mottled, wooden bail and straight spout, "Nesco Ware."
4. Teakettle, light blue and white, large swirl, cover not original, black trim and handle.

Plate 3, Row 4:

1. Teakettle, green and white with green trim, fine mottled.
2. Teakettle, cobalt blue and white with black trim, medium mottled, marked "Elite."
3. Teakettle, cast iron, solid light gray, embossed on cover, "Wrought Iron Range Co., St. Louis, Mo., No. 8." These teakettles were given away as premiums wtih the purchase of a cooking range from this company. Advertising cross collectible. *Note:* This gray teakettle is harder to find than the cobalt blue and white ones.

Plate 4, Row 1:

1. Teakettle, dark lavender shaded, wooden bail.
2. Teakettle, cobalt blue and white with black trim, large swirl, "Azurelite, Enterprise Enamel Company, Bellaire, Ohio."

Plate 4, Row 2:

1. Teakettle, yellow and white with black trim, large swirl, wooden bail, circa 1930's.
2. Teakettle, gray medium mottled, marked "Granite Iron Ware, May 30, 76--July 3, 77."
3. Teakettle, red and white, large mottled, black handle and trim, circa 1960's, lightweight.

Plate 4, Row 3:

1. Teakettle, blue and white, large mottled, embossed on top of teakettle "Savoy." Oval copper hinged cover is riveted to the teakettle, wooden handle and knob. Copper cover dated "Pat'd. 1903."
2. Teakettle, reddish dark brown and white, medium mottled, "Garnet Ware." The small round filler cover with black wooden knob is off-center on top of the teakettle, black weld handle. Geuder Paeschke & Frey Company, "Cream City Ware" Milwaukee. Mark is a circle with a star and the initials of the company in the center.

Plate 4, Row 4:

1. Teakettle, gray and white, large mottled, "Snow on the Mountain."
2. Teakettle, squatty shaped, gray medium mottled, wooden bail missing from wire handle.
3. Teakettle, dark blue and white, black trim, large swirl, wooden bail.

Plate 5, Row 1:

1. Teakettle, dark green and white, large swirl, wire bail with Alaska handle, "Chrysolite."
2. Teakettle, white with fine blue veining, Chicken Wire pattern, "Snow on the Mountain."
3. Teakettle, light blue and white, large swirl.

Plate 5, Row 2:

1. Teakettle, blue, decorated with a black Art Deco pattern trimmed in gold, wire bail Alaska handle, marked "Germany."
2. Teakettle, cobalt blue, decorated with white stripes with yellow shading on bottom.
3. Teakettle, orange, decorated with a black checkered pattern, wire bail with Alaska handle, marked "Made in Germany."

Plate 5, Row 3:

1. Teakettle, cobalt blue and white with black trim and handle, large mottled.
2. Teakettle, white, light blue, dark blue, and brown, very fine speckled, "End of Day."
3. Teakettle, blue and white with blue trim, large swirl, wooden bail.

Plate 5, Row 4:

1. Teakettle, unusual blue and white. *Note:* This color has been applied over original colors from the factory which were brown and white large swirl. The original colors show through enough so you can tell what it was. *Note:* This is referred to as "redipped."
2. Teakettle, gray large mottled, wooden handle and knob.
3. Teakettle, blue and white fine mottled.

257

Section 19

Baking Pans, Roasters and Broilers

Plate 1, Row 1:

1. Oblong baking pan, applied side handle, cobalt blue and white, white inside, black trim, large mottled. *Note:* The author believes this was also used as a cover for a two-piece roaster.
2. Oblong baking pan or stove pan, dark green and white, white inside, large swirl, molded handles, "Chrysolite." *Note:* These were also referred to as stove pans because they were used on top of the stove as well as for baking.
3. Oblong baking pan, gray large mottled, applied side wire handle.

Plate 1, Row 2:

1. Oblong baking pan, brown and white, white inside, large swirl, molded handles.
2. Oblong baking pan, no handles, white, brown, orange, dark blue, gray, yellow, green, and red inside and outside, large swirl, "End of Day."
3. Oblong baking pan, lavender blue and white, white inside, large swirl, molded handles.

Plate 1, Row 3:

1. Oblong baking pan, blue and white, white inside, large swirl, molded handles.
2. Oblong baking pan, exceptionally large, cobalt blue and white, white inside, large swirl, black trim, molded handles.
3. Oblong baking pan, two handled, green and white, white inside, cobalt blue trim, large swirl, "Emerald Ware."

259

Plate 2, Row 1:

1. Oblong baking pan, cobalt blue and white, white inside, medium mottled, riveted handles, triple coated, "Snow on the Mountain," marked "Elite."
2. Oblong baking pan, blue and white, white inside, large swirl, molded handles.
3. Oblong baking pan, cobalt blue and white inside and outside, large swirl, molded handles.

Plate 2, Row 2:

1. Square baking pan, blue and white, white inside, applied wire handles, triple coated, Chicken Wire pattern. Marked with lion standing with his two front paws on a coffee pot and has a letter "B" in the center. "Paragon Ware" imported by New England Enameling Co.
2. Oblong baking pan, gray medium mottled, molded handles, unusual grooved bottom.
3. Oblong baking pan, blue and white, white inside, large swirl, molded handles.

Plate 2, Row 3:

1. Oblong baking pan, light blue and white, white inside, black trim and handles, large swirl, applied handles.
2. Oblong baking pan, blue and white, white inside, large mottled, molded handles.

Plate 3, Row 1:

1. Oblong baking pan, brown and white, white inside, large swirl, molded handles. Note the unusual corrugated bottom.
2. Oblong baking pan, green and white, white inside, large swirl, molded handles, "Emerald Ware."
3. Oblong baking pan, lavender blue, white and gray, white inside, large swirl, molded handles, "End of Day."

Plate 3, Row 2:

Square baking pan, gray medium mottled, applied wire handles.

Plate 3, Row 3:

1. Oblong baking pan, lavender blue and white, white inside, large swirl, molded handles.
2. Oblong baking pan, cobalt blue and white, white inside, black trim, large swirl, applied handles.
3. Oblong baking pan, cobalt blue and white, white inside, large mottled, molded handles.

Plate 4, Row 1:

Three-piece flat-top roaster, blue and white, white inside, black trim and handles, large swirl, white handled insert, metal steam vent on the cover.

Plate 4, Row 2:

1. Three-piece flat-top roaster, deep sea green shading to moss green, white inside, shaded handled insert, metal steam vent on the cover, "Shamrock Ware."
2. Three-piece flat-top roaster, green and white with cobalt blue trim and handles, white inside, large swirl, white handled insert trimmed in cobalt blue, metal steam vent on the cover, "Emerald Ware."

Plate 4, Row 3:

1. Two-piece round roaster, brown and white inside and outside, black trim and handles, large swirl, metal steam vent on cover, riveted handles, and two side wire locks that lock the cover. In the bottom are three little protruding round feet and three indentations which form to hold the liquid in the bottom of the roaster. *Note:* Most of the round roasters the author has seen do not have inserts like the oval ones do.
2. Three-piece oval roaster, brown and white with black trim and handles, large swirl, white handled insert trimmed in black. Bottom of insert has a shell pattern, handles and wire cover locks are riveted, metal steam vent on cover. *Note:* The wire cover locks on the round one are on the front and back sides of the roaster. The oval roaster has them on the ends under the handles. The flat top roasters the author has seen did not have cover locks.

Plate 5, Row 1:

Two-piece oval roaster, blue and white decorated with a fancy scallop design on bottom and cover, blue strap handles, heavyweight. Marked "MC CLARY'S" on the cover under the handle. Center of cover is recessed, bottom has three protruding molded feet. Made in Canada.

Plate 5, Row 2:

1. Three-piece broiler, blue and white inside and outside, trimmed in black, medium mottled, granite top, metal slanted broiling rack and drip pan, Alaska wire spiral handle. Marked "Pat. applied for." *Note:* This was designed for the two front feet to fit in the burner on the New Perfection Oil Cook Stove. Advertised "No smoke or odor from the meat while broiling as neither meat nor drip pan is placed directly over fire. Broil both sides of meat at once." Labeled "New Perfection Broiler" in a triangle. (See Section 12, Plate 2, Row 2, No. 5.)
2. Two-piece oval roaster, gray medium mottled, cover is tapered in with self-basting indentations. *Note:* The indentations were designed so liquids would form on them while food was cooking, basting the food.

Plate 5, Row 3:

1. Two-piece small oval roaster, gray medium mottled. *Note:* This was designed so the top could also be used as a separate baking or serving pan.
2. Coverless roaster, dark brown with a reddish cast and white, medium mottled, applied wire handles. Food was placed in the center to cook and brown. *Note:* This style was believed to brown foods better. The outer deep well held the excess liquids. Marked "Cream City Ware," Milwaukee, Geuder Paeschke & Frey Co., "Garnet."

267

Plate 6, Row 1:

1. Two-piece oval roaster, blue and white with black handles and trim, large swirl, perforated foot, bottom inside part of the roaster is rounded. The perforated foot keeps it from setting directly on the heat thus preventing food from sticking on the bottom and burning.

Plate 6, Row 2:

1. Three-piece roaster, deep violet shaded, white inside, "Thistle Ware."
2. Roaster insert, deep violet shaded (3rd pc.), white inside, handled, "Thistle Ware."

Plate 6, Row 3:

1. Three-piece oval roaster, small size, blue and white, white inside, black trim, fine mottled, white handled insert. Roaster embossed "LISK" on the cover. Two metal steam vents on cover with wire handles for opening or closing vents. Vents dated "Pat. May 2, 1911." Made by The Lisk Manufacturing Co. of Canandaigua, N.Y. which was famous for its Lisk Self Basting Roasters.
2. Three-piece oval roaster, medium size, blue and white inside and outside, black trim, medium mottled, white handled insert. Roaster embossed "LISK" on the cover, two metal steam vents on cover with metal handles for opening and closing vents on the cover. Vents dated "Pat. May 2, 1911 made by Lisk." *Note:* The author has seen this roaster in four different sizes. There is one larger than the medium one pictured. Besides these three, there is a salesman sample.

Plate 7, Row 1:

1. Three-piece oval roaster, cobalt blue and white with black trim and handles, steam vent and cover locks, large swirl, handled insert with a shell-shaped bottom, white trimmed in black.
2. Two-piece round roaster, light blue and white, white inside, black trim and handles, large swirl, self basting cover has indentations.

Plate 7, Row 2:

1. Two-piece oval roaster, blue and white with black trim, large swirl.
2. Two-piece oval flat-top roaster. As taken from an old ad, "U.S. Light Blue Mottled Triple Coated Enamel with pure White acid-proof lining." Self-basting, handles on top permit raising of top without removing from oven. Each piece can be removed separately thus making a three-in-one article. No. 100 size 11½" x 15" x 7".

Plate 7, Row 3:

1. Three-piece flat-top roaster, cobalt blue and white, white inside, large swirl, metal steam vent on cover.
2. Roaster insert handled (3rd pc.), cobalt blue and white outside, white inside, large swirl. _Note:_ The inserts are usually white, not in color.

Section 20

Measures, Colanders, Strainers, Steamers, Rice Balls, Poachers, Sectioned Pans, Cookers

Plate 1, Row 1:

1. Measure, brown and white with dark blue trim, large swirl, riveted lip and strap handle.
2. Measure, blue and white, light blue trim, large mottled.
3. Measure, "old red and white," large mottled, seamless lip.
4. Measure, blue and white, blue trim, large swirl, seamless lip.
5. Measure, blue and white, black trim and handle, medium mottled, riveted lip and handle.
6. Measure, cobalt blue and white, black trim, large swirl, seamed lip.

Plate 1, Row 2:

1. Measure, green and white, dark blue trim and handle, large swirl, seamless, "Emerald Ware."
2. Measure, cobalt blue and white, Chicken Wire pattern, "Paragon Ware."
3. Measure, cobalt blue and white, medium mottling.
4. Measure, unusual green and white, black trim and handle, large mottled.
5. Measure, cobalt blue and white, black trim, large swirl, "Azurelite."
6. Measure, gray mottled, seamed lip, "Agate Ware."
7. Measure, brown and white, large swirl, redipped over cobalt blue and white.

Plate 1, Row 3:

1. Measure, blue and white, dark blue trim, large mottled, seamed lip.
2. Measure, black and white outside, gray and white inside, fine mottled.
3. Measure, bright lavender shaded, black trim and handle, riveted lip and handle.
4. Measure, blue and white large swirl, seamless, "Lava Ware."
5. Measure, green shaded, seamless, "Shamrock Ware."
6. Measure, aqua green and white, cobalt blue trim, large swirl.
7. Measure, cobalt blue and white, black trim and handle, large swirl.

Plate 1, Row 4:

1. Measure, aqua green and white, cobalt blue trim, large swirl.
2. Measure, black and white inside and outside, large swirl.
3. Measure, blue and white inside and outside, blue trim and handle, fine mottled.
4. Measure, deep violet shaded, seamless, "Thistle Ware."
5. Measure, brown and white, Relish pattern.
6. Measure, gray, unusual type mottling, cobalt blue trim and handle.
7. Measure, solid blue, with floral decoration, cobalt blue trim and handle.

Plate 2, Row 1:

1. Measure, gray mottled, riveted spout and handle.
2. Measure, blue and white, black trim, large swirl, riveted spout.
3. Measure, large mottled, embossed "1 GAL. LIQ'D." Labeled "Royal Granite." National Enameling and Stamping Co.
4. Measure, cobalt blue and white, black trim and handle, large swirl.
5. Measure, gray mottled, seamed body and lip, riveted handle.

Plate 2, Row 2:

1. Tumbler-shaped measure, lipped and handled, white with black trim and handle, marked inside " 2 oz. to 16 oz."
2. Graduated lipped dry measure, blue and white fine mottled.
3. Graduated lipped tall-style dry measure, blue and white medium mottled.
4. Graduated lipped dry measure, white with green veins, large mottled, marked Elite."
5. Cup style measure, solid red, white inside, marked "0.51."

Plate 2, Row 3:

1. Measure, solid cobalt blue, white inside, seamed, strap handle.
2. Measure, solid blue, white inside, dark cobalt blue trim.
3. Measure, blue, decorated with pink roses, numbered 929.
4. Measure, blue, decorated with pink roses, numbered 928. *Note:* The author believes these are part of a set.
5. Measure, solid cobalt blue, white inside, riveted spout and handle.

Plate 2, Row 4:

1. Measure, "old red and white" medium mottled, seamless lip, seamed body.
2. Measure, cobalt blue and white, black trim and handle, large swirl, seamed lip and body.
3. Measure, blue, red, and white, dark blue trim, large swirl, "End of Day."
4. Measure, green and white, cobalt blue trim, large swirl, "Emerald Ware."
5. Measure, black and white inside and outside, large mottled, "Snow on the Mountain."

Plate 3, Row 1:

1. Measure, gray large mottled, seamed lip and body, riveted handle.
2. Measure, gray mottled, lip is applied with four rivets, handle is also riveted.
3. Seamless vinegar measure, gray large mottled, riveted strap handle with extra inside piece added to the handle, marked "Granite Iron Ware."
4. Seamless vinegar measure, gray large mottled, riveted handle, marked "Granite Iron Ware." Trademark on every piece.
5. Agate "Favorite" measure, gray mottled, advertised in 1884 L. & G. Mfg. Co. Catalogue. Unusual round, flared lip does not taper down, but continues all around the measure. Top part of the handle is applied to the back part of lip.
6. Seamless vinegar measure, gray medium mottled, rolled riveted handle, marked "Granite Steelware. Nesco."

Plate 3, Row 2:

1. One cup measure, gray medium mottled, embossed "For Household Use Only."
2. Measure, gray mottled, embossed "For Household Use Only," seamed with riveted handle.
3. Measure, gray mottled, embossed "For Household Use Only," seamed with riveted handle.
4. Measure, labeled "EL-an-GE Mottled Gray Ware 2 qt. N.Y.C. apprd. D8."
5. Measure, gray mottled, embossed "1 pt. Liq'd," seamed with weld handle.
6. Measure, gray large mottled, embossed "1 pt. Liq'd U.S. Standard." Labeled "Nesco Pure Greystone Enameled Ware Patented July 20, 1909 and Dec. 9, 1912."
7. Measure, gray mottled, embossed "¼ Qt. Liq'd."

Plate 3, Row 3:

1. Measure, gray large mottled, seamed with strap handle.
2. Measure, gray medium mottled, marked "General Steel Ware's Ltd. 1 qt."
3. Measuring cup, gray medium mottled, embossed measurements "¼ cup, ⅓ cup, ½ cup, ⅔ cup, ¾ cup." Handle is applied up under the top rolled edge.
4. Measure, gray large mottled, embossed "1 Qt. Liq'd."
5. Measure, light gray medium mottled, marked "McClary Mfg. Co. 1 Quart London, Ont."
6. Measuring cup, gray medium mottled, riveted handle, embossed on top side of cup "Quarters, and Thirds."
7. Measure, gray large mottled, seamed with strap riveted handle.

Plate 3, Row 4:

1. Four-cup graduated lipped dry measure, gray large mottled, seamless.
2. Graduated lipped dry measure, gray large mottled, embossed on one side "For Household Use Only," on the other side embossed "½ pt., 1 pt., 1½ pt., 1 qt."
3. Graduated lipped dry measure, gray medium mottled, embossed "For Household Use Only 1 qt. Liq'd."
4. Graduated lipped dry measure, gray large mottled, emobssed "½ pt., 1 pt., 1½ pt. 1 qt."
5. Graduated lipped dry measure, gray mottled, seamed, riveted handle, marked "Extra Agate Nickel Steel Ware, L. & G. Mfg. Co."

Plate 4, Row 1:

1. Colander, cobalt blue and white, black trim and handles, large swirl, footed, deep.
2. Colander, unusual green and white, cobalt blue trim and handles, large swirl, footed, deep.
3. Colander, brown and white, brown trim and handles, large swirl, footed, deep.

Plate 4, Row 2:

1. Colander, mottled gray, deep with three applied feet, strap handles, fancy perforations.
2. Handled gravy or soup strainer, gray medium mottled, screen bottom.
3. Colander, light blue and white inside and outside, dark blue trim and handles, large swirl, deep, bottom has three rounded indentations that protrude out to form the molded feet.

Plate 4, Row 3:

1. Strainer, eight-sided, dark blue and white, medium mottled, three spatula feet, brass eyelet for hanging.
2. Teardrop sink strainer, dark cobalt blue and white, medium mottled, seamed perforated front and bottom. The rolled top edge supports the wire hanger.
3. Round strainer, three applied feet, blue and gray inside and outside, large mottled.

Plate 4, Row 4:

1. Colander, dark green and white inside and outside, dark blue trim and handles, large mottled, footed, deep.
2. Handled gravy or soup strainer, gray large mottled, screen bottom.
3. Colander, blue and white inside and outside, black trim and handles, large swirl, footed, deep.

Plate 5, Row 1:

1. Colander, footed, violet blue shading to light violet blue.
2. Handled strainer, white, kettle hook on opposite end to hold strainer in place, marked "G.B.N." in a three leaf clover.
3. Colander, deep sea green to moss green, footed, deep, "Shamrock Ware."

Plate 5, Row 2:

1. Colander, cobalt blue and white with black trim and handles, large swirl, footed.
2. Sink strainer, gray medium mottled, rounded with two sides shaped to fit the corner of sink. Three indentations protrude to form the molded feet.
3. Colander, cobalt blue and white, black trim and handles, large swirl, footed, shallow.

Plate 5, Row 3:

1. Colander, shaded green and ivory, black trim and handles, footed, "Old Ivory Ware."
2. Handled strainer with kettle hook, white with blue veining, perforated bottom, Chicken Wire pattern.
3. Colander, gray large mottled, footed, shallow.

Plate 5, Row 4:

1. Colander, blue and white inside and outside, black trim and handles, large mottled, footed, deep. La Lance and Grosjean's 1884 catalogue advertises these as hotel colanders because of their exceptionally large size. *Note:* Colanders with colors inside and outside are more in demand and usually demand a higher price.
2. Square sink strainer, mottled gray, perforated side and bottom, rolled top edge supports wire that goes around the strainers top that form corner loops for hanging.
3. Colander, blue and white inside and outside, black trim and handles, large swirl, footed, deep, seamed.

Plate 6, Row 1:

1. Gravy strainer, gray mottled, deep, footed, perforated tin bottom insert. Marked "Extra Agate Nickel Steel Ware, L. & G. Mfg. Co."
2. Colander, cobalt blue and white, dark blue trim and handles, medium mottled, footed, deep, marked "Elite Austria No. 30."
3. Handled strainer with kettle hook, white with cobalt blue trim, fancy perforated bottom and sides.

Plate 6, Row 2:

1. Triangular sink strainer, gray medium mottled, seamed, extended rivets on the bottom form the three little feet.
2. Triangular sink strainer, gray large mottled, fancy perforations on sides and bottom, three small loop-shaped feet.
3. Teardrop sink strainer, gray large mottled, rolled top edge supports wire that goes around the strainer's top edge and forms a loop for hanging.

Plate 6, Row 3:

1. Colander, dark green and white inside and outside, cobalt blue trim, large mottled, footed, deep.
2. Handled strainer with kettle hook, white with blue veining, Chicken Wire pattern.
3. Colander, blue and white inside and outside, black trim and handles, large swirl, footed.

Plate 6, Row 4:

1. Colander, white with cobalt blue trim and handles, footed, deep, fancy perforations.
2. Colander, gray large mottled, footed, shallow, fancy perforations. Note the numerous styles of perforations in colanders and strainers.
3. Colander, unusual blue and white inside and outside, dark blue handles and trim, large mottled, footed.

Plate 7, Row 1:

1. Colander, green and white, white inside, dark blue trim and handles, large swirl, footed.
2. Colander, cobalt blue and white, white inside, black trim, medium mottled, footed, deep, fancy perforations, marked "W. MORSE OMEGA." The author has never seen another piece with this mark.
3. Strainer, blue and white, white inside, medium mottled, cone-shaped with two handles, marked "Elite."

Plate 7, Row 2:

1. Handled strainer, blue and white, white inside, large swirl, riveted hollow handle and kettle hook.
2. Triangular wire footed strainer, gray and white, medium mottled. Rolled-top edge supports wire that goes around the strainer's top edge to form a loop for hanging. The removable wire foot slides into two attached sections, back of strainer is seamed.
3. Covered sink strainer, white, with blue trim. The hinged cover swings up to cover the strainer or under the strainer to make a drip tray. Perforated bottom has three indentations that protrude to form the feet.

Plate 7, Row 3:

1. Eight-sided strainer with handle, gray large mottled, three spatula-shaped feet attached to the bottom drain pan.
2. Triangular sink strainer, white with dark blue trim, wire fits over the corner of the rolled edge on the sink. The wire can be used on either the right or left side because the left side also has holes for the wire to fit into.
3. Handled strainer with kettle hook, green and white, white inside, large mottled, marked "Elite."

Plate 7, Row 4:

1. Colander, footed, advertised as "Harmonizing Colors." "Vollrath Ware," Sheboygan, Wisconsin.
2. Handled gravy strainer with kettle hook, gray large mottled, perforated tin bottom and riveted handle.
3. Colander, blue and white, blue trim, medium mottled, footed, deep, fancy perfora tions.

285

Plate 8, Row 1:

1. Covered strainer with matching perforated graniteware cover, light gray and dark blue, fine mottling, wire bail, collapsible wire feet. When the wire feet are squeezed, the feet fold up on the strainer's side.
2. Handled strainer with three ring feet, gray medium mottled, fancy perforated bottom and sides.
3. Covered strainer with matching perforated graniteware cover, white, wire bail, collapsible wire feet, smaller size than No. 1. Note the different way the wire feet are applied to the body in comparison to No. 1 on this row.

Plate 8, Row 2:

1. Strainer insert, gray medium mottled, fancy perforated sides and bottom, marked "L. & G. Mfg. Co." Note the shape of the wire bail. This is part of a two-piece cooker.
2. Rice ball, light gray and white, fine mottled, perforated, back side is hinged for opening, front part has a latch for closing. *Note:* Rice is placed in the ball and dropped by the chain in boiling water to cook.
3. Rice ball, gray large mottled, fancy perforations. The tension from the heavy bailhandle holds the two sections together.

Plate 8, Row 3:

Egg poacher with tin cover, black and white large mottled. This type includes a tin insert that holds the five graniteware egg poacher cups. These cups can be round or flat on the bottom. The other style the author has seen has only graniteware egg poacher cups, the rest of the unit is tin. The tin cover has a Cat's Eye knob and is embossed "Buffalo Steam Egg Poacher."

Plate 8, Row 4:

1. Upcooker, gray large mottled, has perforated cover that has a ring handle. *Note:* These were used for boiling milk or other liquids. The perforated cover kept the milk or liquid from boiling over on the stove because the boiling liquid would run back through the holes in the perforated cover.
2. Asparagus boiler with white handled insert, green and white, large mottled, marked "Elite Austria."
3. Upcooker, gray Relish pattern. Note center hole in cover where funnel fits. Funnel is used to add more liquid.

287

Plate 9, Row 1:

1. Fish kettle or poacher, blue and white, white inside, dark blue trim and handles, fine mottled.
2. Double saucepan, blue and white with dark blue trim and handle, medium mottled, seamed with riveted handle. *Note:* There should be two of these handled saucepans in this type set. These sets came with either tin or granite covers. They were designed to fit on one burner of the stove to conserve fuel.

Plate 9, Row 2:

1. Double saucepan set with matching granite covers, solid blue.
2. Fish kettle or poacher, gray large mottled, handled perforated insert, marked "Granite Iron Ware," trademark on every piece.

Plate 9, Row 3:

1. Fish kettle or poacher with white handled perforated insert, white with blue veining, Chicken Wire pattern, marked "ROSVA RNENANTA GERMANY."
2. Triple saucepan set with matching covers, green and white large mottled, marked "Elite Austria." *Note:* There should be three of these handled sauce pans with this set. These were designed to fit on one burner to conserve fuel.

Plate 9, Row 4:

1. Fish kettle or poacher with white handled perforated insert, light blue and white large mottled, marked "Elite Austria."
2. Fish kettle or poacher, white, unusual wire bail handles, seamed, marked "H.M. Government."

289

Section 21

Double Boilers, Kettles, Oval Shirred Egg Plates, Sauce Pans, Spaghetti or Potato Kettles, Cruller or Potato Friers, Fruit Kettle, Mush Mugs, Covers and Lid Rack

Plate 1, Row 1:

1. Double boiler with matching granite cover, green and white with cobalt blue trim, white inside, large swirl, "Emerald Ware." The Strong Manufacturing Co., Sebring, Ohio. Old trade catalogs advertise these as rice, milk, or farina boilers. Called double boilers by today's collectors.
2. Double boiler, green and white with green trim, large mottled, marked "Elite Austria." Note extra tipping handle on lower part of boiler.

Plate 1, Row 2:

1. Double boiler, blue and white with black trim and handles, large swirl. Note unusual shape.
2. Double boiler, blue and white with black trim and handles, large swirl.

Plate 1, Row 3:

1. Double boiler, blue and white with black trim and handles, large mottled, "Snow on the Mountain."
2. Double boiler, gray medium mottled, matching granite cover, flared bottom. Both the insert and bottom are marked "Extra Agate NIckel Steel Ware, L. & G. Mfg. Co."
3. Double boiler, green shaded, seamless, "Shamrock Ware."

Plate 1, Row 4:

1. Double boiler, cobalt blue and white with black trim and handles, large swirl, seamless. *Note:* Bottom section is "Belle" shaped.
2. Double boiler, blue and white with black trim and handles, large swirl, "Belle" shaped.

Plate 2, Row 1:

1. Double boiler, aqua green and white with cobalt blue trim and handles, large swirl, flared, seamed bottom.
2. Double boiler, blue, cobalt blue, and white with cobalt blue trim and handles, large mottled, flared, seamed bottom, "End of Day." "Royal Granite Steel Ware, Crown Industries, Binghamton, N.Y."

Plate 2, Row 2:

1. Double boiler, green and white with black trim and handles, large swirl, seamless. Note convex-shaped bottom.
2. Double boiler, white with cobalt blue trim and handles. Inside top part of boiler marked "For Household Use Only, Pints ¼ and ½ pints, cups ½ and 1 cup."
3. Double boiler, cobalt blue and white with black trim and handles, large swirl, flared, seamed bottom. Labeled "Monogram Ware," triple coated. "John Dunlop Co., Pittsburgh, Pa., Enamel Ware Guaranteed Acid Proof."

Plate 2, Row 3:

1. Double boiler, red and white with black trim and handles, large swirl, black bakelite knob, seamless, heavy, circa 1930's.
2. Double boiler, dark green and white with cobalt blue trim and handles, large swirl, flared bottom, seamed, "Chrysolite."

Plate 2, Row 4:

1. Double boiler, blue and white, large swirl, "Lava Ware," The Cleveland Stamping and Tool Co., Cleveland, Ohio.
2. Double boiler, brown and white with dark brown trim and handles, white inside, large swirl.

Plate 3, Row 1:

1. Covered convex kettle or sauce pan, blue and white with black side handles and trim, large swirl, seamless.
2. Lipped preserving kettle, cobalt blue and white, large swirl, seamless, wire bail, pierced ear on back for hanging.

Plate 3, Row 2:

1. Covered Berlin-style kettle, brown and white, white inside, dark brown trim, large swirl, seamless, wire bail and wooden knob.
2. Covered Berlin-style kettle or handled bean pot, blue and white with black side handles and trim, large swirl, seamless.
3. Covered Berlin-style kettle, green and white with cobalt blue trim, large swirl, seamless, wire bail and matching granite cover, spun knob, "Emerald Ware."

Plate 3, Row 3:

1. Covered small kettle, gray large mottled, fancy black wooden bail.
2. Oval shirred egg plate, blue and white with cobalt blue trim, white inside, medium mottled.
3. Lipped sauce pan, brown and white with black trim and handle, large swirl.

Plate 3, Row 4:

1. Oval shirred egg plate, gray medium mottled, marked "Granite Steel Ware, Pat. Oct. 9, '84 and July 2, '86."
2. Covered Berlin-style sauce pan, green and white large swirl, heavy, round cobalt blue handle and trim, seamless, "Emerald Ware."
3. Covered convex sauce pan, lavender cobalt blue and white with black trim and handle, large swirl, seamelss, unusual wire handle on cover is marked "Pat. PD'G."
4. Oval-shirred egg plate, light blue and white with dark blue trim, large swirl, not old, lightweight, circa 1960's.

Plate 4, Row 1:

1. Lipped preserving kettle, blue and white with black trim and back tipping handle, large mottled, wooden bail.
2. Two-handled pan, pink and white, cobalt blue trim, white inside, large mottled, marked "A.W. 20." Looks like a top part of a double boiler.
3. Lipped preserving kettle, cobalt blue and white with black trim, large swirl, wooden bail and black tipping handle.

Plate 4, Row 2:

1. Covered Berlin-style kettle, cobalt blue and white, large swirl, seamless, wire bail and matching granite cover with spun knob.
2. Covered two-handled kettle, white, decorated with grapes and leaves with light green shading around the decoration, trimmed with brown and light green.
3. Covered Berlin-style kettle, bluish gray and white inside and outside, large swirl, dark blue trim, wooden bail.

Plate 4, Row 3:

1. Lipped preserving kettle, blue and white, large swirl, wooden bail.
2. Covered Berlin-style kettle or bean pot, cobalt blue and white with black trim, large swirl, matching granite cover, spun knob and wire bail.
3. Lipped saucepan, blue and white with black trim and handle, large swirl, seamless.

Plate 4, Row 4:

1. Covered Berlin-style kettle, cobalt blue and white, large swirl, matching granite cover, seamless wooden bail.
2. Covered Berlin-style kettle, green and white, large swirl, matching granite cover, spun knob, seamless, "Emerald Ware."
3. Covered convex kettle, reverse cobalt blue and white with cobalt blue trim, large swirl, wooden bail. *Note:* The author refers to this color as "Reverse cobalt blue and white" because it appears the cobalt blue was applied first with the white over it.

Plate 5, Row 1:

1. Lipped preserving kettle, green and white with cobalt blue trim, large swirl, back tipping handle, wooden bail, "Emerald Ware."
2. Covered Berlin-style kettle, blue and white with black trim, large swirl, matching granite cover, wooden knob and wire bail.
3. Lipped preserving kettle, brown and white with dark brown trim, large swirl, wire bail and back tipping handle.

Plate 5, Row 2:

1. Oblong, deep stove pan, gray large mottled, seamless.
2. Covered Berlin-style kettle, blue and white with light blue trim, fine mottled, granite cover, spun knob, wooden bail, marked "Elite Austria 14."
3. Oblong shallow stove pan, cobalt blue and white, white inside with dark blue trim, large swirl, seamless.

Plate 5, Row 3:

1. Maslin-style kettle, black and white, large swirl, heavy bail, "Eboney Ware."
2. Small covered kettle, gray large mottled.
3. Covered Berlin-style kettle, charcoal gray and light gray, dark blue trim, large mottled, wire bail.

Plate 5, Row 4:

1. Berlin-style sauce pan, blue and white with rolled black handle and trim, large swirl, seamless.
2. Convex sauce pan, blue and white with black flat handle and trim, large swirl, seamless.

Plate 6, Row 1:

1. Deep stove kettle, blue and white with light blue trim, white inside, medium mottled, wire bail, back metal tipping handle is embossed "Solid Steel." Handle is de-signed to hold cover on when pouring. Some granite or tin covers have the slit for the metal handle to fit down in.
2. Berlin-style spaghetti or potato kettle, blue and white, medium mottled, matching granite cover. *Note:* The bail is designed to hold cover secure when handle is raised. Back tipping handle. Perforated straining spout has a hinged flip cover.

Plate 6, Row 2:

1. Berlin-style spaghetti or potato kettle, blue and white, medium mottled, tin cover, wooden bail, back tipping handle. Note how metal cover on tapered spout is hinged.
2. Berlin-style kettle, old red and white with red trim, large mottled, riveted wire ears, marked "Elite Austria 16," "Snow on the Mountain."
3. Convex-style spaghetti or potato kettle, bluish gray and light gray with cobalt blue trim, medium mottled, wire bail and metal back pull-up handle that fits into cover groove to hold cover secure while pouring. On the front of the tin cover is an added perforated piece that fits inside the kettle spout for straining because the kettle spout does not have a perforated strainer.

Plate 6, Row 3:

1. Windsor-style spaghetti or potato kettle, white with fine blue flecks and black trim, wooden bail, riveted spout and ears and back metal tipping handle.
2. Lipped preserving kettle, solid cobalt blue outside, wooden bail, back tipping handle.
3. Straight-style spaghetti or potato kettle, blue and white with blue trim, large swirl, back tipping handle, tin cover. Note the different shaped spouts on the spaghetti kettles.

Plate 6, Row 4:

1. Covered stove pot, gray mottled, seamless flat bottom, wire bail, riveted flat ears.
2. Covered stove pot, reddish brown densely speckled with white inside and outside, medium mottled, seamless, wire bail. "Cream City Garnet Ware," Geuder-Paeschke & Frey Co. Manufacturers, Milwaukee, U.S.A.
3. Covered stove pot, brown and white Relish pattern, seamless flat bottom, wire bail, riveted flat ears.

Plate 7, Row 1:

1. Covered convex-style kettle, cobalt blue and white, black trim, large swirl, riveted wire-shaped ears, wooden bail.
2. Berlin-style kettle, dark green and white, cobalt blue trim, large swirl, seamless, tin cover, wire bail, "Chrysolite."
3. Covered Berlin-style kettle, brown and white, white inside, dark brown trim, large swirl, seamless, wire bail, wooden knob.

Plate 7, Row 2:

1. Berlin-style kettle, gray medium mottled, wire bail, tin cover. Labeled "Leader Pure Enameled Ware. 6. Easy to clean as China. Sanitary Durable, Made in U.S.A."
2. Lipped preserve kettle, green and white, white inside, black trim, large swirl, riveted ears, wire bail, pierced ear for hanging.
3. Lipped preserve kettle, aqua green and white, cobalt blue trim, large swirl, back tipping handle.

Plate 7, Row 3:

1. Berlin-style kettle, cobalt blue and white, fine Chicken Wire pattern, marked "Elite."
2. Lipped -handle sauce pan, cobalt blue and white, white inside, black trim and handle, large swirl, seamless.
3. Covered shallow two-handled pan, cobalt blue and white, white inside, black trim, large swirl, "Azurelite."

Plate 7, Row 4:

1. Covered Berlin-style kettle, blue and white, white inside, black trim and handles, large swirl, "Columbian Ware."
2. Mush mug or camp mug, light blue and white, light blue trim, medium swirl. *Note:* These were used for warming and cooking food as well as coffee.
3. Mush mug or camp mug, blue and white, black trim, large swril.

Plate 8, Row 1:

1. Cruller or potato frier (fryer), light gray mottled. *Note:* The food is placed for deep frying in the handled perforated basket. The bottom part holds the frying fat, much like today's deep fryers.
2. "Agate" cruller or potato frier (fryer), gray large mottled, marked "Agate Nickel Steel Ware," L. & G. Mfg. Co. Note the difference in the way the handles are applied.

Plate 8, Row 2:

1. Covered convex-style kettle, light blue and white, white inside, black trim, large swirl, wire bail.
2. Covered Berlin-style kettle or bean pot, cobalt blue and white, black trim, large swirl.
3. Berlin-style kettle or bean pot, blue and white, cobalt blue trim and handles, fine mottled, two side handles, tin cover with Cat's Eye knob.

Plate 8, Row 3:

1. Lipped preserving kettle, cobalt blue and white, white inside, large swirl, bail handle, pierced ear for hanging,
2. Lipped preserving kettle, gray large mottled, wire bail, back pouring handle, riveted ears.
3. Lipped preserving kettle, cobalt blue and white, white inside, large swirl, bail handle, pierced ear for hanging.
4. Lipped preserving kettle, light blue and white, white inside, large swirl, bail handle, pierced ear for hanging.

Plate 8, Row 4:

1. Maslin-style kettle, blue and white, black trim, large swirl, wooden bail, "Azure Ware."
2. Berlin-style kettle, cobalt blue and white with black trim, large swirl.
3. "Agate" seamless flaring preserving kettle, advertised in the Agate Cookbook, January 1, 1890.

Plate 9, Row 1:

1. Dome-shaped cover, cobalt blue and white, medium mottled, center metal steam vent and top handle.
2. Dome-shaped cover, blue and white, large mottled.
3. Lid with applied long handle, white with light blue veining, "Snow on the Mountain."

Plate 9, Row 2:

Dome-shpaed cover, brown and white large swirl, wooden knob.

Plate 9, Row 3:

1. Cover, lavender blue and white, large swirl, wire handle embossed "Pat. PD'G," unusual shape.
2. Dome-shaped cover, cobalt blue and white, large swirl.
3. Lid with applied long handle, white with light blue veining, "Snow on the Mountain."

Plate 9, Row 4:

Dome-shaped cover, light blue and white, large swirl.

Plate 9. Row 5:

1. Grooved lid with hook wire handle, gray medium mottled, applied with rivets.
2. Small handihook lid, gray medium mottled, "Republic Metalware Company." Note the grooves in the lids made to fit different size pans.

Plate 9, Row 6:

1. Large handihook lid, gray large mottled.
2. Lid rack, green with white flecks. Rack is tapered to hold different size covers. "Speckled pattern."

Section 22

Dinner Buckets, Covered Buckets, and Chestnut Roaster

Plate 1, Row 1:

1. Round miner's dinner bucket, deep violet shaded, white inside, seamless, "Thistle Ware." Has food tray inside top section, cover fits down inside of the top edge.
2. Round miner's dinner bucket, light blue and white, white inside, large swirl, seamed, food tray and dessert tray. Cover not original.
3. Round miner's dinner bucket, blue and white, white inside, large swirl, seamed, food tray and dessert tray. Cover fits over the top edge. *Note:* This type cover was also used to hold food for serving when removed from the dinner bucket.

Plate 1, Row 2:

1. Round miner's dinner bucket, gray medium mottled, seamed, food and dessert tray, cover fits over top edge.
2. Chestnut roaster, light gray and white, medium mottled, latched perforated cover. Added rim on bottom part is also perforated around the lower edge for heat to escape, thus not burning the chestnuts. *Note:* The author believes this had versatile uses and was also used as a lunch bucket to heat foods such as soups, etc.
3. Round miner's dinner bucket, gray large mottled, seamed, food and dessert tray, cover fits over top edge. Note the size difference from No. 1 on this row.

Plate 1, Row 3:

1. Oval dinner bucket with food insert, blue and white, white inside, black trim, large swirl, cover fits down inside top edge of food insert.
2. Oval dinner bucket with food insert, cobalt blue and white, white inside, black trim, large swirl, "Azurelite, Enterprise Enamel Company, Bellaire, Ohio."
3. Oval dinner bucket with food insert, blue and white, large swirl. Labeled "Venetian Ware White Lined. Guaranteed absolutely Pure. Federal Enameling and Stamping Company, Pittsburgh, Pa."

Plate 1, Row 4:

1. Stack dinner carrier, white, red, cobalt blue, green, and light blue, cobalt blue trim, large swirl, lightweight, "End of Day." Has four food containers held together with a metal carrier marked "14 C.M.-3." The bottom section of the handle flips down on the cover holding the food containers secure when carrying. The author believes this to be circa 1950's.
2. Stack dinner carrier, white with black trim, two food containers, metal holder with wooden bail.
3. Stack dinner carrier, blue and white, white inside, blue trim, large mottled, metal holder with wooden bail. Marked with a lion standing on a coffee pot with his two front paws. "Paragon Ware," New England Enameling Co.

Note: The author thought a breakdown of some of the dinner buckets, showing how parts are assembled, is essential to learning what they include.

Plate 2, Row 1:

Round miner's dinner bucket, blue and white, large swirl, seamed. Includes wihte food insert, dinner bucket with long wooden bail. *Note:* The long bail was designed to secure the cover that fits over the top edge of dinner bucket when raised for carrying. Cover also used as food container, white dessert tray. *Note:* The dessert trays are shallow whereas the food inserts are deep. A Coonley Manufaturing Co. ad stated that coffee went in the bottom section under the food tray on this style.

Plate 2, Row 2:

Oblong dinner bucket, gray large mottled, seamed body, self-locking bail, granite dessert tray, tin cup that fits down into removable granite coffee flask. Labeled "Royal Enameled Ware," National Enameling and Stamping Company, Inc. *Note:* This type bail holds the cover secure when handle is raised for carrying.

Plate 2, Row 3:

Oval dinner bucket, blue and white, white inside, black trim, large swirl, cover fits down inside food insert. *Note:* Food insert is almost as deep as dinner bucket. The ridge around the center of the food insert holds it up in the bucket making room in the bottom for food also.

Plate 2, Row 4:

Round miner's dinner bucket, gray large mottled, cover, dessert tray, food insert, bucket with wooden bail.

311

Plate 3, Row 1:

1. Oval dinner bucket, gray large mottled, seamed with cover that fits over the top edge of dinner bucket, handled granite cup, tin dessert tray and tin food insert, wooden bail. *Note:* This bucket has the different handled granite cup that fits over the top whereas No. 3 on this row has the tin cup that fits down into the top.
2. Oblong dinner bucket, cobalt blue and white, black trim, large swirl, seamed. Removable seamed coffee flask with tin cup that fits down into the neck of the coffee flask, and dessert tray.
3. Oblong dinner bucket, gray large mottled, seamed, self-locking bail. Granite pie tray, tin cup that fits down into re movable granite coffee flask. Labeled "Royal Enamel Ware," National Enameling and Stamping Company, Inc.

Plate 3, Row 2:

1. Covered bucket or berry bucket, brown and white, white inside, black trim, large swirl, tin cover with wooden knob, wire bail.
2. Covered bucket, brown and white, white inside, black trim, large swirl, tin cover with wooden knob, wire bail.
3. Covered bucket, brown and white, white inside, black trim, large swirl, tin cover with wooden knob, wire bail.

Plate 3, Row 3:

1. Covered bucket, blue and white, dark blue trim, medium mottled, matching granite cover.
2. Covered bucket, blue and white with some gray in the white swirl, large swirl, "End of Day."
3. Covered bucket, gray mottled, matching granite cover.
4. Covered bucket, blue and white, large swirl, matching granite cover.

Plate 3, Row 4:

1. Covered bucket, green and white with green trim, medium mottled, matching granite cover, marked "Elite Austria."
2. Covered bucket, gray mottled, matching granite cover.
3. Covered bucket, light blue and white, white inside, fine mottled, matching granite cover.
4. Covered bucket, white with black trim.
5. Covered bucket, light brown, white, yellow, dark blue, and pink, large mottled, "End of Day," matching granite cover. Marked "Purity Ware B.E.G."

Plate 4, Row 1:

1. Oblong dessert tray, white with black trim.
2. Oblong dinner bucket, cobalt blue and white, white inside, black trim, large swirl, seamed.
3. Removable seamed coffee flask with tin cup that fits down into the neck of coffee flask.

Plate 4, Row 2:

Oval dinner bucket, gray large mottled, seamed, tin food insert, granite cover and handled cup that fits over the top of the cover, tin dessert tray.

Plate 4, Row 3:

1. Stack dinner carrier, blue and white large mottled, metal holder with wooden bail, four food containers, "Paragon Ware." *Note:* The cover is also used for serving food when removed from the dinner bucket.
2. Oval dinner bucket, blue and white large swirl, tin cover, dinner bucket with wooden bail. Food insert labeled "Venetian Ware," White Lined Federal Enameling & Stamping Co., Pittsburgh, Pa.

Plate 4, Row 4:

1. Covered bucket, deep sea green shading to a moss green, "Shamrock Ware," distributed by Norvell Shapleigh Hardware Co., St. Louis.
2. Covered bucket, gray large mottled, tin cover and bail.
3. Covered bucket, blue shading to a lighter blue, matching granite cover, wooden bail.
4. Covered bucket, blue and white with dark blue trim, medium mottled, tin cover, wire bail.
5. Covered bucket, brown shading to a lighter brown, white inside, matching granite cover.

315

Plate 5, Row 1:

1. Covered bucket, black and white inside and outside, large swirl, tin cover, wooden bail.
2. Covered bucket, light blue and white, black trim, large swirl, matching granite cover, wooden bail. Note the two small extra riveted front and back wire-type ears on top part of the bucket.
3. Covered bucket, dark blue and white, black trim, large swirl, matching granite cover.

Plate 5, Row 2:

1. Covered bucket, green and white, blue trim, large swirl, matching cover, "Emerald Ware" made by The Strong Manufacturing Company, Sebring, Ohio.
2. Covered bucket, cobalt blue and white, black trim, large mottled, "Azurelite," Enterprise Enamel Company, Bellaire, Ohio.
3. Covered bucket, light blue and white, black trim, large swirl.
4. Covered bucket, cobalt blue and white, white inside, black trim, large swirl.

Plate 5, Row 3:

1. Covered bucket, light blue and white, black trim, unusual wavey-type mottling, wire bail.
2. Covered bucket, gray medium mottled, seamless with wire bail and tin cover.
3. Covered bucket, deep reddish brown and white, fine mottled, marked "McIntosh Ware" in a diamond. 2.
4. Covered bucket, light blue and white with blue trim, fine mottled.
5. Covered bucket, light blue, cobalt blue, and white, cobalt blue trim, large mottled, "End of Day," "Granite Steel Ware," Crown Industries, Binghamton, N.Y.

Plate 5, Row 4:

1. Covered bucket, light blue and white, black trim, large mottled.
2. Covered bucket, blue and white, black trim, large swirl.
3. Covered bucket, green and white, black trim, large swirl, "Emerald Ware."
4. Covered bucket, cobalt blue and white, large swirl.

Plate 6, Row 1:

1. Covered bucket, black and white inside and outside, large mottled.
2. Covered bucket, labeled "Iron Gray" Enamel Ware, Banner Stamping Co. Paper label shows a picture of an anvil.
3. Covered bucket, cobalt blue and white, black trim, large swirl.
4. Covered bucket, advertised as "Azure Marble Enamel," Pure White Azure Blue Marbelized Figure. Rich black handle and edges.

Plate 6, Row 2:

1. Covered bucket, lavender blue and white, black trim, large swirl.
2. Covered bucket, unusual green and white, black trim, large swirl.
3. Covered bucket, green and white, dark blue trim, large swirl, "Emerald Ware."
4. Covered bucket, dark green and white, black trim, large swirl, "Chrysolite."
5. Covered bucket, cobalt blue and white, black trim, large swirl.

Plate 6, Row 3:

1. Covered bucket, light blue and white, black trim and knob, large swirl.
2. Covered bucket, gray large mottled, wire bail, tin cover, wooden knob.
3. Covered bucket, gray large mottled, matching granite cover.
4. Covered bucket, blue and white fine mottled, brass bail, decorated with gold bands and girl's name "Inez."
5. Covered bucket, blue and white, black trim and knob, large swirl, "Columbian Ware," Bellaire Stamping Co., Bellaire Ohio.

Plate 6, Row 4:

1. Covered bucket, blue and white, black trim, large swirl.
2. Covered bucket, cobalt blue and white, black trim, large swirl.
3. Covered bucket, light blue and white, black trim, large swirl.
4. Covered bucket, cobalt blue and white, large swirl.
5. Covered bucket, dark green applied over an original "Chrysolite" color, redipped.

Section 23

Clocks, Candlesticks, Lamps, Pocket Match Holders, Matchboxes, Petroleum Jug, Stoves, Table Top Stoves with Matching Teakettles, Toasters, Oven Thermometers, Coal Scuttles, Trivets, Foot Warmers

Plate 1, Row 1:

Clock, school house style, dark blue shading to a lighter blue, beveled glass window
covering pendulum, marked "8 day Germany."

Plate 1, Row 2:

1. Clock, green and dark green mottled, marked "8 day Germany."
2. Clock, mountain scene, marked "8 day Germany."

Plate 1, Row 3:

Alarm clock, light gray on cast iron, advertises Westinghouse Automatic Electric Range.
Marked "Made in U.S.A. Patented April 27, 1920, other Pat. Pending." *Note:* This was
given as a premium with the purchase of a Westinghouse Automatic Electric Range.
Advertising cross-collectible.

Plate 1, Row 4:

1. Clock, blue delft style scene, marked "8 day Germany."
2. Clock, white, decorated with cobalt blue design.

Plate 1, Row 5:

Clock, light green and dark green, decorated, marked "8 day Germany."

Plate 2, Row 1:

1. Candlestick or chamberstick, scalloped style, white shading to a deep maroon, decorated with gold trim, numbered 449-16.
2. Oil lamp, "Gone With the Wind" style, lavender and white Relish pattern, melon shaped with fancy pewter embossed protection bands, brass holder and fount with metal base. *Note:* One company advertises their ware as an improvement, as far as durability of material, over glass lamps because of their breaking and causing accidents.
3. Candlesticks, pair, white on cast iron, 7⅞" tall, 3½" base diameter.

Plate 2, Row 2:

1. Candlestick, white with fine blue flecks, speckled pattern.
2. Candlestick, white shading to brilliant cobalt blue.
3. Match holder, single pocket, solid blue on cast iron.
4. Candlestick, gray and white mediium mottled.
5. Candlestick, blue and white with cobalt blue trim, fine mottled.

Plate 2, Row 3:

1. Candlestick, white with cobalt blue decoration.
2. Matchbox, blue, decorated with a checkered design. "ALLUMETTES" is "matches."
3. Candlestick, gray large mottled, beehive shape.
4. Matchbox, white, decorated with red and gray checkered pattern, black trim, scratch pad on cover.
5. Candlestick, scalloped style, cobalt blue, gray, and white, large swirl, finger ring and thumb rest, "End of Day."

Plate 3, Row 1:

1. Candlestick, scalloped style, solid blue, finger ring and thumb rest.
2. Table lamp, electric, white, decorated with cobalt blue pattern. Looks like peacocks and an urn, brass footed pedestal and top attachment, shade not original. Marked "MARTEPOM."
3. Lamp, bracket style, white with fine blue veins, large mottled. *Note:* The author believes this type was meant to fit into a wall-style bracket.
4. Candlestick, gray medium mottled.

Plate 3, Row 2:

1. Candlestick, shell-shaped, gray medium mottled, marked "Extra Agate," L. & G. Mfg. Co. *Note:* The handle is not applied but molded in a one-piece bottom.
2. Candlestick, blue and white, light blue trim, large swirl, finger ring with a flat thumb rest.
3. Double pocket match holder, solid light gray on cast iron. *Note:* The top pocket holds the unused matches and the bottom pocket holds the used ones.
4. Twin pocket match holder, gray medium mottled, "Granite Steel Ware," Kieckhefer. *Note:* The rough section between the two pockets is for striking matches. The author is aware of two styles. The other style has a star impressed on the lower front section of each pocket.
5. Candlestick, blue and white medium mottled.
6. Candlestick, cobalt blue and white large swirl, finger ring and thumb rest.

Plate 3, Row 3:

1. Petroleum jug, gray and white Relish pattern, wire bail and side handle. *Note:* This is used to hold oil for filling oil lamps.
2. Candlestick, light blue and white, dark blue trim, large swirl, finger ring and flat thumb rest.
3. Candlestick, dark blue and white large swirl.
4. Matchbox, blue and gray, blue trim, medium swirl with embossed fancy back.

Plate 4:

Combination wood and and gas kitchen range, all original, royal blue and white with nickel-plated trim, top warming oven. Marked "Perfect 0 Pat. May 8, 1917." *Note:* Display of granite ware on stove described and priced elsewhere in this book.

Plate 5:

Oil or kerosene stove, royal blue and black with nickel-plated trim, advertises Shapleigh Hardware Co., St. Louis, U.S.A., "Bluebelle." Reg. U.S. Pat. Off. No. 30. The three chimneys on the burners are shaded "Bluebelle Ware."

Section 23, Plate 4

Section 23, Plate 5

Plate 6, Row 1:

Twin table top oil stove, six burners, light gray and white, large swirl, fancy embossed metal parts, embossed "Georg Haller Ottensen."

Plate 6, Row 2:

1. Table top oil stove, two burners, dark green trimmed with gold. *Note:* This stove has the bottom drip tray that the stove sits on. Most of the time this part is missing. The fancy embossed metal parts on the stove are enameled green embossed with "Georg Haller Ottensen Hamburg. O.R.G. 3191."
2. Hot plate, electric, single burner, gray and white medium mottled.
3. Table top oil stove, single burner, dark green with gold trim, marked "Original Haller" in gold.

Plate 6, Row 3:

1. New Perfection toaster, solid blue, dated November 27, 1912. Ad in 1917 New Perfection Oil Cook Stoves Catalog reads, "New Perfection toaster. Four large pieces of bread may be toasted at one time. The heat is evenly distributed over entire toasting surface."
2. New Perfection toaster, solid light green. This one is not dated. There are at least two styles of these. The other style has the wooden handle on the side instead of the corner.

Plate 7, Row 1:

1. Oven thermometer, white. *Note:* These are placed in ovens for regulating the right degree of heat for cooking individual items because many wood-burning stoves did not have oven thermometers that told the exact degree of heat. Instead, they read "Warm, Medium, and Hot," or "1 - 2 - 3."
2. Table top oil stove, single burner, brick red, matching pit bottom teakettle.
3. Table top oil stove, three burners, solid robin egg blue, matching pit bottom teakettle, fancy embossed metal. Top part where teakettle fits has three different size removable rings for different size pots. Metal rings marked "Georg Haller," teakettle marked "G.H." in circle.
4. Oven thermometer, white. *Note:* There are two holes near the top of the thermometer. A fork prong was inserted in them for lifting the thermometer out of the hot oven.

Plate 7, Row 2:

1. Armstrong electric table top stove, white with nickel-plated metal parts. Includes four-cup egg poacher, griddle, broiling pan, and toaster that browns both sides of the bread at once. Pat Oct. 9–17, April 23–18, No. 8–A, Standard Stamping Co., Huntington, W. Va., U.S.A.
2. Oven thermometer, red, advertises "Good Housekeeping Institute conducted by Good Housekeeping Magazine." Advertising cross collectible.
3. Table top oil stove, single burner, bluish-gray and white medium mottled, fancy embossed metal marked "Georg Haller Original." *Note:* Gray and white Relish pattern pit bottom teakettle does not match the stove.

Plate 7, Row 3:

1. Hot plate, electric, solid light green. Made by Westinghouse Electric & Mfg. Co., Mansfield Works, Mansfield, Ohio, dated Pat. 9–11–06.
2. Oven thermometer, white with black, advertises Swans Down Cake Flour, No. 3666. Advertising cross collectible. *Note:* This might have been a promotional "give-away."
3. Oven thermometer, cream with a green porcelain-type base. Made by Taylor Instrument Co., Rochester, N.Y. The upper section of the thermometer unscrews from the porcelain-type base for cleaning.
4. Hot plate, electric, white and green, speckled pattern.

Plate 8, Row 1:

Floor model gas heater, gray and white Relish pattern, fancy perforations on top and sides.

Plate 8, Row 2:

1. Floor model oil stove, solid blue with nickel-plated metal parts, fancy perforated removable lid on top. Top of stove has a handle for lifting the inner section out of enamel frame.
2. Coal scuttle, white, decorated with a blue floral design, cast iron base and feet.
3. Coal scuttle, solid gray, has handles for lifting and pouring coal on fire.

Plate 8, Row 3:

1. Whistling tea kettle, solid blue, black bottom. Labeled "Gay-La. Singing Kettle by Federal. The most sanitary whistling tea kettle made, completely Porcelain Enameled inside and out, holds 2 qts."
2. Handled sauce pan, pink, black trim and handle. Labeled "Vogue Enameled Ware. Titanium added for extra life. Federal Enameling & Stamping Co., Pittsburgh, U.S.A."
3. Twin electric hot plate, blue and white fine mottled, marked "Bersted Mfg. Co., Dated November 27, 1912." *Note:* One switch operates both burners.
4. Coffee biggin, black and white fine mottled, aluminum biggin and spreaders.
5. Double boiler, black and white inside and ouside, large swirl, seamless, chrome-plated cover with wooden knob.
6. Twin electric hot plate, green and white top, large swirl, black trim and handles, chrome-plated legs. Embossed "twin hot plate Proctor No. 404." Made by "Proctor & Schwartz Electric Co., Cleveland, Ohio U.S.A."

Plate 9, Row 1:

1. Trivet, aqua blue with three molded feet on cast iron, marked "F. & W. ETI."
2. Trivet, white with a perforated center and three applied feet.
3. Handled trivet, white, decorated with a duck scene, three molded feet.

Plate 9, Row 2:

1. Insert for No. 3 on this row, dark gray, perforated bottom. This holds hot coals to keep food warm.
2. Trivet, light green with three molded feet.
3. Food warmer, gray and white Relish pattern, perforated sides, pewter claw feet and handles, fancy perforated nickel-plated detachable top.

Plate 9, Row 3:

1. Foot warmer, light green on cast iron, wooden bail, perforated top and sides, four fancy molded feet. *Note:* These held hot coals and were used for warming feet.
2. Trivet, light blue, perforated tulip pattern, three molded feet.
3. Foot warmer, blue on cast iron, perforated top and sides, wooden bail, four molded feet. Embossed "GODIN 2 CIE A GUISE AISNE BIE. S.G.D.G. No. 5."

Plate 9, Row 4:

1. Food warmer, cobalt blue, gray, and white, large swirl, "End of Day," two pieces, cover and sides perforated, three applied feet, fancy embossed metal handles.
2. Foot warmer, green on cast iron, wooden bail. *Note:* This style has a collar base instead of feet.
3. Handled trivet, white, decorated with a dark blue windmill scene.

Section 24

Household and Personal Items, Washboards, Dishwasher, Enamel Cleansers,Clothes Boilers, Suds Dipper, Flasks, Toaster, Nut Crackers, Soap Saver, Starch Cannister, Stack Ice Box Containers, Spoon Rests, Handled Griddle Cleaner, Thermos, Dust Pans, Irons, Cuspidors, Comb Cases, Dish Pans

Plate 1, Row 1:

1. Washboard, cobalt blue with metal soap saver.
2. Washboard, charcoal gray and white, medium mottled. Marked "Pearl Enamel Washboard" wears like Granite. SMP "Qualtiy." Made in Canada by General Steel Wares Limited.

Plate 1, Row 2:

1. Enamel cleanser, "Mule–Kick" Made by J.S. Sexauer Mfg. Co., San Francisco, New York, and Niagara Falls, Ont., Pat. May 14, 07.
2. Electric dishwasher, three piece, bottom section is green and white fine mottled, copper cover with brass handles, wire dish drainer. Applied metal tag reads "Sterro Electric Dish–Washer. 'VIDRIO' Products Corp., Chicago, Ill., Made in U.S. America." *Note:* Items in metal dish drainer priced elsewhere in book.
3. Soap for cleaning enamel ware, "Day and Frick, Philadelphia, Pa., Soap Grit, Type 1, for cleaning and polishing glass, enamel ware and all metal surfaces."

Plate 1, Row 3:

1. Washboard, charcoal gray and white medium mottled, marked "Empire Enamel." Manufactured by The Canadian Woodenware Co., Winnepeg, St. Thomas, Montreal.
2. Washboard, black and white medium mottled. Marked "National Washboard Co. No. 818, Trade Mark Reg. U.S. Pat. Off., Made in U.S.A. Chicago–Saginaw–Memphis." *Note:* The author believes this is a salesman sample.

Plate 1, Row 4:

1. Covered clothes boiler, white, trimmed and lettered in reddisdh brown, small size.
2. Covered oblong clothes boiler, cobalt blue and white, white inside, large mottled. *Note:* This was placed on the stove, filled with water, and brought to a boil. Clothes were then added to be sterilized.

Plate 2, Row 1:

1. Suds dipper, gray medium mottled, seamless, tubular open end handle. *Note:* This was used to dip suds from wash tubs, etc.
2. Clothes boiler, black and white with black lettering, medium mottled. *Note:* Cover is missing.
3. Powder cannister, white with white clamp-on porcelain stopper. Shown in Matthai-Ingram catalog. Not sure what type powder it held.

Plate 2, Row 2:

1. Coffee flask, light blue and white fine mottled, seamed. *Note:* Metal top is missing. *Special note:* This flask was photographed only as an example of a rare shape and color. Basically, the poor condition destroys the value. Had it been in good plus condition, it would have had a value of $285.00.
2. Coffee flask, gray medium mottled with cork-lined screw top, seamed, marked "L. & G. Mfg. Co." in an oval.
3. Flask, light gray and white fine mottled, seamed.
4. Flask, cobalt blue, cork stopper with ring, seamed.
5. Coffee flask, gray large mottled, cork-lined screw top, seamed.
6. Coffee flask, solid blue with cork-lined screw top, seamed.

Plate 2, Row 3:

1. Electric toaster, charcoal gray and white medium mottled, fancy perforated metal inner holder. *Note:* The two wire toast holders have a green pottery-type knob for grasping when placing bread in the toaster.
2. Dog nutcracker on cast iron, light gray dog with blue standard. *Note:* Nuts are cracked by raising the dog's tail and placing nut in dog's mouth. Cross collectible.
3. Starch cannister, brick red outside, white inside. Held starch in powder form, marked "Elite Austria."
4. Soap saver, solid brick red, fancy perforated, hinged center latch, top ring with chain. *Note:* Scrap pieces of soap were placed in the soap saver and used for soaking clothes.

Plate 2, Row 4:

1. Stack refrigerator containers, white and light green large swirl, seamless.
2. Cat spoon rest on cast iron, gray with black ears and whiskers.
3. Horse spoon rest on cast iron, gray and white large mottled, three molded feet and hook on back for hanging. Made by "Prizer Stove Co., Reading, Pennsylvania" as a premium in the 1920's. This company went out of business in the 1940's.
4. Nutcracker, solid light green.
5. Handled griddle cleaner, white on cast iron, replaceable wick-like fabric adheared on bottom for cleaning griddles.
6. Thermos, white with black trim. *Note:* Shaped a lot like a coffee carrier. The difference is the cover serves as a handled drinking cup.

Plate 3, Row 1:

1. Dust pan, dark blue with black applied handle, seamless.
2. Coleman gas iron, solid blue, wooden handle, nickel-plated metal parts. Marked "Coleman Lamp and Stove Co., Wichita, Kan., Toronto, Canada. Instant light. Model 4A, Made in U.S.A. Pat.* 1718473."
3. Dust pan, white with fine blue veins, seamed with applied handle, Chicken Wire pattern.

Plate 3, Row 2:

1. Dust pan, light gray medium mottled, riveted handle, ridged bottom.
2. Electric iron, light gray and white medium mottled, wooden handle, nickel-plated metal parts. Note finger rest. Marked "Magnet." Made in England by the General Electric Co., Ltd.
3. Ant cup, gray large mottled. *Note:* One of these was placed under each leg of a piece of furniture. The leg rested on the inner–raised section of the ant cup. Water was placed in outer inside rim. This kept ants from crawling up the legs of furniture that held food.
4. Dust pan, dark gray and white, medium mottled, seamless with applied handle.

Plate 3, Row 3:

1. Dust pan, solid blue, seamless with applied handle.
2. Dust pan, gray and white medium mottled, seamless with molded handle.
3. Electric iron, green and white fine mottled, embossed "The Rhythm No. 3750 Radiation."
4. Dust pan, gray large mottled, ridged bottom and applied riveted handle. Note fluted top corners.

Plate 4, Row 1:

1. Cuspidor, dark green and white, white inside, black trim, large swirl, seamed. "Chrysolite" distributed by Hibbard, Spencer, Bartlett & Co., Chicago, Ill.
2. Cuspidor, light blue and white trimmed in black, large swirl, seamless.
3. Cuspidor, cobalt blue with white and green veins inside and outside, medium mottled, seamed, "End of Day."

Plate 4, Row 2:

1. Cuspidor, two pieces, also called hotel cuspidors. Blue and white, white inside, black trim, medium mottled, seamless.
2. Comb case, gray large mottled, embossed star on inside of back, and on both ends. Embossed "Comb Case" on lower front.
3. Cuspidor, blue and white large swirl, black trim, seamed.

Plate 4, Row 3:

1. Cuspidor, cobalt blue and white large swirl, black trim, seamed.
2. Spit cup, light blue and white, seamless, hinged cover with thumb rest and handle, large mottled. "Snow on the Mountain," marked "Austria.10."
3. Cuspidor, gray medium mottled, seamed.
4. Cuspidor, cobalt blue and white medium swirl, black trim, seamed.

Plate 4, Row 4:

1. Cuspidor, two pieces, brown and white, white inside, black trim, large swirl, seamless.
2. Comb case, gray medium mottled, embossed on inside of back "THE JEWEL." Lower front part, embossed "COMB CASE."
3. Cuspidor, two piece, deep, cobalt blue and white, white inside, black trim, large swirl, seamless.

Plate 5, Row 1:

Handled dishpan, inside view, white with black lettering and gold decoration. Advertises "Lisk Enameled Ware," blue and white fine mottled outside. Advertising cross-collectible.

Plate 5, Row 2:

1. Handled dishpan, white, light blue, light green, and brown, large swirl, black trim and handles, "End of Day."
2. Handled dishpan, blue and white with dark blue trim and handles, large swirl.

Plate 5, Row 3:

Oval foot tub, cobalt blue and white large swirl, black trim, eyelet for hanging.

Plate 6, Row 1:

1. Handled dishpan, white, light blue, and gray large swirl, black trim and handles, "End of Day."
2. Handled dishpan, cobalt blue and white large swirl, black trim and handles. *Note:* This dishpan has riveted tubular handles.

Plate 6, Row 2:

1. Handled dishpan, cobalt blue and white large swirl, black trim and handles.
2. Dishpan, red and white inside and outside, black trim, large swirl, circa 1960's, lightweight.

Plate 6, Row 3:

1. Dishpan, brown and white outside, white inside, brown trim, large swirl, circa 1970's, lightweight.
2. Handled dishpan, dark green and white large swirl, dark blue trim and handles, "Chrysolite."

347

Plate 1:

Checkerboard, 19" x19", cobalt blue, white, red, green, yellow, dark brown, medium brown, beige, and light blue, "End of Day," large swirl, black on back, triple coated. The Checkerboard part is raised slightly from the border. Each square of the checkerboard has an individual look, as if each one was placed separately. The border has four diamond-shaped designs. This is an extraordinary piece of granite ware. The author believes this is of foreign origin.

Plate 2, Row 1: (on opposite page)

1. Wicker picnic basket, some of the contents include silverware and one granite plate. Basket labeled "Reg. trade mark SIRRAM M. LTD. B." *Note:* See rows 2 and 3 for rest of contents.

Plate 2, Row 2:

1. Salt shaker, nickel plated.
2. Tumbler, nickel plated.
3. Granite saucer, blue outside, white inside.
4. Granite cup, blue outside, white inside.
5. Granite plate, blue outside, white inside.
6. Granite plate, inside view, white, outside is blue.
7. Granite cup and saucer, blue outside, white inside.
8. Tin insert, hinged cover, one side marked "Tea," the other side, "Sugar."

Plate 2, Row 3:

1. Cream flask, white granite, screw-on, nickel-plated top and attached chain.
2. Butter dish, nickel-plated cover embossed "BUTTER." There are two of these. *Note:* These are ceramic.
3. Fuel can, metal.
4. Teakettle, blue granite. *Note:* The teakettle's nickel-plated stopper and spout stopper have a cork applied to the bottom section of the stopper where it fits into the teakettle. Thus the teakettle can be filled with water and carried without spilling. A brass chain connects to both stoppers and to a metal tag with embossed instructions reading "Caution before lighting stove, remove both stoppers." Marked "PATENT, SIRRAM REG."
5. Stove with alcohol burner, marked "SIRRAM REG. 247422." Burner marked "SIRRAM REG. 542349."
6. Covered container, white granite with nickel-plated cover and bands.

Plate 3, Row 1:

1. Pedestal vase, blue shaded, white inside, decorated with flowers and gold bands, lettered "Sainte Barbe."
2. Vase, shaded red to black, red inside, marked "Germany."
3. Pedestal vase, blue shaded, white inside, decorated with flowers and gold bands, also lettered.

Plate 3, Row 2:

1. Wine cooler or pedestal vase, yellow and white inside and outside, large swirl, black trim, circa 1960's, lightweight.
2. Hanging wall vase, cream and dark maroon large swirl, back of vase is riveted on heavy base metal, cross collectible.
3. Vase, blue and white with black trim, large swirl.

Plate 3, Row 3:

1. Ashtray and cigar nipper. Ashtray is white with blue border, center serves as cigar nipper. To snip off the end of a cigar, pull up the knob on top of the post, place the end of the cigar in the hole, and press down. On the underside of the ashtray is a round cup that screws on and off and holds the cigar ends. Marked "D.R.G.M."
2. Ashtray, white, pink, and green, large swirl, "End of Day."
3. License plate, red and white, circa 1900's, marked "L. & G. Mfg. Co." *Note:* This has no year imprinted on it. Cross collectible.

Section 26

Child's Items, Miniatures and Salesman's Samples, Child Feeding Sets, Child Starter Sets, Table, Stoves, Trays, Chamber Pots, Utensils, Graters, Dust Pan, Crumb Tray, Roasters, Teakettles, Pails, Irons, Cuspidors, Tea Sets, Molds, Funnels, Place Card Holders, Clocks, Pitcher and Bowl Sets, Advertising, Wash Basins

Plate 1, Row 1:

1. Child's two-piece feeding set, green, decorated with white and yellow chickens. Note the two handled cup. This was for the child to hold with both hands. The two-handled cups are not often found. Marked "Made in Germany." *Note:* The smaller size sets are feeding sets, and the larger size sets are starter sets.
2. Child's feeding dish, pink, decorated with Humpty Dumpty, marked "KOCHUMS SWEDEN. 18 C.M."
3. Child's two-piece feeding set, blue, decorated with a girl feeding a duck.
4. Child's cup, blue, decorated with a girl having a tea party with a bear.
5. Child's plate, white, decorated with frolicking teddy bear, dog, and kitten. Advertises "MOLENAARS KINDERMEEL." Advertising cross collectible.

Plate 1, Row 2:

1. Child's two-piece feeding set, pink with orange trim, decorated with a rabbit.
2. Child's plate, blue, decorated with a girl having a tea party with a bear. *Note:* The author doesn't believe this went with No. 4 on Row 1 of this plate because the coloring is different and it's marked "G.W. Co. N.Y., Made in Germany."
3. Child's mug, green, decorated with a girl and lamb with nursery rhyme "Mary had a little lamb."
4. Child's feeding dish, yellow, decorated with a boy riding a dog. Marked "Elite, Czechoslovakia. Rg'd. 37140."
5. Child's two-piece feeding set, mug and cereal bowl, blue trimmed with a darker blue, decorated with a duck swimming with an umbrella.

Plate 1, Row 3:

1. Child's table with chair, white trimmed in dark blue, decorated with ABC's, numbers, circus scene, and nursery rhymes. *Note:* There should be another chair with the set.

Plate 2, Row 1:

1. Child's starter plate, part of a two-piece starter set, white trimmed in black, decorated with "The Campbell Kids." Signed "g.g. Drayton." *Note:* There is a mug that goes with this set. Cross collectible.
2. Salesman's sample "Hearth Style" wood-burning stove, blue with fine white flecks, speckled pattern, embossed "Karr Range Co., Belleville, Ill." *Note:* This stove has original working parts.
3. Child's starter plate, white trimmed in black, decorated with "The Campbell Kids." *Note:* There is a mug that goes with this set. This plate is not signed. Cross collectible.

Plate 2, Row 2:

1. Child's miniature electric toy stove, yellow with nickel-plated warming shelf and legs, cross collectible.
2. Child's starter plate, white trimmed in brown decorated with two girls walking their doll, marked "Made in Austria." These are a series of sets. *Note:* The author believes these represent some type of child's story.
3. Child's starter mug, white trimmed in brown decorated with four girls walking, marked "Made in Austria."
4. Child's starter plate, white trimmed in brown decorated with four girls walking, marked "Made in Austria."

Plate 2, Row 3:

1. Child's three-piece starter set, red, trimmed in black, decorated with a snowman and a child on a sled, marked "Elite Czechoslovakia Reg'd. 8151K."
2. Child's miniature toy stove, solid light blue body on cast iron with gray top, two removable lids, front metal towel rack. Also has a drop-down oven door on front of stove. 11½" long by 6½" high. Embossed on top of stove "BABY BAUBIN." Cross collectible.

Plate 3, Row 1:

1. Miniature electric range with blue enamel panels, marked "EMPIRE" under warming shelf, cross collectible.
2. Advertising booklet for No. 1 on this row. Booklet reads "The only Practical Miniature Electric Range is the Empire. Empire furnishes two models of miniature electirc ranges. The larger model has two side ovens. The smaller one has a large single oven. Both are as efficient for all cooking and baking as any large range. These toys are instructive. They teach girls to cook and bake in a practical way. The ovens are large enough for small cakes, pies, potatoes and other dishes. The cooking top is roomy too. The legs, door frames, cooking top and shelf are heavily Nickel-plated and sturdily constructed. Body is Black Japanned finish. The heating element is designed to give economical operation and even temperatures to both ovens. It operates on standard electirc light socket. Made by Metal Ware Corporation, Chicago, Ill., Two Rivers, Wis."

Plate 3, Row 2:

1. Child's potty, cobalt blue and white with black trim, large swirl.
2. Child's sectioned tray, white, decorated with Sunbonnet Babies, numbers, and alphabet. Marked "Patents PEN'D." *Note:* This is a cross collectible because of the great desirabliity of Sunbonnet Babies to collectors. Made in 1915 by Lisk Manufacturing Co., Canandaigua, N.Y.
3. Child's covered potty, white with greeen trim, labeled "Savory Ware" No. 01 PORCELAIN ENAMEL ON INGOT IRON. ARMCO."

Plate 3, Row 3:

1. Child's feeding dish, white with dark blue trim decorated with a girl holding a spoon, looks like a Campbell Kid, marked "KOCKUMS KER. SWEDEN. 18CM."
2. Child's tray, cream trimmed in black, decorated with Bo Peep and a lamb, signed "Edna Lewis ©."
3. Child's two-piece starter set, cream trimmed in green, decorated with a decal of Orphan Annie and her dog, Sandy. Advertises "Ovaltine," "Didja Ever Taste Anything So Good as Ovaltine?" and "It's Good For Yuh Too." Signed "Harold Gray." Cross collectible because of great desirability of Orphan Annie items and also as an advertising item for Ovaltine.

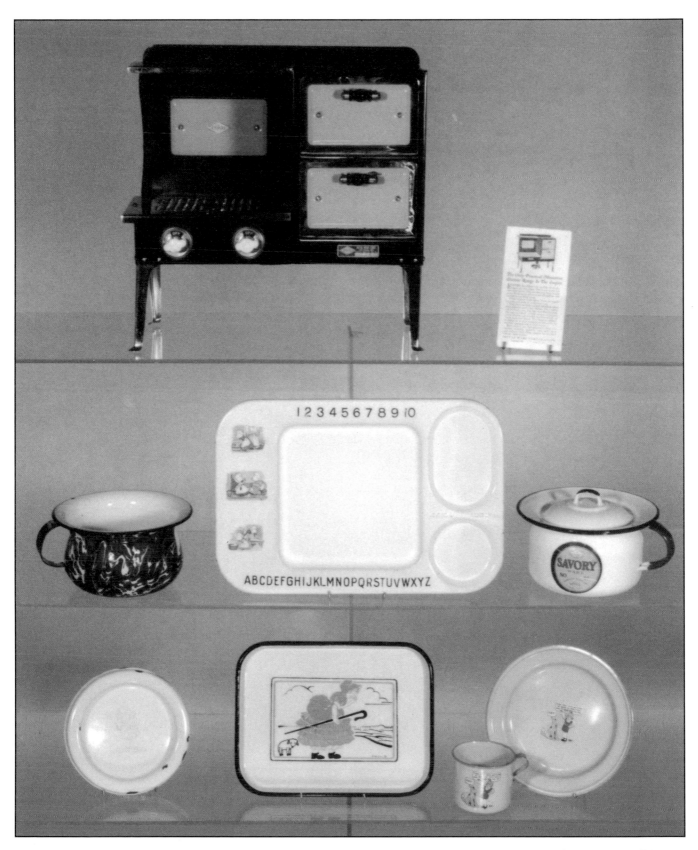

Section 26, Plate 3

Plate 4, Row 1:

1. Child's cup and saucer, white decorated with cobalt blue design, cobalt blue trim and handle, marked "Made in Austria."
2. Child's miniature toy stove, doll size, gray with black granite stove top, fancy embossed body, 10½" long, 6" wide, 6¾" high. White granite extension side shelf, four removable lids with lid lifter, water reservoir, hinged oven door and fire door. All parts work. Embossed on back "KEHTON BRAND." Oven door is also embossed "ROYAL." Cross collectible.
3. Embossed alphabet plate, gray, L. & G. Manufacturing Co. *Note:* This plate was also used to teach children their ABC's. It is a cross collectible because of great desirability of alphabet plates.
4. Child's mug, blue and white with black trim, large swirl.

Plate 4, Row 2:

1. Tea set, 13 pieces, white, decorated with red floral and leaf design, includes place setting for four with cups, saucers, covered teapot, covered sugar and creamer. It's interesting to note that in the 1924 Butler Brothers Christmas Wholesale Catalog, the advertisements varied on tea sets. Some included plates while others did not. Also, some sets only came with two cups and saucers while other sets had four or six. This set has the original box with label "G.B.M."
2. Child's plate, white, decorated with red horse and trim.

Plate 4, Row 3:

1. Child's three-piece starter set, blue, decorated with children carrying dolls and an umbrella, includes plate, saucer and cup. Marked "Elite Czechoslovakia."
2. Child's three-piece starter set, pink, decorated with a girl and her dog frolicking, marked "Elite Czechoslovakia."

Plate 5, Row 1:

1. Handled skimmer, dark blue.
2. Handled skimmer, dark blue. Note the different shaped handles on No. 1 & 2.
3. Grater, white, trimmed in light blue.
4. Dustpan, white, with light blue handle.
5. Spoon, blue and white, fine mottled.
6. Spatula or turner, blue and white, fine mottled.
7. Ladle, blue and white, fine mottled.
8. Grater, blue and white, fine mottled.
9. Colander, blue and white inside and outside, fine mottled, footed with two handles.
10. Handled strainer, blue and white inside and outside, fine mottled, with kettle hook on opposite end.

Plate 5, Row 2:

Tea set, white, trimmed in red, service for four including plates, cups, saucers and covered coffee pot. *Note:* The shape and design of the tea sets were traditional of that particular era.

Plate 5, Row 3:

1. Teakettle, solid blue outside, white inside.
2. Salesman sample plate, red and white, with black trim, large swirl inside and outside, circa 1960's. *Note:* The author believes one purpose for these salesman sample pieces was for salesmen or jobbers to give these pieces to customers to get their reactions on how well a particular item might sell for color, shape and durability.
3 Miniature candlestick, white, trimmed in gold, finger ring and thumb rest.
4. Tea set, 13 pieces (continued on row 4). White, trimmed in cobalt blue, service for four incudes cups, saucers, and plates plus a covered sugar, creamer and teapot. *Note:* Numerous sets were advertised in different sizes. Sets were purchased by individuals for special uses. For instance, the larger sets were used for fun or to teach little girls how to prepare liquids and foods as well as teaching etiquette in serving.

Plate 6, Row 1:

1. Child's fry pan, red, trimmed in black, white inside.
2. Cooking set (continued on Row 2), light gray, trimmed in royal blue, two handled kettle, baking pan, lipped sauce pan, handled pudding pan, and mixing bowl. The pie plate is missing. *Note:* These sets were used to teach little girls how to cook.

Plate 6, Row 3:

1. Roaster, dark blue with white flecks, speckled pattern, Centennial souvenir. *Note:* This roaster was given away as a promotional souvenir to celebrate The Columbian Enameling & Stamping Company's first 100 years, 1871 to 1971. This is an advertising cross collectible because of its desirability to both advertising and enamel ware collectors.
2. Roaster insert and covered roaster, oval salesman's sample, cobalt blue and white inside and outside, black trim and handles, large swirl, white handled insert with black trim and handles.

Plate 6, Row 4:

1. Covered roaster with handled insert, Speckled pattern, salesman's sample. All pieces are black and white flecked, inside and outside, embossed on cover is "LISK." Cover also has two metal steam vents. These are replicas of the original "LISK" large roasters that the Lisk Manufacturing Co., Canandaigua, N.Y. was famous for. *Note:* The author was told by a former employee of the factory that these sample roasters were actually salesman samples given to little girls as a premium when their mothers purchased a certain amount of granite ware.
2. Insert and covered roaster, salesman's sample, white insert with dark blue trim. Covered roaster, blue and white with black trim, fine mottled. Roaster embossed on cover "LISK."

Plate 7, Row 1:

1. Covered handled sauce pan, dark charcoal gray and white, large mottled.
2. Teakettle, dark charcoal gray and white, large mottled, "Belle" shaped.
3. Lipped preserve kettle, black outside, white inside. Labeled "The Pennsylvania and Atlantic Seaboard Hardware Ass'n., Inc. 22nd Exhibition Souvenir, Philadelphia, Pa., Februbary 12–13–`14–15–16, 1925. "NESCO." Note ears that hold wire bail from resting on kettle. Advertising cross collectible.
4. Salesman's sample water pail, gray with wooden bail, marked "Royal Granite Steel Ware."

Plate 7, Row 2:

1. Covered sugar, gray and white inside and outside, fine mottled.
2. Long handled strainer, cobalt blue, white inside, fancy perforated rounded bottom.
3. Preserve kettle, solid blue, wire bail.
4. Covered handled sauce pan, blue and white inside and outside, large mottled.

Plate 7, Row 3:

1. Child's electric iron, solid light blue, marked "Gold Seal."
2. Cuspidor, salesman's sample, white, red, light blue, dark blue and maroon, inside and outside, large swirl, heavy metal base, "End of Day."
3. Child's electric iron, solid green, marked "Ideal." *Note:* These irons were actually used to teach children how to do ironing.
4. Miniature coffee pot, solid light blue with riveted spout, strap handle and back seam. *Note:* The pots with the coffee pot spouts are harder to find than with the gooseneck spouts.

Plate 7, Row 4:

Domestic science cook set, gray medium mottled, oblong baking pan, long handled sauce pan, cake pan, preserve kettle with wire bail, and lipped fry pan. *Note:* Pudding pan is missing. The author has seen this set in two different sizes, this being the largest.

Plate 8, Row 1:

1. Cup and saucer, blue and white, fine mottled.
2. Plate, blue and white, fine mottled.
3. Cup and saucer, blue and white, fine mottled.
4. Coffee pot, blue and white, fine mottled.
5. Oval platter, blue and white, fine mottled.
6. Pudding pan, cobalt blue and white, black trim, large swirl.
7. Percolator funnel, solid cobalt blue and white, riveted handle.
8. Wash basin, salesman's sample, cobalt blue and white, white inside, black trim, large mottled.

Plate 8, Row 2:

1. Partial tea set, large size, part of 12-piece set. Advertised in Butler Brothers Wholesale Catalog, December 1924, as toy tea sets. Shows this set with four cups, saucers, creamer, covered sugar, and teapot. Price of this set then was $4.90.
2. Tea set, 13 pieces (continued on Row 3), includes teapot, cover, underplate, creamer, open sugar, four cups, and saucers. White with cobalt blue bands and gold trim, marked "Germany." Note the different sizes of these two sets on Row 2.

Plate 8, Row 3:

1. Salesman's sample wash basin, black and white inside and outside, fine mottled.
2. Partial tea set, part of a 13-piece set, shaded blue and white.
3. Wash basin, salesman's sample, blue and white, white inside, black trim, fine mottled.

Plate 8, Row 4:

1. Partial tea set, part of a 12-piece set, solid blue, cover is missing on sugar bowl.
2. Cup, white, blue, yellow, and brown, large swirl, "End of Day."
3. Pitcher, gray and white, medium mottled.
4. Tube mold, turban style, gray and white, fine mottled, ring for hanging.
5. Funnel, gray and white inside and ouside, medium mottled.
6. Cup and saucer, dark charcoal gray and light gray medium mottled. Note the unusual small size.
7. Oblong teapot, dark charcoal gray and light gray medium mottled, cover is missing.

367

Plate 9, Row 1:

1. Handled skimmer, gray and white, medium mottled.
2. Perforated spatula or turner, dark gray and white, medium mottled.
3. Ladle, gray and white, medium mottled.
4. Grater, gray and white, medium mottled.
5. Grater, solid dark blue.
6. Grater, gray and white, medium mottled. Note the different shapes of these three graters.
7. Perforated spatula or turner, solid blue.
8. Spatula or turner, solid blue back and handle, white inside.
9. Perforated spatula or turner, bluish gray and white medium mottled.

Plate 9, Row 2:

1. Partial tea set, solid blue, four cups, saucers, teapot and creamer. *Note:* Sugar is missing.
2. Coffee pot, solid blue, riveted spout and handle.
3. Covered sugar, solid blue.
4. Creamer, solid blue, straight sided.
5. Wash basin, salesman's sample, white, dark brown, and blue inside and outside, large swirl, "End of Day."
6. Wash basin, salesman's sample, white, gray, dark blue, light blue inside and outside, large swirl, "End of Day." What could be a better example for salesmen to show colors than this? *Note:* These "End of Day" salesman's sample wash basins generally are colored inside and outside.

Plate 9, Row 3:

1. Preserve kettle, salesman's sample, white with green veining, marked "Elite." *Note:* The author believes this is a salesman's sample because it's identical in characteristics to a large kettle that was seen.
2. Covered stew pan, solid green. *Note:* Handle is missing.
3. Mug, solid green.
4. Plate, solid green.
5. Egg fry pan, solid green, four eyes.
6. Fluted mold, solid green.
7. Crumb tray, solid green. *Note:* There should be a small brush with this used for brushing crumbs off the table.
8. Fry pan, cream and green.

Plate 9, Row 4:

1. Oblong roasting pan, brick red, gray inside.
2. Two handled sauce pan, brick red, white inside.
3. Covered mush mug, brick red, white inside.
4. Creamer, brick red, white inside.
5. Fry pan, brick red, white inside.
6. Plate, brick red, white inside.
7. Teakettle, light brown shaded. *Note:* Cover not original.

Plate 10, Row 1:

1. Creamer, blue, white inside, straight sided.
2. Handled sauce pan, blue, white inside.
3. Handled divided vegetable dish, blue white inside.
4. Two-handled sauce pan, blue, white inside.
5. Small wash basin, blue, white inside, ring for hanging.
6. Funnel, blue, white inside.
7. Oblong roasting pan, blue, white inside, with pouring spout.
8. Large wash basin, blue, white inside, ring for hanging.
9. Egg fry pan, blue, white inside, five eyes.
10. Two-handled roasting pan, blue, white inside.
11. Plate, blue, white inside.

Plate 10, Row 2:

1. Creamer, blue, white inside, straight sided.
2. Platter, blue, white inside.
3. Teapot, blue, white inside.
4. Open sugar, blue, white inside.
5. Large platter, blue, white inside.
6. Pieced scoop, blue, white inside.
7. Fry pan, solid blue.
8. Gravy or sauce bowl, blue, white inside.

Plate 10, Row 3:

1. Covered sauce pan, blue and white, fine mottled.
2. Fry pan, blue and white, fine mottled.
3. Mug, blue and white, fine mottled.
4. Fluted mold, blue and white, fine mottled.
5. Funnel, blue and white, fine mottled.
6. Pail, blue and white, fine mottled.
7. Two-handled sauce pan, blue and white, fine mottled.

Plate 10, Row 4:

1. Two-handled sauce pan, gray and white, medium mottled.
2. Fry pan, gray and white, medium mottled.
3. Wash basin, gray and white, medium fine mottled.
4. Oblong roasting pan, gray and white, medium mottled.
5. Creamer, gray and white, medium mottled.
6. Mug, gray and white, medium mottled.
7. Fluted mold, gray and white, medium mottled.
8. Fry pan, gray and white, Relish pattern.
9. Stew pan, gray and white, medium mottled. Note the depth of this compared to the fry pans.
10. Pail, gray and white medium mottled, wire bail. Note size variations on all these pieces on this page.

Plate 11, Row 1:

1. Cup and saucer, light green, decorated with darker green, red, and white pattern.
2. Tea set, 13 pieces (continued on Row 2). Light blue, decorated with white and dark blue design, includes four cups, saucers, plates, creamer, covered sugar, and teapot. *Note:* An old advertisement states that these sets were also used to serve cocoa and coffee as well as dinners.

Plate 11, Row 2:

1. Pair of place card holders, Victorian style man and woman with pink outfits. *Note:* These were used to hold a personalized card for each place setting at a social dinner.
2. Pair of place card holders, Victorian style man and woman with blue outfits.
3. Creamer and saucer, blue, decorated with a white bow design.

Plate 11, Row 3:

1. Grater, solid green.
2. Cup and saucer, decorated with a green pattern.
3. Plate, dark green and white inside and outside, medium mottled.
4. Cup and saucer, decorated with a green and gold pattern.
5. Cup and saucer, white, decorated with flower pattern.
6. Creamer, white, decorated with flower pattern.
7. Partial tea set, white, decorated with a pink and green checkered design, trimmed in black, two cups, saucers, and covered teapot.

Plate 11, Row 4:

13-piece tea set, brown, decorated with a gold leaf pattern, white inside, includes four cups and saucers, covered teapot, creamer, and covered sugar.

Plate 12, Row 1:

13-piece tea set (continued on Row 2). Cream, decorated with green shamrocks and gold trim.

Plate 12, Row 2:

Partial serving set, white, decorated with gold leaves and trim, includes soup tureen with lid and ladle, gravy boat, and eight plates. *Note:* Divided handled vegetable dish and oval platter are missing.

Plate 12, Row 3:

13-piece tea set (continued on Row 4). Cobalt blue, decorated with children's scenes, trimmed in gold.

Plate 12, Row 4:

Partial tea set, white, decorated with pink flowers and green leaves with brown trim, includes covered sugar, creamer, two cups and saucers. *Note:* The teapot, two cups and two saucers are missing.

Plate 13, Row 1:

13-piece serving set, decorated, includes six cups, saucers, and serving tray. *Note:* This set is heavily enameled over copper. Also note the unusual wire-shaped handles.

Plate 13, Row 2:

Doll's 12-piece tea set, solid blue. This small set was used by little girls when having a party with their dolls. *Note:* The doll-size sets are much harder to come by than the larger ones.

Plate 13, Row 3:

1. Salesman's sample wash basin, cobalt blue and white, white inside, black trim, medium swirl.
2. Salesman's sample wash basin, blue and white, white inside, black trim, fine mottled.
3. 12-piece tea set, solid light blue, includes four cups and saucers, covered teapot, creamer, and open sugar.
4. Salesman's sample wash basin, white and light blue inside and outside, black trim, medium mottled, "Snow on the Mountain."
5. Salesman's sample wash basin, dark purple shaded, white inside, black trim.

Plate 13, Row 4:

1. Saucer, dark blue and white, medium mottled.
2. Plate, dark blue and white, medium mottled.
3. Plate, dark blue and white, medium mottled.
4. Saucer, dark blue and white, medium mottled.
5. Two-handled sauce pan, dark blue and white, medium mottled.
6. Covered mush mug, dark blue and white, medium mottled.
7. Oblong roasting pan, dark blue and white, medium mottled.
8. Handled sauce pan, dark blue and white, medium mottled.

Plate 14, Row 1:

1. Salesman's sample advertising cuspidor, blue and white, white inside, black trim, large mottled. Advertising on inside bottom of cuspidor, "United States Stamping Co., Moundsville, W. Va." Advertising cross collectible.
2. Miniature "Red Riding Hood" clock, marked "Germany." *Note:* This clock also is a cross collectible because of Red Riding Hood's desirability.
3. Fluted mold, solid dark blue.
4. Miniature mountain scene clock, marked "Germany."
5. Child's coffee pot, large gray mottling, seamed, applied strap handle, tin cover with wooden acorn knob, very early.

Plate 14, Row 2:

1. Two-handled sauce pan, brick red, white inside.
2. Melon-shaped mold or patty pan, brick red, white inside. Note: In the La Lance & Grosjean Mfg. Co. Catalog, March 1884, these are referred to as patty pans.
3. "Heart" fluted mold or patty pan, brick red, white inside.
4. "Lobster" fluted mold or patty pan, brick red, white inside.
5. Two-handled bean pot, blue and white, black trim, large mottled.

Plate 14, Row 3:

13-piece tea set, white, decorated with cobalt blue and light blue floral design, includes four cups and saucers, covered sugar, covered teapot and creamer.

Plate 14, Row 4:

1. Advertising Salesman's sample wash basin, solid blue, marked "REED." Advertising for Reed Manufacturing Company, Newark, New York. This company was famous for "Reed" Sanitary Self-Basting Roasters with the name "REED" embossed on the roaster cover.
2. Advertising salesman's sample wash basin, cream and green, marked "LISK." Advertising for The Lisk Manufacturing Company, Canandaigua, N.Y., famous for their "Lisk" Self-Basting Roaster with the name "LISK" embossed on the roaster cover.
3. Two-handled egg plate, blue and white, medium mottled, white inside, cobalt blue trim and handles.
4. Advertising salesman's sample wash basin, solid green, marked "REED."
5. Advertising Salesman's sample wash basin, white, trimmed in black, marked "LISK."

379

Plate 15, Row 1:

1. Fry pan, white, cobalt blue, light blue, pink, yellow and green, white inside, Confetti pattern, "End of Day." *Note:* The author calls this pattern "Confetti" because of the resemblance to the colors of paper confetti.
2. Pitcher, Confetti pattern, "'End of Day."
3. Handled strainer, Confetti pattern, "End of Day."
4. Mixing bowl, Confetti pattern, "End of Day."

Plate 15, Row 2:

1. Scalloped soap dish, Confetti pattern, "End of Day."
2. Water dipper, Confetti pattern, "End of Day."
3. Covered sugar, Confetti pattern, "End of Day."
4. Covered sauce pan, Confetti pattern, "End of Day."

Plate 15, Row 3:

1. Oval platter, Confetti pattern, "End of Day."
2. Pudding pan, Confetti pattern, "End of Day."
3. Cup and saucer, Confetti pattern, "End of Day."
4. Cup and saucer, Confetti pattern, "End of Day."

Plate 15, Row 4:

1. Pitcher and bowl, blue shaded, white inside, black trim.
2. Partial wash set, includes water pail with wooden bail, soap dish, and pitcher and bowl. Pink, decorated with white and maroon checkered border, tirmmed in gold. *Note:* The tumbler and chamber pot are missing.

Section 27

The Hunt Goes On

I hope by the time you have reached this point in the book that I have sparked a "Granite Ware Interest" in each and every one of you. As one can see, the beauty of the colors and shapes in granite ware is unending.

For this reason, I thought this would be an appropriate way to end the book by showing you a few of the things which have surfaced after the official photography was completed. You see, It's still out there! All you have to do is get up at the "crack of dawn" and start driving, only to find out some distance down the road that you missed the buy or find of the day. Now there is something inside of you that says over and over again, "I just have to keep on going and find something today." Soon you are dying of hunger and your feet are killing you! All of a sudden, the unexpected happens - there it is! You make a mad dash! You have found your treasure! Now all the hunger and fatigue seems unimportant because the adrenalin is pumping again! You are on a roll! There is no stopping you now! You knew you could do it!

As I leave you with these thoughts, I wish each and every one of you the "Best that Granite Ware Has To Offer."

Granitely,

Helen Greguire

(Opposite Page)

Plate 1, Row 1:

1. Oil stove teakettle, gray medium mottled, gooseneck spout, tin cover, wooden bail. *Note:* Because this teakettle has the gooseneck spout rather than the straight spout often seen, it would be classified as an extremely rare shape.
2. Small bucket, white with green veining, large mottled, wooden bail, marked "Elite."
3. Four-piece coffee biggin, orange and white, black trim, large mottled, includes cover, pot, granite biggin and perforated spreader, "Snow on the Mountain."
4. Oyster measure, gray large mottled, seamed body, riveted strap handle, labeled "Haberman's Steel Enameled Ware," "Haberman Mfg. Co. Oyster Measure," label shows a teakettle in a diamond. *Note:* This was used for dipping out and measuring the amount of oysters from the containers at the store.
5. Rice or farina boiler, blue and white, white inside, black trim and handle, large swirl, wire bail. *Note:* Popularly known as a double boiler.

Plate 1, Row 2:

1. Teapot, cream and green, only 5½" high with spun cover knob.
2. Teapot, cream and green, 6½" high with open ring cover knob.
3. Cake safe, cream and green, decorated with birds and floral pattern, labeled "Cream City Ware," Geuder, Paeschke, and Frey Company, Milwaukee, Wisconsin.
4. Percolator, electric, cream and green with gray coffee basket, labeled "Polar" Made in U.S.A., Polar Ware Co., Sheboygan, Wisconsin, Pat. July 18, 1916.

Plate 1, Row 3:

1. Molasses pitcher, cobalt blue and white, white inside, large swirl.
2. Chocolate or coffee pot, blue and white, white inside, black trim, medium mottled, weld handle, seamless. Note the unusual shaped, round, seamless bottom.
3. Tumbler, small, white, with green veining and trim, large mottled, marked "Elite."
4. Bread pan, cobalt blue and white, white inside, black trim, large swirl, seamed ends.
5. Partial set of spice cannisters, solid red, white inside, white knobs and white lettering. Embossed "ALLSPICE, CINNAMON, NUTMEG, AND CLOVES. MARKED KOCKUMS, K.E.R. SWEDEN."
6. Coffee pot, light blue and white, white inside, large swirl, dark blue trim, seamed.

383

Price Guide Introduction

What I will try to achieve in this Price Guide is an approximate suggested price for each item even though different areas of the country and abroad demand different prices. Many factors help to determine the price. Some of these include condition, rarity, color, shape, size, age, popularity, dates, types of marks or labels and cross collectibility.

Condition is of prime importance when setting up any price guide. Granite ware is more likely to be found in "Good Plus" condition, meaning all sides should be quite presentable with no more than minor chipping. The piece should also have a good shine to the finish. A pinhole in the bottom could be permissible. The same condition holds for all metal and wood parts. We must remember that granite ware by its very nature was made to be utilitarian. It was both used and abused. This is why I chose to realistically base this guide on "Good Plus" condition.

Even harder to find and commanding a premium over "Good Plus" condition are those "Near Mint" items. They can have limited tiny chips, and again must have a good shine to the finish. All metal and wood parts must be in similar condition. On the other hand, "Mint" pieces are not often found. By "Mint" I mean "like new," including all metal and wood parts. When these "Mint" pieces do surface, they command the largest additional premium of all over "Good Plus." It should be noted that items found in poorer condition than "Good Plus," that is anything lacking at least one good display side, having lots of rust or holes, and lacking a good shine to the finish, fall into a category which leaves it to the discretion of each buyer as to what he or she feels they should pay.

Rarity is determined by availability of a particular color, shape, or size. Certain colors were originally made in very limited quantities. A good example of this is "Old" Red and White Swirl. Shape and size play a very important part in pricing too. Smaller, larger, longer or shorter than usual, or different shapes such as squatty, straight-sided, pedestalled bases, footed or any other shapes not often seen in a particular item, help to increase an item's value.

Popularity can also have a very important effect on the pricing and saleability of an item. Pieces can be popular for one reason or another, such as color, shape or size. Certain items are always highly sought after by collectors such as coffee and teapots, granite ware which can be easily hung for display, miniatures and children's pieces. Dates stamped, embossed or marked on pieces can make a great difference in their value. The type of other marks or labels are also important. Many collectors look for a manufacturer's name or place of manufacture. Additional information on a label, such as color or the name of a particular line, can be most important when it comes to collecting or researching.

Last but not least, cross collectibility adds a degree of importance to granite ware. If a piece has advertising on it for a World's Fair, it then belongs in the advertising category, and is of particular interest to World's Fair collectors as well.

In summary, my personal opinion is that granite ware is only worth what you or anyone else is willing to pay for it. A price guide is meant to be just what it says, "A Guide." In an effort to bring you the closest price on an item, I have compiled price lists from all over the country, going auction prices, antique show prices, dealer's prices, and private sale prices. I have also discussed prices that have been acutally paid for granite ware with hundreds of collectors. I feel prices paid over two years ago to be out of date! My main purpose in trying to reach an appropriate figure is not to outprice granite ware for beginning collectors. On the other hand, I want to be realistic as far as actual going prices are concerned. If a collector after reading this price guide was to see a piece of granite ware for sale at a high price, he or she might well pass it up if the guide had quoted an unrealistic lower price. Remember, suggested prices in this guide are based on "Good Plus" condition unless otherwise stated. I have to decline to assume any responsibility for losses incurred by purchasers or users of this guide.

How to Use the Price Guide

Condition

1. **Mint (M).** No chips and a good shine to the finish. Also, all metal and wooden parts should be mint.
2. **Near Mint (N.M.).** Limited tiny chips and a good shine to the finish. Also, all metal and wooden parts should be Near Mint.
3. **Good Plus (G.P.).** All sides should be quite presentable with minor chipping and a good shine to the finish. Also, all metal and wooden parts should be in Good Plus condition. A pinhole in the bottom could be permissible.

Price Guide Rarity Key*

1. Extremely Rare Color
2. Extremely Rare Shape
3. Extremely Rare Size
4. Rare Color
5. Rare Shape
6. Rare Size

Note:
1. A color which is relatively common on a particular item may in turn be rare on another item.
2. A shape may be rare in a particular size and not rare in another size.
3. Similarly, a size in one shape may be relatively common whereas the same size in another shape may be a rarity, e.g. 1.) A gray pie plate, which is common as opposed to a gray lady finger pan, which is rare; 2.) A miniature mug in comparison with a standard size mug is rare; 3.) A 9" squatty teapot could be rare whereas a 9" straight-sided teapot could be classified as more common.

*Complete sets add 15% more, meaning it should have all its parts including covers.
Labeled, marked and dated pieces usually demand a higher premium.

Section 1

Item	Condition	Rarity	Price
Plate 1, Row 1:			
1. Teapot	(M)		$325.00
2. Teapot	(M)	6	$550.00
3. Teapot	(M)	2	$475.00
4. Teapot	(M)	6	$550.00
5. Teapot	(M)		$295.00
Plate 1, Row 2:			
1. Teapot	(N.M.)		$225.00
2. Teapot	(M)		$295.00
3. Teapot	(M)		$295.00
4. Teapot	(M)	5,6	$550.00
Plate 1, Row 3:			
1. Teapot	(M)	4	$285.00
2. Teapot	(M)		$395.00
3. Teapot	(M)	4	$375.00
4. Teapot	(M)		$295.00
Plate 2, Row 1:			
1. Coffee pot	(M)		$295.00
2. Teapot	(M)		$285.00
3. Coffee pot	(M)		$275.00
4. Teapot	(M)		$295.00
Plate 2, Row 2:			
1. Teapot	(M)		$295.00
2. Teapot	(M)	2	$1395.00
3. Teapot	(M)	5	$425.00
Plate 2, Row 3:			
1. Teapot	(M)		$225.00
2. Coffee pot	(M)		$200.00
3. Coffee pot	(N.M.)		$215.00
Plate 3, Row 1:			
1. Coffee pot	(M)		$295.00
2. Coffee pot	(M)		$225.00
Plate 3, Row 2:			
1. Coffee pot	(M)		$250.00
2. Coffee pot	(M)		$275.00
3. Teapot	(M)		$295.00
Plate 3, Row 3:			
1. Teapot	(M)	5	$395.00
2. Teapot	(M)		$295.00
3. Coffee pot	(M)		$295.00
4. Teapot	(M)	5	$395.00
Plate 4, Row 1:			
1. Teapot	(M)	5	$285.00
2. Coffee pot	(M)		$225.00
3. Coffee pot	(M)		$225.00
Plate 4, Row 2:			
1. Coffee pot	(N.M.)		$225.00
2. Coffee pot	(M)		$255.00
3. Teapot	(M)	4,5	$525.00
Plate 4, Row 3			
1. Teapot	(G.P.)		$195.00
2. Teapot	(N.M.)		$210.00
3. Coffee pot	(M)		$235.00
4. Coffee pot	(M)	4,5	$395.00
Plate 5, Row 1:			
1. Coffee Biggin	(M)	5,6	$295.00
2. Coffee Biggin	(M)	2,3	$595.00
3. Coffee Biggin	(N.M.)	2,3	$395.00
4. Coffee Biggin	(M)		$195.00

Item	Condition	Rarity	Price
Plate 5, Row 2:			
1. Coffee Biggin	(M)	1,2	$595.00
2. Coffee Biggin	(M)	1,2	$495.00
3. Coffee Biggin	(M)	4,5	$285.00
4. Coffee Biggin	(N.M.)	1,2	$595.00
Plate 5, Row 3:			
1. Coffee Biggin	(N.M.)	4,6	$495.00
2. Coffee Biggin	(N.M.)	5	$210.00
3. Coffee Biggin	(M)	2	$495.00
4. Coffee Biggin	(M)	5	$245.00
Plate 6, Row 1:			
1. Coffee Biggin	(N.M.)	2,3	$395.00
2. Coffee Biggin	(M)	2	$495.00
Plate 6, Row 2:			
Coffee Biggin	(M)	2,3	$595.00
Plate 6, Row 3:			
1. Coffee Biggin	(M)		$195.00
2. Coffee Biggin	(M)	5,6	$295.00
Plate 7, Row 1:			
1. Coffee Biggin	(N.M.)	1,2	$595.00
2. Coffee Biggin	(M)	1,2	$550.00
3. Coffee Biggin	(G.P.)	1,2	$595.00
Plate 7, Row 2:			
1. Coffee Biggin	(N.M.)	4,5	$295.00
2. Coffee Biggin	(M)	5	$275.00
3. Coffee Biggin	(N.M.)	5,6	$295.00
4. Coffee Biggin	(M)	2	$295.00
5. Coffee Biggin	(M)	1,2,3	$795.00
Plate 7, Row 3:			
1. Coffee Biggin	(M)		$125.00
2. Coffee Biggin	(M)	5	$135.00
3. Coffee Biggin	(M)		$125.00
4. Coffee Biggin	(G.P.)		$100.00
Plate 8, Row 1:			
1. Coffee Biggin	(N.M.)	4,5	$395.00
2. Coffee Biggin	(N.M.)	5	$295.00
3. Coffee Biggin	(M)	1,2	$495.00
4. Coffee Biggin	(G.P.)	1,2	$565.00
Plate 8, Row 2:			
1. Coffee Biggin	(N.M.)	5	$285.00
2. Coffee Biggin	(M)	1,2	$465.00
3. Coffee Biggin	(M)	4,5	$395.00
4. Coffee Biggin	(M)	4,5	$350.00
Plate 8, Row 3:			
1. Coffee Biggin	(M)	4,5	$425.00
2. Coffee Biggin	(N.M.)	1,5	$425.00
3. Coffee Biggin	(N.M.)	4,5	$395.00
4. Coffee Biggin	(G.P.)	1,2	$565.00
Plate 9, Row 1:			
1. Mugs	(N.M.)	4	ea.$95.00
2. Coffee Boiler	(G.P.)	2,4	$495.00
Plate 9, Row 2:			
1. Mug	(M)	4	$95.00
2. Mug	(M)	4	$95.00
3. Mug	(M)	4,5	$95.00
4. Coffee Roaster	(M)	2	$400.00

Item	Condition	Rarity	Price
Plate 9, Row 3:			
1. Coffee Roaster	(M)	2	$425.00
2. Coffee Roaster	(M)	2	$400.00
Plate 10, Row 1:			
1. Coffee Boiler	(M)		$295.00
2. Coffee Boiler	(N.M.)	1	$2300.00
3. Coffee Boiler	(M)		$225.00
Plate 10, Row 2:			
1. Coffee Boiler	(M)		$200.00
2. Coffee Boiler	(M)	4	$595.00
3. Coffee Boiler	(N.M.)	4	$295.00
Plate 10, Row 3:			
1. Coffee Boiler	(N.M.)	4	$350.00
2. Coffee Boiler	(N.M.)		$225.00
3. Coffee Boiler	(G.P.)		$275.00
Plate 11, Row 1:			
1. Coffee Boiler	(M)		$225.00
2. Coffee Boiler	(N.M.)	5	$275.00
3. Coffee Boiler	(N.M.)		$225.00
Plate 11, Row 2:			
1. Coffee Boiler	(M)	4	$495.00
2. Coffee Boiler	(N.M.)		$295.00
3. Coffee Boiler	(N.M.)	4	$495.00
Plate 11, Row 3:			
1. Coffee Boiler	(N.M.)	4	$495.00
2. Coffee Boiler	(G.P.)		$200.00
3. Coffee Boiler	(N.M.)	4	$525.00
Plate 12, Row 1:			
1. Coffee Boiler	(M)	5,6	$165.00
2. Coffee Boiler	(M)		$195.00
3. Coffee Boiler	(M)	5	$125.00
Plate 12, Row 2:			
1. Teapot	(N.M.)		$165.00
2. Coffee pot	(M)		$250.00
3. Coffee pot	(N.M.)	4	$550.00
4. Coffee pot	(G.P.)		$225.00
Plate 12, Row 3:			
1. Coffee pot	(G.P.)		$145.00
2. Coffee pot	(N.M.)		$195.00
3. Teapot	(N.M.)	4,6	$550.00
4. Coffee pot	(N.M.)	4	$550.00
Plate 13, Row 1:			
1. Teapot	(M)	5,6	$395.00
2. Teapot	(M)	5,6	$395.00
3. Teapot	(N M)	5,6	$350.00
Plate 13, Row 2:			
1. Coffee pot	(G.P.)	4	$185.00
2. Teapot	(M)	5	$350.00
3. Teapot	(M)	5,6	$350.00
4. Teapot	(N.M.)	5	$325.00
Plate 13, Row 3:			
1. Teapot	(M)	4	$125.00
2. Coffee pot	(N.M.)	4	$325.00
3. Teapot	(M)		$265.00
4. Teapot	(G.P.)	4	$225.00

Item	Condition	Rarity	Price
Plate 14, Row 1:			
1. Teapot	(G.P.)	2,3	$395.00
2. Teapot	(N.M.)	4	$475.00
3. Coffee pot	(N.M.)	4	$475.00
4. Coffee pot	(M)		$275.00
Plate 14, Row 2:			
1. Coffee pot	(M)	4	$425.00
2. Coffee pot	(N.M.)		$200.00
3. Coffee pot	(N.M.)	4	$495.00
4. Coffee pot	(G.P.)		$210.00
Plate 14, Row 3:			
1. Coffee pot	(M)	4	$385.00
2. Coffee pot	(N.M.)	4	$265.00
3. Coffee pot	(N.M.)		$225.00
4. Coffee pot	(G.P.)		$225.00
Plate 15, Row 1:			
1. Teapot	(N.M.)	4	$375.00
2. Teapot	(G.P.)		$225.00
3. Teapot	(N.M.)	4,5	$675.00
4. Teapot	(M)		$225.00
Plate 15, Row 2:			
1. Teapot	(N.M.)	4,6	$575.00
2. Teapot	(G.P.)	4,6	$625.00
3. Teapot	(N.M.)	1,2,3	$2,875.00
4. Teapot	(N.M.)	4,6	$395.00
Plate 15, Row 3:			
1. Teapot	(N.M.)	4,5	$495.00
2. Teapot	(G.P.)		$210.00
3. Teapot	(G.P.)	4	$285.00
4. Teapot	(N.M.)	4	$375.00
Plate 16, Row 1:			
1. Coffee pot	(G.P.)		$285.00
2. Coffee pot	(N.M.)	4	$325.00
3. Coffee pot	(M)	4,5	$550.00
4. Coffee pot	(G.P.)		$210.00
5. Teapot	(M)		$285.00
Plate 16, Row 2:			
1. Coffee pot	(N.M.)	4,6	$550.00
2. Coffee pot	(N.M.)	4	$325.00
3. Coffee pot	(M)	4,5	$325.00
4. Coffee pot	(G.P.)	4	$475.00
5. Teapot	(N.M.)		$225.00
Plate 16, Row 3:			
1. Coffee pot	(N.M.)	6	$285.00
2. Teapot	(N.M.)	4	$295.00
3. Coffee pot	(N.M.)		$295.00
4. Coffee pot	(G.P.)	4	$350.00
5. Teapot	(N.M.)	2,3,4	$495.00
Plate 17, Row 1:			
1. Teapot	(M)	4,5	$175.00
2. Teapot	(N.M.)	5	$165.00
3. Coffee pot	(M)	4	$195.00
4. Coffee pot	(M)	4	$225.00
Plate 17, Row 2:			
1. Teapot	(N.M.)	4	$425.00
2. Teapot	(M)	1,2	$395.00
3. Coffee pot	(N.M.)	4	$395.00
4. Teapot	(N.M.)	1,2,3	$495.00

Item	Condition	Rarity	Price
Plate 17, Row 3:			
1. Coffee pot	(G.P.)		$200.00
2. Coffee pot	(M)		$210.00
3. Coffee pot	(M)	4	$225.00
4. Teapot	(G.P.)	5	$225.00
Plate 18, Row 1:			
1. Coffee pot	(M)		$495.00
2. Coffee pot	(N.M.)	1	$1,000.00
3. Coffee pot	(N.M.)		$295.00
Plate 18, Row 2:			
1. Coffee pot	(G.P.)		$195.00
2. Coffee pot	(G.P.)		$275.00
3. Coffee pot	(M)	4	$395.00
4. Teapot	(N.M.)		$285.00
Plate 18, Row 3:			
1. Teapot	(N.M.)	4	$255.00
2. Coffee pot	(G.P.)		$225.00
3. Teapot	(N.M.)		$250.00
4. Coffee pot	(N.M.)	4	$295.00
Plate 19, Row 1:			
1. Coffee pot	(G.P.)		$200.00
2. Coffee pot	(N.M.)		$275.00
3. Coffee pot	(G.P.)		$215.00
4. Coffee pot	(N.M.)	4	$425.00
Plate 19, Row 2:			
1. Teapot	(N.M.)	2,3	$625.00
2. Coffee pot	(M)	4	$425.00
3. Coffee pot	(G.P.)		$295.00
4. Coffee pot	(N.M.)	2,3	$575.00
Plate 19, Row 3:			
1. Teapot	(G.P.)	5	$425.00
2. Coffee pot	(N.M.)	4	$395.00
3. Cofffee pot	(N.M.)	4,5	$595.00
4. Teapot	(G.P.)	5	$325.00
Plate 20, Row 1:			
1. Teapot	(M)		$275.00
2. Teapot	(M)		$250.00
3. Teapot	(M)	4	$325.00
4. Coffee pot	(G.P.)		$200.00
Plate 20, Row 2:			
1. Coffee pot	(N.M.)		$200.00
2. Teapot	(G.P.)		$100.00
3. Teapot	(N.M.)		$325.00
4. Teapot	(M)		$60.00
5. Teapot	(N.M.)		$350.00
Plate 20. Row 3:			
1. Teapot	(M)	4,6	$525.00
2. Teapot	(M)		$450.00
3. Coffee pot	(M)	4	$450.00
4. Coffee pot	(G.P.)		$185.00
5. Coffee pot	(N.M.)	4,6	$400.00
Plate 21, Row 1:			
1. Coffee pot	(G.P.)	5	$295.00
2. Coffee pot	(N.M.)		$325.00
3. Coffee pot	(M)		$365.00
4. Teapot	(N.M.)	5	$395.00

Item	Condition	Rarity	Price
Plate 21, Row 2:			
1. Coffee pot	(G.P.)		$215.00
2. Coffee pot	(M)		$425.00
3. Teapot	(N.M.)	5	$325.00
4. Coffee pot	(N.M.)		$400.00
Plate 21, Row 3:			
1. Teapot	(G.P.)		$295.00
2. Teapot	(G.P.)	4	$395.00
3. Teapot	(N.M.)		$295.00
4. Coffee pot	(N.M.)		$215.00
Plate 22, Row 1:			
1. Coffee pot	(N.M.)		$265.00
2. Coffee pot	(G.P.)		$200.00
3. Coffee pot	(N.M.)		$425.00
Plate 22, Row 2:			
1. Teapot	(N.M.)		$225.00
2. Coffee pot	(M)		$295.00
3. Teapot	(N.M.)	5	$240.00
4. Coffee pot	(M)		$295.00
5. Teapot	(N.M.)		$295.00
Plate 22, Row 3:			
1. Teapot	(N.M.)	4,5	$675.00
2. Coffee pot	(M)		$395.00
3. Coffee pot	(N.M.)	4,5	$525.00
4. Teapot	(G.P.)	4	$395.00
Plate 23, Row 1:			
1. Coffee pot	(M)		$175.00
2. Coffee pot	(M)		$145.00
3. Teapot	(M)	5	$185.00
4. Teapot	(M)		$135.00
Plate 23, Row 2:			
1. Teapot	(M)	5	$135.00
2. Teapot	(M)	5	$135.00
3. Coffee pot	(M)		$125.00
4. Teapot	(N.M.)		$135.00
Plate 23, Row 3:			
1. Coffee pot	(N.M.)		$125.00
2. Teapot	(M)		$135.00
3. Coffee pot	(M)		$135.00
4. Teapot	(M)		$185.00
Plate 24, Row 1:			
1. Teapot	(G.P.)	1,5	$450.00
2. Teapot	(G.P.)	1	$895.00
3. Teapot	(G.P.)	5	$215.00
Plate 24, Row 2:			
1. Teapot	(N.M.)		$165.00
2. Teapot	(G.P.)		$155.00
3. Teapot	(M)	4,5	$185.00
Plate 24, Row 3:			
1. Teapot	(N.M.)	4,5	$175.00
2. Teapot	(G.P.)		$125.00
3. Teapot	(M)	4,5	$195.00
Plate 24, Row 4:			
1. Teapot	(M)	5,6	$165.00
2. Teapot	(G.P.)		$145.00
3. Teapot	(M)		$165.00

Item	Condition	Rarity	Price
Plate 25, Row 1:			
1. Teapot	(N.M.)		$175.00
2. Teapot	(N.M.)		$225.00
3. Teapot	(N.M.)	5	$185.00
Plate 25, Row 2:			
1. Teapot	(G.P.)		$125.00
2. Teapot	(M)	5	$185.00
3. Teapot	(M)	5	$185.00
4. Teapot	(N.M.)		$145.00
Plate 25, Row 3:			
1. Teapot	(N.M.)		$225.00
2. Teapot	(G.P.)		$155.00
3. Coffee pot	(N.M.)		$200.00
Plate 26, Row 1:			
1. Teapot	(G.P.)	4	$135.00
2. Teapot	(M)	5,6	$165.00
3. Teapot	(N.M.)	5	$145.00
4. Teapot	(N.M.)	4,5	$145.00
Plate 26, Row 2:			
1. Teapot	(M)	5,6	$165.00
2. Teapot	(M)		$180.00
3. Teapot	(M)	5,6	$125.00
4. Teapot	(N.M.)	5,6	$165.00
Plate 26., Row 3:			
1. Teapot	(N.M.)	5,6	$185.00
2. Teapot	(G.P.)		$155.00
3. Teapot	(M)	5	$165.00
4. Teapot	(M)	5,6	$135.00
Plate 26, Row 4:			
1. Coffee pot	(G.P.)	5,6	$155.00
2. Teapot	(M)	5,6	$135.00
3. Teapot	(G.P.)	5,6	$115.00
4. Teapot	(N.M.)	5,6	$135.00
5. Teapot	(M)	4,5,6	$195.00
Plate 27, Row 1:			
1. Teapot	(N.M.)	4,5,6	$265.00
2. Teapot	(G.P.)	1,2,3	$425.00
3. Teapot	(G.P.)	4,5,6	$200.00
4. Teapot	(G.P.)	4,5,6	$185.00
5. Teapot	(G.P.)	4,5,6	$250.00
Plate 27, Row 2:			
1. Coffee pot	(M)		$95.00
2. Teapot	(M)	4,5,6	$140.00
3. Coffee pot	(M)	4,5,6	$195.00
4. Coffee pot	(M)	5,6	$75.00
5. Teapot	(N.M.)		$55.00
Plate 27, Row 3:			
1. Teapot	(N.M.)	5,6	$185.00
2. Coffee pot	(N.M.)	4	$425.00
3. Teapot	(M)		$65.00
4. Teapot	(N.M.)		$180.00
5. Teapot	(N.M.)	5,6	$195.00
Plate 27, Row 4:			
1. Coffee pot	(N.M.)	1,3	$295.00
2. Coffee pot	(G.P.)	6	$200.00
3. Coffee pot	(G.P.)		$125.00
4. Teapot	(G.P.)	4,6	$265.00
5. Teapot	(N.M.)	5,6	$155.00

Item	Condition	Rarity	Price
Plate 28, Row 1:			
1. Teapot	(G.P.)	6	$245.00
2. Teapot	(M)	6	$125.00
3. Coffee pot	(N.M.)	6	$115.00
4. Teapot	(N.M.)	6	$180.00
5. Coffee pot	(G.P.)	6	$135.00
Plate 28, Row 2:			
1. Coffee pot	(M)	6	$185.00
2. Coffee pot	(G.P.)	6	$135.00
3. Teapot	(N.M.)	6	$175.00
4. Coffee pot	(G.P.)	6	$155.00
5. Coffee pot	(N.M.)	6	$155.00
Plate 28, Row 3:			
1. Coffee pot	(G.P.)	5,6	$195.00
2. Teapot	(N.M.)	5,6	$145.00
3. Teapot	(M)	5,6	$135.00
4. Teapot	(N.M.)	5,6	$195.00
5. Coffee pot	(M)	5,6	$130.00
6. Coffee pot	(N.M.)	5,6	$130.00
Plate 28, Row 4:			
1. Coffee pot	(G.P.)	4,5,6	$325.00
2. Teapot	(N.M.)	4,5,6	$365.00
3. Teapot	(G.P.)	1,2,3	$295.00
4. Teapot	(G.P.)	4,5,6	$345.00
5. Coffee pot	(N.M.)	4,5,6	$275.00
Plate 29, Row 1:			
1. Coffee pot	(N.M.)	4,5,6	$365.00
2. Coffee pot	(G.P.)	4,6	$175.00
3. Coffee pot	(N.M.)	5,6	$140.00
4. Teapot	(G.P.)	4,5,6	$295.00
Plate 29, Row 2:			
1. Teapot	(N.M.)	5,6	$165.00
2. Teapot	(N.M.)	5,6	$135.00
3. Teapot	(M)		$25.00
4. Teapot	(M)		$65.00
Plate 29, Row 3:			
1. Coffee pot	(G.P.)	4,5,6	$295.00
2. Coffee pot	(G.P.)	2,3	$275.00
3. Teapot	(M)	4,5,6	$495.00
4. Coffee pot	(N.M.)	5,6	$245.00
5. Teapot	(M)	1,2,3	$425.00
Plate 29, Row 4:			
1. Coffee pot	(N.M.)	5,6	$225.00
2. Coffee pot	(N.M.)	5,6	$235.00
3. Teapot	(M)	5,6	$135.00
4. Coffee pot	(G.P.)	5,6	$195.00
5. Teapot	(M)	5,6	$235.00

Section 2

Item	Condition	Rarity	Price
Plate 1, Row 1:			
1. Sugar bowl	(M)	2	$450.00
2. Coffee urn	(M)	1,2,3	$1,595.00
3. Creamer	(M)	2	$450.00
Plate 1, Row 2:			
1. Cereal bowl	(M)	4,5	$165.00
2. Waste bowl	(M)	2	$450.00
3. Waste bowl	(M)	2	$395.00

Item	Condition	Rarity	Price
Plate 1, Row 3:			
1. Sugar bowl	(M)	5	$350.00
2. Creamer	(M)	5	$350.00
3. Sugar bowl	(M)	5	$395.00
Plate 2, Row 1:			
1. Syrup`	(M)	2	$1,050.00
2. Sugar bowl	(M)	5	$565.00
3. Castor set	(M)	2	$3,500.00
4. Sugar bowl	(M)	5	$595.00
5. Creamer	(M)	5	$625.00
Plate 2, Row 2:			
1. Sugar bowl	(M)	5	$295.00
2. Double egg cup	(N.M.)	2,3	$225.00
3. Sugar bowl	(M)	4,5	$425.00
4. Condiment	(G.P.)	5	$150.00
5. Sugar bowl	(M)	5	$350.00
Plate 2, Row 3:			
1. Sugar bowl	(M)	2,3	$395.00
2. Pickle castor	(M)	1,2,3	$2,500.00
3. Creamer	(M)	2,3	$395.00
Plate 3, Row 1:			
1. Syrup	(G.P.)	5	$195.00
2. Creamer	(G.P.)	1,5	$325.00
3. Molasses pitcher	(M)	4,5	$225.00
4. Oval platter	(M)	5	$185.00
5. Spooner	(N.M.)	1,2	$1,550.00
6. Molasses pitcher	(M)	5	$145.00
Plate 3, Row 2:			
1. Syrup	(G.P.)	1,2,3	$900.00
2. Honey pot	(M)	1,2	$595.00
3. Oval platter	(N.M.)	4,5	$395.00
4. Creamer	(N.M.)	4,5	$1,000.00
5. Sugar bowl	(N.M.)	4,5	$525.00
Plate 3, Row 3:			
1. Creamer	(N.M.)	4,5,6	$85.00
2, Mustard or Horseradish pot	(G.P.)	4,5	$195.00
3. Oval platter	(G.P.)	1,5	$975.00
4. Mustard or Horseradish pot	(N.M.)	5	$175.00
5. Creamer	(N.M.)	4,5	$135.00
6. Sugar	(N.M.)	4,5	$135.00
Plate 3, Row 4:			
1. Syrup	(G.P.)	2,3	$650.00
2. Molasses pitcher	(G.P.)		$225.00
3. Oval platter	(M)	4,5	$395.00
4. Molasses pitcher	(N.M.)	1,2,3	$1,000.00
Plate 4, Row 1:			
1. Butterdish	(G.P.)	4,5	$275.00
2. Creamer	(G.P.)	4,5	$95.00
3. Butterdish	(M)	1,2	$695.00
4. Salt/pepper	(M)	1,2,3	ea.$1,325.00
5. Butterdish	(G.P.)	1,2,3	$750.00
Plate 4, Row 2:			
1. Sugar bowl`	(M)	5	$495.00
2. Salt/pepper	(N.M.)	1,2,3	ea.$995.00
3. Butterdish	(N.M.)	2	$1,100.00
4. Creamer	(N.M.)	5	$225.00

Item	Condition	Rarity	Price
Plate 4, Row 3:			
1. Butterdish	(G.P.)	1,2,3	$425.00
2. Salt/pepper	(N.M.)	2	ea.$365.00
3. Butterdish	(G.P.)	1,2	$275.00
4. Egg cup	(M)	5	$110.00
5. Mustard or Horseradish pot	(G.P.)	5	$155.00
6. Butterdish	(N.M.)	5	$185.00
Plate 4, Row 4:			
1. Creamer	(G.P.)	4,5	$145.00
2. Sugar bowl	(M)	4,5	$60.00
3. Butterdish	(M)	5	$165.00
4. Creamer	(G.P.)	4,5	$725.00
5. Sugar bowl	(N.M.)		$525.00
Plate 5, Row 1:			
1. Creamer	(G.P.)	4,5,6	$395.00
2. Sugar bowl	(N.M.)		$125.00
3. Creamer	(M)		$95.00
4. Platter	(M)	5	$155.00
5. Sugar bowl	(M)	2,4	$595.00
Plate 5, Row 2:			
1. Creamer	(G.P.)	1,2	$595.00
2. Gravy or sauce boat	(N.M.)	1,2	$1,550.00
3. Sugar bowl	(G.P.)	1,2	$650.00
4. Creamer	(N.M.)	5	$85.00
Plate 5, Row 3:			
1. Sugar bowl	(G.P.)	4,5	$275.00
2. Sugar bowl	(G.P.)	1,2	$325.00
3. Creamer	(G.P.)	4,5	$85.00
4. Sugar bowl	(G.P.)	4,5	$250.00
Plate 5, Row 4:			
1. Sugar bowl	(G.P.)	4,5	$295.00
2. Creamer	(N.M.)	4,5	$140.00
3. Fruit bowl	(G.P.)	5	$110.00
4. Sugar bowl	(N.M.)	4,5	$250.00
Plate 6, Row 1:			
1. Creamer	(G.P.)	1,5	$425.00
2. Footed gravy or sauce boat	(N.M.)	4,5	$325.00
3. Creamer	(G.P.)	1,2	$795.00
4. Footed gravy or sauce boat	(N.M.)	5	$165.00
Plate 6, Row 2:			
1. Creamer	(M)	5	$165.00
2. Molasses pitcher	(N.M.)	4,5	$265.00
3. Gravy or sauce boat	(N.M.)	2,4	$325.00
4. Molasses pitcher	(G.P.)	4,5	$265.00
Plate 6, Row 3:			
1. Molasses pitcher	(G.P.)	5,6	$255.00
2. Sugar bowl	(G.P.)	4,5	$225.00
3. Egg cup	(M)	5	$95.00
4. Sugar bowl	(N.M.)		$295.00
5. Creamer	(N.M.)	5,6	$125.00
6. Sugar bowl	(G.P.)	5	$295.00
7. Creamer	(N.M.)	5	$85.00
Plate 6, Row 4:			
1. Creamer	(G.P.)	5,6	$135.00
2. Sugar bowl	(M)	4,5	$65.00
3. Syrup	(G.P.)	2	$395.00
4. Creamer	(M)	4,5	$65.00
5. Creamer	(N.M.)	4,5	$235.00

Item	Condition	Rarity	Price
Plate 7, Row 1:			
1. Syrup	(N.M.)	5,6	$215.00
2. Honey pot	(N.M.)	5	$215.00
3. Creamer	(M)	4,5	$425.00
4. Syrup	(M)	1,2	$1,595.00
5. Creamer	(G.P.)	1,5	$375.00
6. Sugar bowl	(G.P.)	5,6	$145.00
Plate 7, Row 2:			
1. Creamer	(N.M.)	5,6	$100.00
2. Sugar bowl	(N.M.)	5,6	$100.00
3. Syrup	(G.P.)	5	$185.00
4. Syrup	(G.P.)	5	$160.00
5. Open sugar	(M)	5,6	$100.00
6. Creamer	(M)	5,6	$100.00
Plate 7, Row 3:			
1. Creamer	(N.M.)	5	$95.00
2. Creamer	(N.M.)	1,5	$465.00
3. Sugar bowl	(N.M.)	5,6	$165.00
4. Sauce or gravy boat	(G.P.)	2,3	$295.00
5. Creamer	(N.M.)	5,6	$165.00
6. Creamer	(G.P.)	5	$75.00
7. Sugar bowl	(N.M.)	1,2	$265.00
Plate 7, Row 4:			
1. Syrup	(G.P.)	1,2	$550.00
2. Creamer	(G.P.)	4,5	$195.00
3. Molasses pitcher	(N.M.)	4,5	$295.00
4. Fruit bowl	(G.P.)	5	$110.00
5. Molasses pitcher	(N.M.)	4,5	$295.00
6. Creamer	(G.P.)	4,5	$185.00
Plate 8, Row 1:			
1. Oblong pudding or vegetable dish	(M)	4,5	$165.00
2. Oval footed soup tureen	(G.P.)	2	$595.00
3. Oblong pudding or vegetable dish	(N.M.)	4	$200.00
Plate 8, Row 2:			
1. Oblong pudding or vegetable dish	(G.P.)		$120.00
2. Oval pudding or vegetable dish	(N.M.)		$125.00
3. Soup tureen	(N.M.)	2,4,6	$295.00
Plate 8, Row 3:			
1. Footed round soup tureen with ladle	(M)	2,4	set $325.00
2. Oblong pudding or vegetable dish	(M)	1,5	$165.00
Plate 8, Row 4:			
1. Oval pudding or vegetable dish	(M)		$85.00
2. Oblong pudding or vegetable dish	(M)		$85.00
3. Footed round soup tureen	(G.P.)	2	$165.00
Plate 9, Row 1:			
1. Chafing dish	(G.P.)	1,2	$425.00
2. Oval soup tureen	(G.P.)	2	$450.00
Plate 9, Row 2:			
1. Footed round soup tureen	(N.M.)	1,2	$595.00
2. Oval pudding or vegetable dish	(N.M.)	4,5	$250.00
3. Chafing dish	(G.P.)	2	$695.00

Item	Condition	Rarity	Price
Plate 9, Row 3:			
1. Oblong pudding or vegetable dish	(N.M.)		$65.00
2. Oval pudding or vegetable dish	(N.M.)	4,5	$195.00
3. Oblong pudding or vegetable dish	(N.M.)	4,5,6	$245.00
Plate 9, Row 4:			
1. Chafing dish	(M)	2	$295.00
2. Footed round soup tureen	(G.P.)	2	$325.00

Section 3

Item	Condition	Rarity	Price
Plate 1, Row 1:			
1. Large mug	(G.P.)	4,6	$150.00
2. Cup	(G.P.)	4	$115.00
3. Coffee urn	(N.M.)		$325.00
4. Cup	(M)		$25.00
5. Mug	(G.P.)		$45.00
Plate 1, Row 2:			
1. Cup	(M)		$30.00
2. Saucer	(M)		$65.00
3. Mug	(N.M.)		$75.00
4. Cup	(M)	6	$75.00
5. Mug	(N.M.)		$25.00
Plate 1, Row 3:			
1. Mug	(G.P.)	5	$55.00
2. Mug	(M)		$35.00
3. Saucer	(M)		$75.00
4. Mug	(G.P.)		$25.00
5. Mug	(M)	4	$165.00
Plate 2, Row 1:			
1. Plate	(M)	4	$35.00
2. Mug	(G.P.)	4	$25.00
3. Mug	(N.M.)	1,2	$395.00
4. Dinner plate	(N.M.)	4	$25.00
5. Mug	(N.M.)	4	$30.00
6. Mug	(M)		$25.00
7. Plate	(M)	4	$30.00
8. Mug	(M)	4	$30.00
9. Mug	(M)	4	$35.00
Plate 2, Row 2:			
1. Cup	(N.M.)	4,5,6	$110.00
2. Plate	(M)	4,5	$125.00
3. Cup	(M)	4,5	$125.00
4. Cup	(M)	4,5	$125.00
5. Saucer	(N.M.)	4,5	$95.00
6. Luncheon plate	(N.M.)	4,5	$115.00
7. Cup	(N.M.)	4,5	$105.00
Plate 2, Row 3:			
1. Mug	(N.M.)		$85.00
2. Saucer	(N.M.)		$20.00
3. Mug	(M)	5	$95.00
4. Saucer	(M)		$35.00
5. Cup	(N.M.)		$55.00
6. Saucer	(M)		$25.00
7. Cup and saucer	(N.M.)		set $105.00
8. Saucer	(N.M.)		$65.00
9. Cup	(N.M.)		$55.00

Item	Condition	Rarity	Price
Plate 2, Row 4:			
1. Mug	(N.M.)	4	$110.00
2. Plate	(M)	4,5	$125.00
3. Mug	(N.M.)	4	$65.00
4. Luncheon plate	(M)	4	$35.00
5. Cup and saucer	(M)	4,5	set$75.00
6. Mug	(M)	4	$75.00
7. Table setting	(N.M.)	4	$395.00
Plate 3, Row 1:			
1. Saucer	(N.M.)	4	$60.00
2. Plate	(N.M.)	4	$65.00
3. Mug	(N.M.)	2,4	$160.00
4. Table setting	(M)		4 pcs.$95.00
5. Table setting	(N.M.)	4	3 pcs.$295.00
Plate 3, Row 2:			
1. Mug	(N.M.)		$65.00
2. Cup	(G.P.)	5	$40.00
3. Three-pc. table setting	(G.P.)	4	3 pc.$295.00
Plate 3, Row 3:			
1. Cup and saucer	(G.P.)	4	set$195.00
2. Saucer	(G.P.)		$45.00
3. Mug	(M)	5	$35.00
4. Cup and saucer	(M)		set$75.00
5. Cup and saucer	(N.M.)		set$145.00
Plate 3, Row 4:			
1. Plate	(G.P.)	5	$45.00
2. Cup and saucer	(N.M.)		set$85.00
3. Plate	(N.M.)		$55.00
4. Cup and saucer	(G.P.)	6	set$50.00
5. Saucer	(N.M.)		$85.00
Plate 4, Row 1:			
1. Soup plate	(M)	4	$45.00
2. Soup plate	(M)		$75.00
3. Soup plate	(M)	4	$30.00
4. Coasters	(M)	1,2	ea.$85.00
Plate 4, Row 2:			
1. Coaster	(N.M.)	1,2	$225.00
2. Soup plate	(G.P.)		$45.00
3. Shot glass	(N.M.)		$155.00
4. Tumbler	(N.M.)	2,3	$145.00
5. Tumbler-shaped medicine cup	(G.P.)		$35.00
6. Soup plate	(G.P.)	1	$185.00
7. Coaster	(N.M.)	1,2	$225.00
Plate 4, Row 3:			
1. Plate	(G.P.)	4,5,6	$110.00
2. Cup	(N.M.)	4,5	$75.00
3. Mug	(M)	1,2,3	$275.00
4. Cup	(M)	1,2,3	$325.00
5. Child's set	(M)	1,2,3	3 pcs.$750.00
6. Mug	(N.M.)	4	$55.00
7. Plate	(M)	4	$35.00
8. Mug	(G.P.)	6	$45.00
Plate 4, Row 4:			
1. Tumbler	(G.P.)	1,2	$450.00
2. Soup plate	(M)	4	$140.00
3. Tumbler	(M)	4,5	$65.00
4. Plate	(G.P.)	4	$110.00
5. Tumbler	(N.M.)	1,2	$495.00
6. Plate	(N.M.)	4	$125.00
7. Tumbler	(M)	4,5	$65.00
Plate 5, Row 1:			
1. Cup and saucer	(G.P.)	5	set$135.00
2. Farmer's cup	(G.P.)	3,4	$75.00
3. Saucer	(G.P.)	4,5	$50.00
4. Tumbler-shaped mug	(N.M.)	5	$85.00
5. Cup and saucer	(G.P.)	4,5	set$95.00
Plate 5, Row 2:			
1. Mug	(G.P.)	4	$135.00
2. Mug	(M)	5	$125.00
3. Saucer	(G.P.)	5	$40.00
4. Mug	(G.P.)	4	$125.00
5. Cup	(G.P.)	2,3	$325.00
6. Mug	(G.P.)	5	$80.00
Plate 5, Row 3:			
1. Tumbler	(M)	5	$110.00
2. Mug	(G.P.)	6	$65.00
3. Tumbler	(G.P.)	4,5	$75.00
4. Mug	(M)	4,5	$250.00
5. Covered soup mug	(M)	2,4	$75.00
6. Child's mug	(G.P.)	6	$55.00
7. Saucer	(M)		$35.00
Plate 5, Row 4:			
1. Mug	(M)	4	$160.00
2. Mug	(M)	5	$105.00
3. Mug	(N.M.)		$80.00
4. Plate	(M)		$40.00
5. Mug	(N.M.)		$35.00
6. Tumbler	(M)	2	$210.00
7. Mug	(N.M.)	4	$155.00
8. Mug	(G.P.)	4	$125.00

Section 4

Item	Condition	Rarity	Price
Plate 1, Row 1:			
Oblong tray	(G.P.)	4,5	$195.00
Plate 1, Row 2:			
1. Corrugated tray	(N.M.)	1,2,3	$425.00
2. Beer stein	(G.P.)	1,2,3	$1,600.00
3. Advertising beer tray	(N.M.)	4,5	$325.00
Plate 1, Row 3:			
1. Round tray	(N.M.)	5	$65.00
2. Round tray	(N.M.)	4,5	$175.00
3. Round tray	(M)		$55.00
Plate 2, Row 1:			
1. Coffee flask	(G.P.)	2	$495.00
2. Coffee flask	(M)	2	$575.00
3. Oblong tray w/handles	(G.P.)	5	$95.00
Plate 2, Row 2:			
1. Tray	(N.M.)		$145.00
2. Coffee flask	(N.M.)	2	$450.00
3. Coffee flask	(M)	2	$525.00
4. Oblong tray	(M)		$225.00
Plate 2, Row 3:			
1. Oval tray	(N.M.)		$165.00
2. Coffee flask	(NM.)	2	$495.00
3. Tray	(N.M.)	4,5	$495.00

Item	Condition	Rarity	Price
Plate 3, Row 1:			
1. Mug	(M)	4,6	$150.00
2. Oblong tray	(M)		$225.00
3. Coffee flask	(G.P.)	1,2	$695.00
Plate 3, Row 2:			
1. Mug	(G.P.)	4,6	$115.00
2. Egg poacher insert	(N.M.)	4,5	ea.$75.00
3. Mug	(G.P.)	4,6	$135.00
4. Chopper	(N.M.)	4,5	2 pc.$135.00
5. Oblong tray	(N.M.)	4,5	$295.00
6. Oyster patty	(G.P.)	2	$325.00
Plate 3, Row 3:			
1. Oblong tray	(N.M.)	4,5	$325.00
2. Coffee flask	(N.M.)	2	$475.00
3. Coffee flaks	(M)	2	$495.00
4. Square tray	(N.M.)		$165.00

Section 5

Item	Condition	Rarity	Price
Plate 1, Row 1:			
1. Round bread box	(G.P.)		$125.00
2. Oblong bread box	(N.M.)		$115.00
Plate 1, Row 2:			
1. Round bread box	(N.M.)	4	$155.00
2. Salt box	(G.P.)	5	$110.00
3. Salt box	(M)	5	$145.00
Plate 1, Row 3:			
1. Salt box	(G.P.)	4,5	$225.00
2. Salt box	(G.P.)	1,5	$395.00
3. Round bread box	(G.P.)		$155.00
Plate 2, Row 1:			
1. Salt box	(G.P.)	1,5	$395.00
2. Salt box	(G.P.)	1,5	$525.00
3. Salt box	(G.P.)	1,5	$395.00
Plate 2, Row 2:			
1. Salt box	(G.P.)	5	$130.00
2. Salt box	(N.M.)	1,5	$495.00
3. Salt box	(N.M.)	1,2	$595.00
Plate 2, Row 3:			
1. Salt box	(N.M.)	5	$145.00
2. Sugar shaker	(G.P.)	1,2	$295.00
3. Sugar shaker	(M)	1,2	$625.00
4. Salt box	(G.P.)	5	$115.00
5. Sugar shaker	(G.P.)	1,2	$275.00
6. Sugar shaker	(M)	2,4	$225.00
Plate 2, Row 4:			
1. Salt box	(G.P.)	5	$195.00
2. Salt box	(M)	5	$225.00
3. Salt box shape	(M)	4,5	$285.00
Plate 3, Row 1:			
1. Sugar cannister	(G.P.)	6	$95.00
2. Flour cannister	(M)	4,5	$325.00
3. Flour cannister	(G.P.)	4,5	$125.00
Plate 3, Row 2:			
1. Meal cannister	(G.P.)	5	$120.00
2. Pepper cannister	(G.P.)	6	$95.00
3. Tea cannister	(N.M.)	4	$165.00
4. Coffee cannister	(M)	5	$135.00

Item	Condition	Rarity	Price
Plate 3, Rows 3 & 4:			
Ten-piece cannisters	(G.P.)	1,5	$750.00 (10 pcs.)
Plate 4, Row 1:			
1. Three-piece cannisters	(N.M.)	1,5	$795.00 (3 pcs.)
2. Three-piece cannisters	(N.M.)	5	$350.00 (3 pcs.)
Plate 4, Row 2:			
Five-piece cannisters	(G.P.)	4,5	$250.00 (5 pcs.)
Plate 4, Row 3:			
1. Four-piece cannisters	(G.P.)	4,5	$260.00 (4 pcs.)
2. Four spice cannisters	(N.M.)	5,6	$260.00 (4 pcs.)
Plate 4, Row 4:			
1. Four spice cannisters plus tea cannister	(M)	4,5,6	$350.00 (5 pcs.)
Plate 5, Row 1:			
1. Holder	(G.P.)	5	$145.00
2. Utility rack	(G.P.)	5	$235.00
3. Holder	(N.M.)	5	$135.00
Plate 5, Row 2:			
1. Utility rack	(G.P.)	5	$235.00
2. Toothbrush holder	(G.P.)	5,6	$145.00
Plate 5, Row 3:			
1. Utility rack	(G.P.)	2,3	$325.00
2. Holder/scouring	(N.M.)	5	$95.00
3. Holder/soap	(G.P.)	5	$85.00
Plate 5, Row 4:			
1. Utility rack	(G.P.)	5	$220.00
2. Mug	(N.M.)		$85.00
3. Holder/onions	(N.M.)	5	$185.00

Section 6

Item	Condition	Rarity	Price
Plate 1, Row 1:			
1. Utensil rack	(M)	4,5	$495.00
2. Skimmer	(N.M.)	1,6	$195.00
3. Utensil rack	(G.P.)	4,5	$320.00
Plate 1, Row 2:			
1. Hand skimmer	(N.M.)	5	$350.00
2. Soup ladle	(N.M.)	1	$495.00
3. Soup ladle	(N.M.)	1	$495.00
4. Utensil rack	(G.P.)	5	$325.00
5. Cocoa dipper	(G.P.)	5,6	$285.00
6. Hand skimmer	(M)	5	$410.00
7. Cocoa dipper	(G.P.)	5	$285.00
Plate 1, Row 3:			
1. Cocoa dipper	(G.P.)	5	$145.00
2. Hand skimmer	(N.M.)	5	$165.00
3. Hand skimmer	(M)	5	$165.00
4. Skimmer	(G.P.)	5	$125.00
5. Skimmer	(N.M.)	5	$140.00
6. Cocoa dipper	(N.M.)	5	$225.00
7. Cocoa dipper	(G.P.)	5	$295.00

Item	Condition	Rarity	Price
Plate 2, Row 1:			
1. Utensil rack	(G.P.)	5	$295.00
2. Soup ladle	(G.P.)	4	$300.00
3. Spoon	(M)		$110.00
4. Spoon and spice rack	(G.P.)	5	$155.00
5. Spoon	(M)		$20.00
6. Spoon	(G.P.)	4,6	$125.00
7. Spoon	(N.M.)		$25.00
Plate 2, Row 2:			
1. Utensil rack	(M)	4	$300.00
2. Utensil rack	(G.P.)	1,5	$475.00
3. Spatula	(G.P.)	6	$75.00
4. Spatula	(N.M.)	5	$95.00
Plate 2, Row 3:			
1. Spoon	(N.M.)		$25.00
2. Soup ladle	(M)		$20.00
3. Fish tool	(N.M.)	5	$125.00
4. Cake turner	(N.M.)	5	$110.00
5. Handled skimmer	(G.P.)	6	$85.00
Plate 3, Row 1:			
1. Handled skimmer	(N.M.)		$35.00
2. Handled skimmer	(N.M.)		$55.00
3. Utensil rack	(G.P.)	5	$295.00
4. Handled skimmer	(G.P.)		$110.00
5. Handled skimmer	(G.P.)		$110.00
Plate 3, Row 2:			
1. Dipper	(G.P.)	5	$95.00
2. Soup ladle	(N.M.)	4	$195.00
3. Soup ladle	(G.P.)		$30.00
4. Soup ladle	(G.P.)	4	$65.00
5. Soup ladle	(N.M.)		$55.00
Plate 3, Row 3:			
1. Spatula	(N.M.)	5	$95.00
2. Spatula	(N.M.)		$85.00
3. Spatula	(N.M.)		$105.00
4. Spatula	(N.M.)		$95.00
Plate 4, Row 1:			
1. Spoon	(G.P.)		$65.00
2. Spoon	(G.P.)		$75.00
3. Spoon	(G.P.)		$40.00
4. Spoon	(G.P.)		$45.00
5. Spoon	(G.P.)	4,6	$125.00
6. Spoon	(N.M.)		$95.00
7. Spoon	(G.P.)	4	$35.00
8. Spoon	(G.P.)		$30.00
Plate 4, Row 2:			
1. Spoon	(G.P.)	1,6	$125.00
2. Spoons	(N.M.)		ea.$20.00
3. Spoon	(G.P.)	6	$65.00
4. Spoon	(G.P.)		$40.00
5. Spoon	(N.M.)	6	$45.00
6. Spoon	(G.P.)		$30.00
7. Spoon	(N.M.)		$35.00
Plate 4, Row 3:			
1. Ice cream spoon	(G.P.)	2	$140.00
2. Cake spoon	(G.P.)	5	$110.00
3. Skimmer	(G.P.)	5	$85.00
4. Spoon	(N.M.)		$125.00
5. Pickle dipper	(M)	2	$95.00
6. Skimmer	(G.P.)	2	$185.00
7. Spoon	(M)	5	$35.00
8. Soup ladle	(N.M.)	5	$125.00

Item	Condition	Rarity	Price
Plate 5, Row 1:			
1. Spoon	(G.P.)	4	125.00
2. Spoon	(G.P.)		$25.00
3. Spoon	(G.P.)		$75.00
4. Spoon	(G.P.)		$110.00
5. Spoon	(G.P.)		$120.00
6. Spoon	(G.P.)		$55.00
7. Spoon	(G.P.)		$35.00
Plate 5, Row 2:			
1. Skimmer ladle	(N.M.)		$135.00
2. Side snipe ladle	(G.P.)	5,6	$65.00
3. Oyster ladle	(G.P.)	5	$65.00
4. Skimmer ladle	(G.P.)		$65.00
5. Oyster ladle	(G.P.)	5	$75.00
6. Ladle	(M)	5	$65.00
7. Skimmer ladle	(N.M.)		$60.00
Plate 5, Row 3:			
1. Spoon	(M)		$45.00
2. Spoon	(M)		$110.00
3. Spoon	(G.P.)	5	$75.00
4. Side snipe ladle	(M)	5,6	$195.00
5. Side snipe ladle	(N.M.)	5	$55.00
6. Spoon	(G.P.)	4	$85.00
7. Tasting spoon	(N.M.)	5	$60.00
Plate 6, Row 1:			
1. Ladle	(G.P.)	4	$95.00
2. Soup ladle	(N.M.)		$75.00
3. Soup ladle	(G.P.)		$75.00
4. Soup ladle	(N.M.)	4	$265.00
5. Soup ladle	(N.M.)		$75.00
6. Soup ladle	(G.P.)		$30.00
7. Soup ladle	(G.P.)		$65.00
Plate 6, Row 2:			
1. Handled skimmer	(M)		$135.00
2. Spatula	(G.P.)	1,5	$185.00
3. Spatula	(G.P.)	5	$75.00
4. Spatula	(G.P.)	1,5	$195.00
5. Spatula	(G.P.)	4,5	$135.00
6. Spatula	(G.P.)	5	$55.00
7. Handled skimmer	(G.P.)		$40.00
Plate 6, Row 3:			
1. Handled skimmer	(G.P.)	4	$110.00
2. Handled skimmer	(M)		$25.00
3. Handled skimmer	(G.P.)	4	$75.00
4. Handled skimmer	(N.M.)		$65.00
5. Handled skimmer	(N.M.)		$60.00

Section 7

Item	Condition	Rarity	Price
Plate 1, Row 1:			
1. Biscuit sheet	(N.M.)	1,2	$2,550.00
2. Rolling pin	(M)	1,2	$975.00
3. Biscuit cutter	(G.P.)	2	$625.00
4. Biscuit cutter	(N.M.)	2	$525.00
Plate 1, Row 2:			
1. Pudding pan	(M)	4	$225.00
2. Custard cup	(N.M.)	4,5	$110.00
3. Custard cup	(N.M.)	5	$85.00
4. Custard cup	(M)	5	$55.00
5. Pudding pan	(M)	4	$125.00

Item	Condition	Rarity	Price
Plate 1, Row 3:			
1. Pudding pan	(M)	4	$125.00
2. Egg separator	(G.P.)	1,2	$795.00
3. Butter melting set	(M)	5	3 pcs.$115.00
4. Cake pan	(G.P.)	1	$325.00
Plate 1, Row 4:			
1. Custard cup	(M)	4,5	$45.00
2. Jelly roll pan	(M)		$125.00
'3. Custard cup	(M)	4,5	$85.00
4. Egg separator	(G.P.)	1,2	$495.00
5. Bread pan	(G.P.)	2	$185.00
6. Custard cup	(N.M.)	4,5	$165.00
Plate 2, Row 1:			
1. Lady finger pan	(M)	1,2,3	$2,750.00
2. Lady finger pan	(M)	2	$295.00
3. Lady finger pan	(M)	1,2	$2,750.00
Plate 2, Row 2:			
1. Bread pan	(G.P.)	1	$210.00
2. Bread pan	(N.M.)		$65.00
3. Bread pan	(G.P.)	4	$225.00
4. Bread pan	(N.M.)		$45.00
Plate 2, Row 3:			
1. Tube cake mold	(G.P.)	4,5	$285.00
2. Tube cake mold	(N.M.)	4,5	$350.00
3. Tube cake mold	(M)	4,5	$310.00
Plate 2, Row 4:			
1. Pie plate	(M)	4	115.00
2. Lady finger pan	(G.P.)	2,3	$285.00
3. Pie plate	(N.M.)	4	$115.00
Plate 3, Row 1:			
1. Biscuit sheet	(G.P.)	2	$295.00
2. Pudding pan	(N.M.)		$65.00
3. Jelly roll pan	(M)		$95.00
4. Custard cup	(G.P.)	4,5	$135.00
Plate 3, Row 2:			
1. Grooved tray	(N.M.)	5	$110.00
2. Muffin cup	(G.P.)	5	$65.00
3. Lady finger pan	(N.M.)	2,4	$285.00
4. Muffin cup	(G.P.)	5	$65.00
5. Jelly roll pan	(N.M.)		$95.00
Plate 3, Row 3:			
1. Pudding pan	(M)		$95.00
2. Tart or muffin cup	(M)	5	$75.00
3. Pudding pan	(M)		$25.00
4. Bread pan	(N.M.)	5	$195.00
Plate 3, Row 4:			
1. Jelly roll pan	(M)		$85.00
2. Muffin cup	(M)	5	$95.00
3. Pudding pan	(M)		$65.00
4. Shallow tube pan	(M)	4,5	$285.00
Plate 4, Row 1:			
1. Pie plate	(G.P.)		$85.00
2. Pudding pan	(M)	4	$245.00
3. Pie plate	(G.P.)	4	$85.00
4. Pudding pan	(M)	4	$210.00
5. Pie plate	(N.M.)	4	$115.00

Item	Condition	Rarity	Price
Plate 4, Row 2:			
1. Tube cake mold	(N.M.)	4,5	$295.00
2. Tart pan	(G.P.)	5	$65.00
3. Tube cake pan	(N.M.)		$65.00
4. Tube cake pan	(M)	4,5	$275.00
5. Tart pan	(M)	5	$65.00
Plate 4, Row 3:			
1. Pudding pan	(G.P.)		$130.00
2. Pie plate	(M)		$35.00
3. Custard cup	(M)	5	$35.00
4. Tube cake mold	(G.P.)	4,5	$275.00
Plate 4, Row 4:			
1. Bread pan	(G.P.)		$60.00
2. Pie plate	(G.P.)		$40.00
3. Bread pan	(N.M.)	5	$165.00
Plate 5, Row 1:			
1. Pie plate	(N.M.)		$75.00
2. Pie plate	(N.M.)		$115.00
3. Tube cake pan	(G.P.)		$275.00
4. Pie plate	(M)		$25.00
5. Pie plate	(N.M.)	4	$85.00
Plate 5, Row 2:			
1. Tart pan	(M)		$45.00
2. Tube cake pan	(G.P.)	4,5	$310.00
3. Pie plate	(N.M.)		$75.00
4. Pie plate	(N.M.)	4	$75.00
Plate 5, Row 3:			
1. Muffin pan	(M)	4	$525.00
2. Pudding pan	(M)	1	$225.00
Plate 5, Row 4:			
1. Muffin pan	(G.P.)	4,6	$395.00
2. Muffin pan	(G.P.)		$145.00
3. Muffin pan	(N.M.)		$65.00
Plate 6, Row 1:			
1. Muffin pan	(G.P.)	4	$295.00
2. Muffin pan	(G.P.)	5	$195.00
3. Muffin pan	(G.P.)	5	$195.00
4. Muffin pan	(G.P.)	4	$295.00
Plate 6, Row 2:			
1. Muffin pan	(G.P.)		$65.00
2. Muffin pan	(N.M.)		$75.00
Plate 6, Row 3:			
Muffin pan	(N.M.)		$75.00
Plate 6, Row 4:			
1. Muffin pan	(N.M.)	4	$395.00
2. Muffin pan	(N.M.)	5	$135.00
Plate 7, Row 1:			
1. Muffin pan	(N.M.)	4,6	$595.00
2. Muffin pan	(G.P.)	5	$195.00
3. Muffin pan	(G.P.)	4,6	$400.00
Plate 7, Row 2:			
1. Muffin pan	(G.P.)	5	$135.00
2. Muffin pan	(N.M.)	4,6	$610.00
3. Muffin pan	(G.P.)		$45.00
Plate 7, Row 3:			
1. Muffin pan	(G.P.)	5,6	$150.00
2. Muffin pan	(N.M.)		$75.00

Item	Condition	Rarity	Price
Plate 8, Row 1:			
1. Muffin pan	(N.M.)	4	$495.00
2. Muffin pan	(N.M.)	5,6	$165.00
3. Muffin pan	(M)	4	$525.00
Plate 8, Row 2:			
1. Muffin pan	(N.M.)		$75.00
2. Muffin pan	(N.M.)	5	$155.00
3. Muffin pan	(G.P.)	5,6	$175.00
Plate 8, Row 3:			
1. Muffin pan	(N.M.)		$75.00
2. Muffin pan	(N.M.)	4	$345.00
3. Muffin pan	(N.M.)	4	$265.00
Plate 9, Row 1:			
1. Muffin pan	(G.P.)	5	$120.00
2. Muffin pan	(N.M.)	4,6	$650.00
3. Muffin pan	(N.M.)	4,6	$595.00
Plate 9, Row 2:			
1. Muffin pan	(G.P.)	5	$125.00
2. Muffin pan	(N.M.)	4,5	$325.00
3. Muffin pan	(G.P.)	5	$135.00
Plate 9, Row 3:			
1. Muffin pan	(G.P.)	5,6	$195.00
2. Muffin pan	(G.P.)	5,6	$225.00
3. Muffin pan	(G.P.)	5,6	$195.00
Plate 10, Row 1:			
1. Muffin pan	(N.M.)	5,6	$145.00
2. Muffin pan	(N.M.)	4,6	$225.00
3. Muffin pan	(G.P.)	5,6	$135.00
Plate 10, Row 2:			
1. Muffin pan	(M)	4,6	$310.00
2. Muffin pan	(G.P.)	5	$135.00
Plate 10, Row 3:			
1. Muffin pan	(G.P.)	4	$155.00
2. Cornstick pan	(M)	1,2	$345.00
3. Muffin pan	(N.M.)	4	$175.00
Plate 10, Row 4:			
1. Muffin pan	(G.P.)	5,6	$135.00
2. Muffin pan	(N.M.)	2,3	$325.00
3. Muffin pan	(N.M.)	5,6	$130.00
Plate 11, Row 1:			
1. Bread pan	(G.P.)	4	$245.00
2. Bread raiser	(N.M.)	4	$395.00
3. Bread pan	(N.M.)		$75.00
Plate 11, Row 2:			
1. Bread raiser	(N.M.)	4	$425.00
2. Bread raiser	(N.M.)		$215.00
Plate 11, Row 3:			
1. Bread raiser	(G.P.)		$195.00
2. Bread pan	(G.P.)		$20.00
3. Bread pan	(G.P.)		$25.00

Item	Condition	Rarity	Price
Plate 1, Row 1:			
1. Cereal bowl	(N.M.)		$65.00
2. Dough or salad bowl	(G.P.)	6	$70.00
3. Cereal bowl	(N.M.)		$65.00
Plate 1, Row 2:			
Mixing bowls	(M)		set$125.00
Plate 1, Row 3:			
1. Mixing or serving bowl	(N.M.)	4	$30.00
2. Mixing bowl	(N.M.)	4	$95.00
3. Mixing bowl	(M)	1,5	$185.00
Plate 1, Row 4:			
1. Serving bowl	(N.M.)		$65.00
2.-4. Bowls	(M)	4	ea.$35.00
5. Bowl	(G.P.)		$110.00
Plate 2, Row 1:			
1. Salad or mixing bowl	(G.P.)	4	$240.00
2. Serving bowl	(M)	4	$135.00
3. Salad or mixing bowl	(M)	4,6	$350.00
Plate 2, Row 2:			
1.-3. Bowls	(N.M.)	4	3 pcs.$110.00
4. Bowl	(M)		$25.00
Plate 2, Row 3:			
1. Dessert bowl	(G.P.)	5	$65.00
2. Bowl	(N.M.)		$25.00
3. Bowl	(N.M.)		$25.00
4. Salad or mixing bowl	(M)	4	$350.00
Plate 2, Row 4:			
1. Dough or salad bowl	(N.M.)	4,6	$65.00
2. Soup bowl	(M)	4,5	$110.00
3. Mixing bowl	(G.P.)	5	$65.00
4. Soup bowl	(M)		$75.00
Plate 3, Row 1:			
1. Mold	(M)		$75.00
2. Rabbit mold	(N.M.)	2	$225.00
3. Tube mold	(N.M.)		$75.00
4. Rabbit mold	(N.M.)	2,4	$245.00
5. Mold	(M)		$65.00
Plate 3, Row 2:			
1. Fish mold	(N.M.)	5	$175.00
2. Mold	(N.M.)	5	$175.00
3. Fish mold	(M)	5	$190.00
Plate 3, Row 3:			
1. Melon mold	(M)		$110.00
2. Melon mold	(M)		$125.00
3. Melon mold	(M)		$125.00
4. Melon mold	(M)	4	$155.00
5. Melon mold	(M)	6	$125.00
Plate 3, Row 4:			
1. Turk's head turban mold	(M)		$110.00
2. Ice cream mold	(G.P.)	5	$55.00
3. Turk's head tube-style turban mold	(G.P.)	4	$295.00
4. Ice cream mold	(G.P.)	5	$60.00
5. Turk's head turban mold	(M)	1	$325.00

Item	Condition	Rarity	Price

Plate 4, Row 1:

Item	Condition	Rarity	Price
1. Turk's head tube-style turban mold	(M)		$135.00
2. Turk's head scalloped turban mold	(M)	5,6	$125.00
3. Ring-shaped mold	(N.M.)	2	$295.00
4. Scalloped mold	(M)	5,6	$135.00
5. Turk's head tube-style turban mold	(G.P.)	4	$145.00

Plate 4, Row 2:

Item	Condition	Rarity	Price
1. Oval mold	(G.P.)		$85.00
2. Turk's head turban mold	(G.P.)	5,6	$65.00
3. Shell-shaped mold	(G.P.)	2	$110.00
4. Ring mold	(N.M.)	4	$110.00

Plate 4, Row 3:

Item	Condition	Rarity	Price
1. Ribbed tube-style mold	(M)		$95.00
2. Oval mold	(M)	5,6	$85.00
3. Turk's head tube-style turban mold	(M)		$95.00
4. Shell mold	(M)	4,5,6	$135.00
5. Turk's head tube-style turban mold	(G.P.)		$85.00

Plate 4, Row 4:

Item	Condition	Rarity	Price
1. Round tube mold	(M)	4	$225.00
2. Oval fluted shallow mold	(G.P.)	5,6	$55.00
3. Melon mold	(M)	1	$185.00
4. Oval fluted mold with strawberry imprint	(G.P.)	1,5	$175.00
5. Turk's head tube-style turban mold	(G.P.)	4	$110.00

Plate 5, Row 1:

Item	Condition	Rarity	Price
1. Turban-style ice cream mold	(G.P.)	5	$95.00
2. Turban-style ice cream mold	(G.P.)	5	$95.00
3. Ribbed-style tube mold	(M)	4	$325.00
4. Turk's head tube-style turban mold	(N.M.)		$75.00

Plate 5, Row 2:

Item	Condition	Rarity	Price
1. Turk's head tube-style turban mold	(G.P.)	1	$395.00
2. Oval fluted mold with strawberry imprint	(M)	5	$265.00
3. Oval fluted mold with rabbit imprint	(M)	1,5	$395.00
4. Turk's head turban mold	(M)	4	$325.00
5. Turk's head turban mold or muffin cup	(M)	5,6	$125.00

Plate 5, Row 3:

Item	Condition	Rarity	Price
1. Tube mold	(M)	1	$335.00
2. Turk's head turban mold	(N.M.)	1,5,6	$135.00
3. Oval ribbed mold	(N.M.)		$85.00
4. Round fluted mold	(M)	5,6	$85.00
5. Round fluted mold with flower imprint	(M)	1,2	$365.00

Plate 5, Row 4:

Item	Condition	Rarity	Price
1. Oval fluted mold with grape imprint	(G.P.)	2	$135.00
2. Shell mold	(G.P.)	5,6	$95.00
3. Oval fluted mold with corn imprint	(M)	5	$195.00

Plate 5, Row 4 (Continued):

Item	Condition	Rarity	Price
4. Turk's head turban-style mold	(M)		$135.00
5. Round fluted mold	(G.P.)	5,6	$110.00
6. Oval fluted mold with wheat imprint	(M)	5	$195.00
7. Oblong shell mold	(G.P.)	5,6	$85.00

Section 9

Plate 1, Row 1:

Item	Condition	Rarity	Price
1. Flat Ideal grater	(N.M.)	2	$525.00
2. Food grinder	(M)	4	$165.00
3. Grater	(G.P.)	4,5	$325.00
4. Grater	(M)	5	$325.00

Plate 1, Row 2:

Item	Condition	Rarity	Price
1. Grater	(M)		$125.00
2. Revolving grater	(N.M.)	4,5	$195.00
3. Revolving grater	(G.P.)		$175.00
4. Revolving grater	(G.P.)	4	$175.00
5. Flat grater	(M)	5	$175.00

Plate 1, Row 3:

Item	Condition	Rarity	Price
1. Large grater	(G.P.)	6	$130.00
2. Noodle cutter	(N.M.)	2	$225.00
3. Revolving grater	(M)	6	$295.00
4. Grater	(G.P.)	4	$110.00

Plate 1, Row 4:

Item	Condition	Rarity	Price
1. Grater	(N.M.)		$120.00
2. Grater	(G.P.)		$75.00
3. Grater	(G.P.)	6	$105.00

Plate 2, Row 1:

Item	Condition	Rarity	Price
1. Batter jug	(N.M.)	5	$310.00
2. Batter jug	(M)	1,5	$475.00

Plate 2, Row 2:

Item	Condition	Rarity	Price
1. Large spouted batter jug	(N.M.)	2	$525.00
2. Batter jug	(N.M.)	5	$310.00

Plate 2, Row 3:

Item	Condition	Rarity	Price
1. Short style batter jug	(N.M.)	5,6	$310.00
2. Small batter jug	(M)	5	$335.00
3. Batter jug	(M)	5	$310.00

Plate 3, Row 1:

Item	Condition	Rarity	Price
1. Spice scoop	(G.P.)	2,3	$265.00
2. Spice scoop	(N.M.)	2,3	$325.00

Plate 3, Row 2:

Item	Condition	Rarity	Price
1. Grocer's scoop	(G.P.)	5	$155.00
2. Grocer's scoop	(G.P.)	5	$140.00
3. Large grocer's scoop	(N.M.)	5	$165.00
4. Grocer's scoop	(G.P.)	5	$145.00
5. Grocer's scoop	(G.P.)	5	$140.00

Plate 3, Row 3:

Item	Condition	Rarity	Price
1. Thumb scoop	(N.M.)	4,5	$115.00
2. Thumb scoop	(G.P.)	1,5	$335.00
3. Candy scoop	(N.M.)	2,5	$275.00
4. Scoop	(G.P.)	5,6	$140.00
5. Agate seamless scoop	(G.P.)	2	$260.00
6. Scoop	(G.P.)	5,6	$95.00
7. Scoop	(G.P.)	5,6	$125.00
8. Scoop	(M)	5,6	$185.00

Item	Condition	Rarity	Price
Plate 3, Row 4:			
1. Scoop	(N.M.)	5	$165.00
2. Small thumb scoop	(G.P.)	5,6	$135.00
3. Scoop	(G.P.)	5	$135.00
4. Druggist's scoop	(G.P.)	5	$135.00
5. Large scoop	(N.M.)	4,5	$165.00
6. Candy scoop	(N.M.)	5	$275.00
7. Candy scoop	(M)	5	$225.00
8. Tea scoop	(G.P.)	5	$180.00
Plate 3, Row 5:			
1. Thumb scoop	(M)	5	$195.00
2. Thumb scoop	(G.P.)	5	$165.00
3. Thumb scoop	(M)	5	$195.00
4. Thumb scoop	(G.P.)	5	$175.00
5. Thumb scoop	(M)	5	$195.00
6. Thumb scoop	(G.P.)		$175.00
7. Flat bottom thumb scoop	(G.P.)	5	$275.00

Section 10

Item	Condition	Rarity	Price
Plate 1, Row 1:			
1. Butter churn	(G.P.)	1,2	$1,175.00
2. Milk pan	(N.M.)	4	$145.00
3. Hand skimmer	(M)	5	$410.00
Plate 1, Row 2:			
1. Milk pitcher	(G.P.)	1,2	$795.00
2. Butter churn	(N.M.)	2	$2,650.00
Plate 2, Row 1:			
1. Buttermilk churn	(G.P.)	2	$1,295.00
2. Brass scale	(N.M.)		$55.00
3. Butter churn	(G.P.)	1,2	$1,275.00
Plate 2, Row 2:			
1. Butter churn	(G.P.)	5	$1,795.00
2. Scale tray	(N.M.)	4	w/scale $395.00
3. Scale tray	(N.M.)	1	w/scale $550.00
4. Butter churn	(G.P.)	1	$750.00
Plate 3, Row 1:			
1. Chocolate or coffee pot	(G.P.)	2	$225.00
2. Oval butter kettle or carrier	(N.M.)	6	$275.00
3. Chocolate or coffee pot	(G.P.)	2	$225.00
Plate 3, Row 2:			
1. Oval butter kettle or carrier	(N.M.)	4	$350.00
2. Oval butter kettle or carrier	(N.M.)	4	$350.00
Plate 3, Row 3:			
1. Oval butter kettle or carrier	(N.M.)		$250.00
2. Steam coffee pot	(M)	2,4	$375.00
3. Steam coffee pot holder	(G.P.)	2	$85.00

Section 11

Item	Condition	Rarity	Price
Plate 1, Row 1:			
1. Milk can	(N.M.)	4,6	$1,195.00
2. Milk can	(N.M.)	4,6	$995.00
3. Milk can	(N.M.)	4,6	$595.00

Item	Condition	Rarity	Price
Plate 1, Row 2:			
1. Cream can	(M)	4,6	$795.00
2. Milk can	(N.M.)		$395.00
3. Milk can	(N.M.)	4,6	$1,165.00
4. Cream can	(M)		$185.00
Plate 1, Row 3:			
1. Coffee carrier	(G.P.)	5	$175.00
2. Coffee carrier	(G.P.)	1,5	$395.00
3. Milk can	(M)		$185.00
4. Coffee carrier	(N.M.)	5	$295.00
Plate 1, Row 4:			
1. Boston milk can	(N.M.)	4,5	$195.00
2. Milk can	(N.M.)	5,6	$595.00
3. Boston milk can	(G.P.)	5	$125.00
Plate 2, Row 1:			
1. Coffee carrier	(G.P.)	5	$265.00
2. Coffee carrier	(N.M.)	5	$295.00
3. Coffee carrier	(N.M.)	5,6	$265.00
4. Coffee carrier	(N.M.)	5	$210.00
5. Coffee carrier	(N.M.)	1,5	$595.00
Plate 2, Row 2:			
1. Cream can	(N.M.)	5,6	$125.00
2. Cream can	(M)	4	$195.00
3. Cream can	(N.M.)	4	$1,395.00
4. Cream can	(M)	4	$195.00
5. Cream can	(M)	4	$1,450.00
6. Cream can	(N.M.)		$110.00
Plate 2, Row 3:			
1. Boston cream can	(N.M.)	5,6	$195.00
2. Boston cream can	(N.M.)	1,5	$1,000.00
3. Boston cream can	(M)	5	$145.00
4. Boston cream can	(G.P.)	4,5	$285.00
5. Boston cream can	(N.M.)	4,5	$195.00
Plate 2, Row 4:			
1. Boston cream can	(G.P.)	5	$265.00
2. Boston milk can	(G.P.)	4,5	$235.00
3. Boston cream can	(N.M.)		$175.00
4. Boston milk can	(G.P.)	4,5	$695.00
5. Boston cream can	(N.M.)	4,5	$235.00
Plate 3, Row 1:			
1. Boston milk can	(N.M.)	5,6	$525.00
2. Milk can	(M)		$85.00
3. Milk can	(G.P.)	4,6	$750.00
Plate 3, Row 2:			
1. Milk can	(M)	4	$595.00
2. Cream can	(M)		$110.00
3. Cream can	(M)		$55.00
4. Milk can	(M)		$165.00
Plate 3, Row 3:			
1. Cream can	(M)	5,6	$195.00
2. Cream can	(G.P.)	4	$175.00
3. Cream can	(M)	4	$225.00
4. Cream can	(M)	4	$295.00
5. Cream can	(M)	5,6	$155.00
Plate 3, Row 4:			
1. Milk can	(N.M.)	4	$995.00
2. Milk can	(M)	4	$695.00
3. Milk can	(M)	4	$595.00

Item	Condition	Rarity	Price
Plate 4, Row 1:			
1. Milk can	(N.M.)	5,6	$295.00
2. Milk can	(N.M.)	5	$135.00
3. Milk can	(G.P.)	4,6	$975.00
Plate 4, Row 2:			
1. Milk can	(N.M.)		$295.00
2. Coffee carrier	(M)	5	$195.00
3. Coffee carrier	(G.P.)	1,5	$895.00
4. Coffee carrier	(G.P.)	5	$175.00
5. Cream can	(G.P.)		$165.00
Plate 4, Row 3:			
1. Boston cream can	(G.P.)	4,6	$275.00
2. Cream can	(N.M.)		$395.00
3. Cream can	(N.M.)		$165.00
4. Cream can	(N.M.)	4,6	$1,200.00
5. Cream can	(N.M.)	5,6	$175.00
Plate 4, Row 4:			
1. Milk can	(M)		$80.00
2. Boston milk can	(G.P.)	2	$325.00
3. Milk can	(G.P.)	5	$110.00
4. Milk can	(M)	4	$995.00
Plate 5, Row 1:			
1. Milk can	(N.M.)	4	$575.00
2. Milk can	(N.M.)	4,6	$265.00
3. Cream can	(G.P.)	5,6	$155.00
4. Milk can	(M)	1	$1,095.00
Plate 5, Row 2:			
1. Cream can	(G.P.)	4,5	$525.00
2. Milk can	(G.P.)		$70.00
3. Milk can	(N.M.)	4	$975.00
4. Milk can	(N.M.)	4	$250.00
Plate 5, Row 3:			
1. Cream can	(M)		$200.00
2. Cream can	(G.P.)	4	$895.00
3. Cream can	(M)	5,6	$325.00
4. Cream can	(M)	4	$1,000.00
5. Cream can	(N.M.)		$495.00
6. Cream can	(N.M.)	4	$395.00
Plate 5, Row 4:			
1. Cream can	(N.M.)		$395.00
2. Milk can	(M)	4	$295.00
3. Milk can	(N.M.)	4	$210.00
4. Cream can	(G.P.)		$195.00

Section 12

Item	Condition	Rarity	Price
Plate 1, Row 1:			
1. Counter-top family scale	(G.P.)	2	$340.00
2. Wash basin	(N.M.)	5	$185.00
3. Ashtray	(N.M.)	1	$285.00
4. Bean scoop	(N.M.)	2,3	$350.00
Plate 1, Row 2:			
1. Ashtray	(N.M.)	1	$225.00
2. Ice cream scoop	(G.P.)	2,3	$495.00
3. Plate	(M)	1,2,3	$350.00
4. Bowl	(N.M.)	5	$225.00
5. Mug	(N.M.)	2	$175.00

Item	Condition	Rarity	Price
Plate 1, Row 3:			
1. Ashtray	(M)	4	$185.00
2. Ashtray	(G.P.)	5	$130.00
3. Tray-type ashtray	(M)	1,6	$285.00
4. Mug	(N.M.)	2	$195.00
5. Ashtray	(M)		$155.00
Plate 2, Row 1:			
1. 50th Anniversary catalog	(M)		$265.00
2. Box of Mendets	(N.M.)		$30.00
3. 1919 ad	(M)		$95.00
Plate 2, Row 2:			
1. Card of Mendets	(M)		$25.00
2. Pamphlet cookbook	(M)		$95.00
3. Ad	(G.P.)		$30.00
4. Trade card	(M)		$30.00
5. New Perfection advertising pamphlet	(M)		$55.00
Plate 2, Row 3:			
1. 1925 magazine ad	(M)		$40.00
2. Kalamazoo Stove ad	(M)		$40.00
3. Magazine ad	(M)		$40.00
Plate 3, Row 1:			
Oval advertising tray	(N.M.)	2	$1,275.00
Plate 3, Row 2:			
1. Oval sign	(G.P.)	2	$975.00
2. Oval sign	(G.P.)	2	$1,000.00

Section 13

Item	Condition	Rarity	Price
Plate 1:			
Ten-piece pitcher and bowl set	(N.M.)	5	set $975.00
Plate 2, Row 1:			
Squatty pitcher and bowl	(N.M.)	5	$465.00
Plate 2, Row 2:			
1. Squatty pitcher and bowl	(G.P.)	4,5	$200.00
2. Pitcher and bowl	(M)		$100.00
Plate 2, Row 3:			
1. Pitcher and bowl	(M)	6	$110.00
2. Squatty pitcher and bowl	(N.M.)	5	$225.00
Plate 3, Row 1:			
1. Hanging soap dish	(G.P.)		$60.00
2. Body pitcher	(G.P.)	1,2	$975.00
3. Body pitcher	(N.M.)	1,2	$950.00
4. Hanging soap dish	(G.P.)		$45.00
Plate 3, Row 2:			
1. Water pail	(M)		$200.00
2. Hanging soap dish	(G.P.)	1	$265.00
3. Pitcher and bowl	(N.M.)	1	2 pr. $1,200.00
Plate 3, Row 3:			
1. Water pail	(N.M.)	4	$135.00
2. Pitcher with ice lip	(M)	2	$265.00
3. Water pail	(M)		$245.00

Item	Condition	Rarity	Price
Plate 4, Row 1:			
1. Bed pan	(N.M.)	4,5	$85.00
2. Chamber pot	(N.M.)		$65.00
3. Hanging soap dish with insert	(G.P.)	2	2 pc.s $95.00
Plate 4, Row 2:			
1. Covered toothbrush holder	(G.P.)	5	$65.00
2. Hanging soap dish	(N.M.)	4	$195.00
3. Child's potty	(N.M.)		$235.00
4. Shell-shaped soap dish	(G.P.)	5	$115.00
5. Open toothbrush holder	(M)	5	$195.00
Plate 4, Row 3:			
1. Hanging soap dish	(M)	4	$200.00
2. Hanging soap dish	(G.P.)	4	$175.00
3. Covered toothbrush holder	(G.P.)	1,5	$265.00
4. Chamber pot	(N.M.)		$165.00
Plate 4, Row 4:			
1. Hanging soap dish	(M)		$55.00
2. Large covered chamber pot	(M)		$325.00
3. Bathtub-style soap dish	(G.P.)	2	$285.00
4. Hanging soap dish	(G.P.)	4	$225.00
Plate 5, Row 1:			
1. Water pail	(N.M.)		$200.00
2. Oval-shaped water carrier	(N.M.)	1,2	$695.00
Plate 5, Row 2:			
1. Water pail	(N.M.)	4	$295.00
2. Oval-shaped water carrier	(G.P.)	6	$110.00
3. Water pail	(M)		$185.00
Plate 5, Row 3:			
1. Water pail	(M)	4	$325.00
2. Large water pail	(M)	4	$325.00
Plate 6, Row 1:			
1. Large water carrier	(G.P.)	2,4	$795.00
2. Water pail	(N.M.)	4	$155.00
Plate 6, Row 2:			
1. Water pail	(M)	4	$135.00
2. Small pail	(G.P.)	6	$95.00
3. Water pail	(G.P.)	4	$125.00
Plate 6, Row 3:			
1. Small water pail	(M)	4	$150.00
2. Water carrier	(G.P.)	2	$325.00
Plate 7, Row 1:			
1. Chamber pail	(N.M.)		$185.00
2. Hanging tumbler holder	(M)		$30.00
3. Chamber pail	(N.M.)	4	$250.00
Plate 7, Row 2:			
1. Chamber pail	(N.M.)	4	$575.00
2. Hanging tooothbrush holder	(N.M.)		$30.00
3. Hanging soap or sponge dish	(G.P.)		$25.00
4. Chamber pail	(N.M.)	4	$165.00

Item	Condition	Rarity	Price
Plate 7, Row 3:			
1. Slop bucket	(N.M.)	4,5	$295.00
2. Hanging soap dish	(G.P.)	5	$35.00
3. Slop bucket	(G.P.)	1	$495.00

Section 14

Item	Condition	Rarity	Price
Plate 1, Row 1:			
1. Windsor dipper	(N.M.)	4	$145.00
2. Shaving basin	(G.P.)	5	$90.00
3. Windsor dipper	(G.P.)	4	$310.00
Plate 1, Row 2:			
1. Large wash basin with eyelet	(G.P.)	4	$195.00
2. Windsor dipper	(N.M.)	4	$130.00
3. Large wash basin with eyelet	(N.M.)	4	$175.00
Plate 1, Row 3:			
1. Flared dipper	(M)	4,5	$110.00
2. Medium wash basin	(G.P.)		$65.00
3. Flat hook-handled dipper	(G.P.)	4	$110.00
4. Medium wash basin	(G.P.)	4	$75.00
5. Flat-handled dipper	(G.P.)	4	$95.00
Plate 2, Row 1:			
1. Windsor dipper	(M)	4	$145.00
2. Large wash basin	(N.M.)	1	$135.00
3. Flared dipper	(N.M.)	4,5	$95.00
Plate 2, Row 2:			
1. Small wash basin	(M)		$80.00
2. Wash basin	(M)		$45.00
3. Wash basin	(M)		$85.00
Plate 2, Row 3:			
1. Deep wash basin	(N.M.)	4	$115.00
2. Wash basin	(G.P.)	4	$85.00
3. Small wash basin	(N.M.)	4,6	$195.00
Plate 2, Row 4:			
1. Windsor dipper	(N.M.)	4	$125.00
2. Windsor dipper	(G.P.)	4	$95.00
Plate 3, Row 1:			
1. Flat hook-handle dipper	(M)	4	$135.00
2. Shallow wash basin	(M)	4	$195.00
3. Dipper	(N.M.)		$40.00
4. Wash basin	(M)		$110.00
5. Dipper	(G.P.)	4,5	$185.00
Plate 3, Row 2:			
1. Large flared dipper	(M)	3,4	$595.00
2. Large wash basin	(G.P.)	1	$295.00
3. Dipper	(G.P.)	6	$115.00
Plate 3, Row 3:			
1. Large wash basin	(N.M.)		$45.00
2. Large wash basin	(G.P.)	4	$95.00
Plate 4, Row 1:			
1. Wash basin	(G.P.)	4	$125.00
2. Flat hook-handled dipper	(G.P.)		$85.00
3. Wash basin	(G.P.)	4	$185.00

Item	Condition	Rarity	Price
Plate 4, Row 2:			
1. Flared dipper	(G.P.)	4	$95.00
2. Large wash basin	(M)	1	$425.00
3. Flat hook-handled dipper	(G.P.)	4	$125.00
Plate 4, Row 3:			
1. Footed wash basin	(N.M.)	2	$135.00
2. Flared dipper	(N.M.)	4	$145.00
3. Wash basin	(N.M.)	4	$145.00
Plate 5, Row 1:			
1. Flared flat-handled dipper	(G.P.)		$80.00
2. Flat-handled dipper	(G.P.)	4	$125.00
3. Wash basin	(G.P.)	4	$155.00
4. Flat hook-handled dipper	(N.M.)		$110.00
5. Flat-handled dipper	(G.P.)	4,5	$125.00
Plate 5, Row 2:			
1. Wash basin	(G.P.)		$45.00
2. Large wash basin	(N.M.)		$125.00
3. Child's wash basin	(N.M.)	3	$115.00
Plate 5, Row 3:			
1. Wash basin	(G.P.)		$85.00
2. Wash basin	(G.P.)		$85.00
3. Wash basin	(G.P.)		$75.00
Plate 5, Row 4:			
1. Flat hooked-handled dipper	(N.M.)	4	$115.00
2. Flared dipper	(G.P.)	4	$110.00
Plate 6: Row 1:			
1. Water pitcher	(M)	4	$650.00
2. Water pitcher	(N.M.)	1	$3,000.00
3. Water pitcher	(M)	4	$650.00
Plate 6, Row 2:			
1. Water pitcher	(G.P.)	4,5	$175.00
2. Milk pitcher	(N.M.)	4,6	$195.00
3. Milk pitcher	(N.M.)	4,6	$195.00
4. Water pitcher	(G.P.)	4	$350.00
Plate 6, Row 3:			
1. Convex water pitcher	(M)	2,4	$395.00
2. Milk pitcher	(N.M.)	5	$175.00
3. Clover leaf convex pitcher	(G.P.)	5	$185.00
Plate 6, Row 4:			
1. Water pitcher	(G.P.)		$140.00
2. Water pticher	(G.P.)	1	$350.00
3. Water pliicher	(N.M.)		$225.00
Plate 7, Row 1:			
1. Water pitcher	(N.M.)	4	$195.00
2. Water pitcher	(N.M.)	4	$295.00
3. Water pitcher	(G.P.)	4	$625.00
Plate 7, Row 2:			
1. Water pitcher	(G.P.)	4	$625.00
2. Water pitcher	(N.M.)		$195.00
3. Water pitcher	(G.P.)	4	$485.00
4. Water pitcher	(G.P.)	4	$395.00
Plate 7, Row 3:			
1. Water pitcher	(N.M.)	4	$275.00
2. Pump or bellboy pitcher	(N.M.)	2,4	$210.00
3. Clover leaf convex pitcher	(G.P.)	5	$295.00
4. Water pitcher	(G.P.)	4	$185.00
Plate 7, Row 4:			
1. Water pitcher	(G.P.)		$160.00
2. Water pitcher	(N.M.)	5	$210.00
3. Water pitcher	(M)		$175.00
4. Milk pitcher	(M)	6	$195.00
Plate 8, Row 1:			
1. Body pitcher	(G.P.)	1,5	$295.00
2. Body pitcher	(N.M.)	4,5	$325.00
Plate 8, Row 2:			
1. Water pitcher	(G.P.)	1	$385.00
2. Water pitcher	(G.P.)	1	$495.00
3. Water pitcher	(G.P.)	1	$595.00
Plate 8, Row 3:			
1. Water pitcher	(G.P.)	4	$175.00
2. Milk pitcher	(M)	4,6	$180.00
3. Water pitcher	(G.P.)	4	$140.00
Plate 9, Row 1:			
1. Water pitcher	(M)	4	$325.00
2. Water pitcher	(G.P.)	4	$180.00
3. Water pitcher	(G.P.)	4	$295.00
Plate 9, Row 2:			
1. Water pitcher	(M)	4	$325.00
2. Footed water pitcher	(G.P.)	5	$225.00
3. Water pitcher	(M)	4	$425.00
Plate 9, Row 3:			
1. Water pitcher	(N.M.)	4	$175.00
2. Water pitcher	(G.P.)	4	$175.00
3. Water pitcher	(N.M.)	4	$150.00
Plate 10, Row 1:			
1. Water pitcher	(G.P.)	1	$3,450.00
2. Water pitcher	(G.P.)	4	$625.00
3. Water pitcher	(N.M.)	4	$525.00
4. Water pitcher	(N.M.)	4	$325.00
Plate 10, Row 2:			
1. Convex agate water pitcher	(G.P.)	5	$175.00
2. Milk pitcher	(N.M.)	5	$165.00
3. Milk pitcher	(M)	5	$175.00
4. Convex agate water pitcher	(M)	5	$225.00
5. Milk pitcher	(G.P.)	4,5,6	$225.00
Plate 10, Row 3:			
1. Water pitcher	(M)	4	$325.00
2. Milk pitcher	(G.P.)	6	$160.00
3. Water pitcher	(G.P.)	4	$295.00
4. Milk pitcher	(G.P.)	6	$165.00
5. Water pitcher	(G.P.)		$250.00
Plate 10, Row 4:			
1. Water pitcher	(M)		$285.00
2. Water pitcher	(N.M.)	2	$325.00
3. Water pitcher	(G.P.)		$175.00
4. Water pitcher	(M)		$225.00

Item	Condition	Rarity	Price
Plate 11, Row 1:			
1. Water pitcher	(N.M.)		$75.00
2. Collar base water pitcher	(G.P.)	4,5,6	$250.00
3. Water pitcher	(N.M.)		$185.00
Plate 11, Row 2:			
1. Water pitcher	(N.M.)	4	$325.00
2. Water pitcher	(G.P.)	4	$395.00
3. Water pitcher	(G.P.)	4	$495.00
Plate 11, Row 3:			
1. Water pitcher	(N.M.)	4	$240.00
2. Water pitcher	(M)		$85.00
3. Water pitcher	(M)		$295.00
Plate 12, Row 1:			
1. Water cooler	(G.P.)	4,5	$625.00
2. Water cooler	(N.M.)	4,5	$750.00
Plate 12, Row 2:			
1. Rooster weather vane	(G.P.)	2	$650.00
2. Cylinder-shaped water cooler	(G.P.)	2	$1495.00
3. Cylinder-shaped gas water heater	(N.M.)	2	$395.00

Section 15

Item	Condition	Rarity	Price
Plate 1:			
Lavabo and basin	(N.M.)	1,2	$1,295.00
Plate 2:			
1. Lavabo and basin	(G.P.)	2	$625.00
2. Lavabo and basin	(G.P.)	2	$625.00
Plate 3:			
1. Lavabo and basin	(G.P.)	1,2	$525.00
2. Lavabo and basin	(G.P.)	2,4	$340.00
Plate 4:			
1. Douche	(G.P.)	2	$395.00
2. Lavabo and basin	(G.P.)	1,2	$1,245.00

Section 16

Item	Condition	Rarity	Price
Plate 1, Row 1:			
1. Funnel	(G.P.)	1	$210.00
2. Funnel	(G.P.)	4	$185.00
3. Large squatty-shaped funnel	(N.M.)	4,6	$265.00
4. Funnel	(N.M.)		$35.00
5. Funnel	(G.P.)	4	$185.00
Plate 1, Row 2:			
1. Squatty-shaped funnel	(G.P.)		$40.00
2. Squatty-shaped funnel	(N.M.)	4,6	$175.00
3. Funnel	(G.P.)		$65.00
4. Funnel	(N.M.)	5	$55.00
5. Large squatty-shaped funnel	(G.P.)		$75.00
6. Squatty-shaped funnel	(N.M.)		$30.00

Item	Condition	Rarity	Price
Plate 1, Row 3:			
1. Large squatty-shaped funnel	(G.P.)	4,6	$245.00
2. Funnel	(N.M.)		$45.00
3. Squatty-shaped funnel	(N.M.)	4	$140.00
4. Large squatty-shaped funnel	(G.P.)	4,6	$225.00
Plate 2, Row 1:			
1. Fruit jar filler	(N.M.)	4	$145.00
2. Fruit jar filler	(G.P.)		$35.00
3. Large fruit jar filler	(N.M.)	4,6	$275.00
4. Fruit jar filler	(M)		$45.00
5. Fruit jar filler	(N.M.)	4	$155.00
Plate 2, Row 2:			
1. Percolator funnel	(M)	4,5	$185.00
2. Large percolator funnel	(G.P.)	1,6	$225.00
3. Percolator funnel	(N.M.)		$185.00
Plate 2, Row 3:			
1. Fruit jar filler	(N.M.)		$120.00
2. Fruit jar filler	(N.M.)	4	$145.00
3. Fruit jar filler	(G.P.)	4	$130.00
4. Fruit jar filler	(G.P.)	1	$225.00
Plate 2, Row 4:			
1. Fruit jar filler	(G.P.)		$35.00
2. Fruit jar filler	(G.P.)	4	$145.00
3. Fruit jar filler	(G.P.)	4	$140.00
4. Fruit jar filler	(N.M.)		$40.00
Plate 3, Row 1:			
1. Funnel	(G.P.)	4	$125.00
2. Funnel	(N.M.)	4	$265.00
3. Squatty-shaped funnel	(G.P.)	1,6	$275.00
Plate 3, Row 2:			
1. Funnel	(M)		$55.00
2. Funnel	(N.M.)	1	$1,875.00
3. Funnel	(G.P.)	5	$55.00
4. Squatty-shaped funnel	(N.M.)	4	$495.00
Plate 3, Row 3:			
1. Small squatty-shaped funnel	(N.M.)	4,6	$260.00
2. Squatty-shaped funnel	(N.M.)	4	$115.00
3. Large funnel	(N.M.)		$95.00
4. Squatty-shaped funnel	(G.P.)	4	$230.00
5. Small funnel	(G.P.)		$65.00

Section 17

Item	Condition	Rarity	Price
Plate 1, Row 1:			
1. Fry pan	(G.P.)	4	$140.00
2. Fry pan	(M)	4	$125.00
3. Fry pan	(N.M.)	4	$235.00
Plate 1, Row 2:			
1. Fry pan	(G.P.)	4	$190.00
2. Fry pan	(N.M.)	4	$275.00
3. Fry pan	(M)	4	$295.00
Plate 1, Row 3:			
1. Small fry pan	(G.P.)	4	$135.00
2. Fry pan	(M)	4	$170.00
3. Small fry pan	(G.P.)		$140.00

Item	Condition	Rarity	Price
Plate 2, Row 1:			
1. Fry pan	(M)	4	$285.00
2. Fry pan	(M)	4	$295.00
3. Fry pan	(M)	4	$225.00
Plate 2, Row 2:			
1. Fry pan	(N.M.)		$35.00
2. Fry pan	(G.P.)	4	$125.00
3. Fry pan	(N.M.)	4	$165.00
4. Fry pan	(M)	2	$215.00
Plate 2, Row 3:			
1. Fry pan	(N.M.)	4	$265.00
2. Fry pan	(N.M.)	4,6	$195.00
3. Fry pan	(G.P.)	4	$185.00
Plate 3, Row 1:			
1. Fry pan	(M)	4	$125.00
2. Fry pan	(N.M.)	4	$185.00
3. Fry pan	(G.P.)	4	$130.00
Plate 3, Row 2:			
1. Fry pan	(G.P.)	4	$225.00
2. Small fry pan	(G.P.)	6	$75.00
3. Fry pan	(M)	4	$295.00
4. Egg dish	(N.M.)	3,4	$285.00
5. Fry pan	(N.M.)	4	$395.00
Plate 3, Row 3:			
1. Fry pan	(N.M.)	4	$225.00
2. Fry pan	(G.P.)	4	$135.00
3. Fry pan	(G.P.)	4	$195.00
Plate 4, Row 1:			
1. Oval griddle	(G.P.)	2	$295.00
2. Two-handled egg plate or pan	(N.M.)	4	$125.00
3. Two-handled egg plate or pan	(M)	4,6	$135.00
4. Two-handled egg plate or pan	(G.P.)	1	$195.00
Plate 4, Row 2:			
1. Oval-handled pan	(G.P.)		$95.00
2. Two-handled egg plate or pan	(M)	1	$325.00
3. Two ear-type handled egg plate or pan	(N.M.)		$120.00
4. Oblong griddle	(N.M.)	2	$635.00
Plate 4, Row 3:			
1. Fry pan	(M)	4	$125.00
2. Egg fry pan	(N.M.)	5	$295.00
3. Two-handled egg plate or pan	(G.P.)	4	$195.00
Plate 5, Row 1:			
1. Shallow stew pan	(G.P.)	4	$225.00
2. Deep stew pan	(N.M.)	4,6	$210.00
3. Shallow stew pan	(G.P.)	4	$210.00
Plate 5, Row 2:			
1. Shallow stew pan	(G.P.)	4	$110.00
2. Shallow stew pan	(N.M.)	4	$115.00
Plate 5, Row 3:			
1. Deep stew pan	(G.P.)	4	$180.00
2. Deep stew pan	(G.P.)	4	$150.00
3. Deep stew pan	(G.P.)	4	$145.00

Item	Condition	Rarity	Price
Plate 5, Row 4:			
1. Deep stew pan	(G.P.)	4	$115.00
2. Shallow stew pan	(G.P.)	4	$120.00

Section 18

Item	Condition	Rarity	Price
Plate 1, Row 1:			
1. Tea steeper or baby food cup	(M)	4	$225.00
2. Tea steeper	(M)		$125.00
3. Tea strainer	(N.M.)	1,5	$255.00
4. Tea steeper	(G.P.)	1	$425.00
5. Tea steeper	(M)	4	$185.00
Plate 1, Row 2:			
1. Tea steeper	(G.P.)	4	$145.00
2. Tea steeper	(G.P.)	4,5	$195.00
3. Tea strainer	(N.M.)	1,5	$195.00
4. Tea strainer	(M)	4	$145.00
5. Tea steeper	(N.M.)	1	$450.00
6. Tea steeper	(N.M.)	4	$195.00
Plate 1, Row 3:			
1. Tea steeper	(M)	4	$435.00
2. Tea steeper	(N.M.)		$75.00
3. Tea strainer	(N.M.)	4	$145.00
4. Tea strainer	(N.M.)		$75.00
5. Tea steeper	(G.P.)	4	$195.00
6. Tea steeper	(N.M.)	6	$135.00
Plate 1, Row 4:			
1. Tea strainer	(N.M.)	5	$50.00
2. Tea steeper	(N.M.)	4	$395.00
3. Tea strainer	(M)	4	$155.00
4. Tea strainer	(G.P.)		$45.00
5. Tea steeper	(G.P.)		$150.00
6. Tea strainer	(M)		$55.00
Plate 2, Row 1:			
1. Teakettle	(G.P.)	2,3,4	$295.00
2. Teakettle	(G.P.)	2,6	$270.00
3. Teakettle	(N.M.)	1,2,3	$365.00
Plate 2, Row 2:			
1. Teakettle	(M)	4,5,6	$195.00
2. Teakettle	(G.P.)	4	$75.00
3. Teakettle	(G.P.)	4,5	$70.00
4. Teakettle	(M)	5,6	$95.00
Plate 2, Row 3:			
1. Teakettle	(N.M.)	6	$225.00
2. Teakettle	(N.M.)	1	$1,195.00
3. Teakettle	(M)	1,2,3	$525.00
4. Teakettle	(G.P.)	4,6	$395.00
Plate 2, Row 4:			
1. Teakettle	(N.M.)	4	$295.00
2. Teakettle	(G.P.)	4	$230.00
Plate 3, Row 1:			
1. Teakettle	(G.P.)	4	$310.00
2. Teakettle	(M)	1,2	$625.00
3. Teakettle	(G.P.)	4	$325.00

Item	Condition	Rarity	Price
Plate 3, Row 2:			
1. Teakettle	(N.M.)	6	$225.00
2. Teakettle w/insert	(N.M.)	2	$295.00
3. Teakettle	(M)	5	$275.00
4. Teakettle	(M)	2	$295.00
Plate 3, Row 3:			
1. Oil stove teakettle	(N.M.)	5	$245.00
2. Teakettle	(N.M.)	1,3	$695.00
3. Oil stove teakettle	(G.P.)	5	$265.00
4. Teakettle	(G.P.)	4,6	$155.00
Plate 3, Row 4:			
1. Teakettle	(G.P.)	4	$165.00
2. Teakettle	(N.M.)	4	$275.00
3. Teakettle	(N.M.)	4	$225.00
Plate 4, Row 1:			
1. Teakettle	(N.M.)	4	$240.00
2. Teakettle	(N.M.)	4	$465.00
Plate 4, Row 2:			
1. Teakettle	(M)	4	$195.00
2. Teakettle	(G.P.)	2	$225.00
3. Teakettle	(M)	4	$145.00
Plate 4, Row 3:			
1. Teakettle	(G.P.)	2,3,4	$325.00
2. Teakettle	(G.P.)	2,3,4	$275.00
Plate 4, Row 4:			
1. Teakettle	(G.P.)	4	$155.00
2. Teakettle	(G.P.)	2,3	$265.00
3. Teakttle	(G.P.)	4	$295.00
Plate 5, Row 1:			
1. Teakettle	(G.P.)	1	$750.00
2. Teakettle	(G.P.)	4	$180.00
3. Teakettle	(N.M.)	4	$435.00
Plate 5, Row 2:			
1. Teakettle	(M)	4	$120.00
2. Teakettle	(N.M.)	4	$120.00
3. Teakettle	(M)	4	$145.00
Plate 5, Row 3:			
1. Teakettle	(G.P.)	4	$395.00
2. Teakettle	(G.P.)	4,6	$210.00
3. Teakettle	(N.M.)	4	$275.00
Plate 5, Row 4:			
1. Teakettle	(G.P.)	4	$235.00
2. Teakettle	(G.P.)	6	$210.00
3. Teakettle	(G.P.)	4	$165.00

Section 19

Item	Condition	Rarity	Price
Plate 1, Row 1:			
1. Oblong baking pan	(G.P.)	4	$135.00
2. Oblong baking pan	(N.M.)	4	$245.00
3. Oblong baking pan	(M)		$55.00
Plate 1, Row 2:			
1. Oblong baking pan	(N.M.)	4	$285.00
2. Oblong baking pan	(G.P.)	1,5	$625.00
3. Oblong baking pan	(N.M.)	4	$165.00

Item	Condition	Rarity	Price
Plate 1, Row 3:			
1. Oblong baking pan	(G.P.)		$85.00
2. Oblong baking pan	(M)	4,6	$325.00
3. Oblong baking pan	(G.P.)	4	$285.00
Plate 2, Row 1:			
1. Oblong baking pan	(N.M.)	4	$155.00
2. Oblong baking pan	(G.P.)		$85.00
3. Oblong baking pan	(N.M.)	4	$130.00
Plate 2, Row 2:			
1. Square baking pan	(G.P.)	4	$115.00
2. Oblong baking pan	(G.P.)		$40.00
3. Oblong baking pan	(G.P.)		$110.00
Plate 2, Row 3:			
1. Oblong baking pan	(M)		$165.00
2. Oblong baking pan	(N.M.)		$140.00
Plate 3, Row 1:			
1. Oblong baking pan	(N.M.)	4,5	$295.00
2. Oblong baking pan	(N.M.)	4	$325.00
3. Oblong baking pan	(M)	4	$250.00
Plate 3, Row 2:			
Squre baking pan	(G.P.)		$40.00
Plate 3, Row 3:			
1. Oblong baking pan	(G.P.)		$110.00
2. Oblong baking pan	(G.P.)	4	$260.00
3. Oblong baking pan	(N.M.)	4	$250.00
Plate 4, Row 1:			
Three-piece flat-top roaster	(N.M.)	4	$375.00
Plate 4, Row 2:			
1. Three-piece flat-top roaster	(N.M.)	4	$195.00
2. Three-piece flat-top roaster	(G.P.)	4	$325.00
Plate 4, Row 3:			
1. Two-piece round roaster	(N.M.)	4	$350.00
2. Three-piece oval roaster	(G.P.)	4	$285.00
Plate 5, Row 1:			
Two-piece oval roaster	(M)	4	$225.00
Plate 5, Row 2:			
1. Three-piece broiler	(M)	2,4	$395.00
2. Two-piece oval roaster	(G.P.)		$40.00
Plate 5, Row 3:			
1. Two-piece small oval roaster	(M)	5,6	$195.00
2. Coverless roaster	(N.M.)	5	$165.00
Plate 6, Row 1:			
Two-piece oval roaster	(M)	4,5	$395.00
Plate 6, Row 2:			
1. Three-piece roaster	(G.P.)	4	$140.00
2. Roaster insert	(G.P.)	4	$95.00
Plate 6, Row 3:			
1. Three-piece oval roaster	(N.M.)	4,6	$325.00
2. Three-piece oval roaster	(G.P.)	4	$135.00

Item	Condition	Rarity	Price
Plate 7, Row 1:			
1. Three-piece oval roaster	(N.M.)	4	$350.00
2. Two-piece round roaster	(M)	4	$195.00
Plate 7, Row 2:			
1. Two-piece oval roaster	(G.P.)	4,6	$185.00
2. Two-piece oval flat-top roaster	(G.P.)	2,4	$295.00
Plate 7, Row 3:			
1. Three-piece flat-top roaster	(N.M.)	4	$245.00
2. Roaster insert	(M)	4	$125.00

Section 20

Item	Condition	Rarity	Price
Plate 1, Row 1:			
1. Measure	(N.M.)	4	$625.00
2. Measure	(G.P.)	4,6	$195.00
3. Measure	(G.P.)	1	$425.00
4. Measure	(N.M.)	4	$295.00
5. Measure	(N.M.)	4	$185.00
6. Measure	(N.M.)	4	$550.00
Plate 1, Row 2:			
1. Measure	(M)	4	$795.00
2. Measure	(N.M.)	4,6	$210.00
3. Measure	(M)	4	$225.00
4. Measure	(G.P.)	4	$215.00
5. Measure	(N.M.)	4	$395.00
6. Measure	(N.M.)	5,6	$225.00
7. Measure	(N.M.)	4	$365.00
Plate 1, Row 3:			
1. Measure	(G.P.)	4	$165.00
2. Measure	(G.P.)	4	$85.00
3. Measure	(G.P.)	4	$185.00
4. Measure	(N.M.)	4	$795.00
5. Measure	(M)	4	$250.00
6. Measure	(G.P.)	4	$295.00
7. Measure	(G.P.)	4	$575.00
Plate 1, Row 4:			
1. Measure	(G.P.)	4	$220.00
2. Measure	(G.P.)	4	$85.00
3. Measure	(N.M.)	4	$120.00
4. Measure	(G.P.)	4	$165.00
5. Measure	(G.P.)	4	$170.00
6. Measure	(N.M.)	4	$145.00
7. Measure	(G.P.)	4	$75.00
Plate 2, Row 1:			
1. Measure	(N.M.)	6	$225.00
2. Measure	(M)	4	$295.00
3. Measure	(M)		$250.00
4. Measure	(G.P.)	4	$325.00
5. Measure	(N.M.)	6	$225.00
Plate 2, Row 2:			
1. Tumbler-shaped measure	(M)	5	$45.00
2. Graduated lipped dry measure	(G.P.)	4	$165.00
3. Graduated lipped tall-style measure	(G.P.)	4,5	$165.00

Item	Condition	Rarity	Price
Plate 2, Row 2 (continued)			
4. Graduated lipped dry measure	(G.P.)	4	$145.00
5. Cup-style measure	(G.P.)	4,5	$80.00
Plate 2, Row 3:			
1. Measure	(M)	4,6	$195.00
2. Measure	(M)	4	$165.00
3. Measure	(N.M.)	4	$140.00
4. Measure	(G.P.)	4	$125.00
5. Measure	(M)	4,6	$210.00
Plate 2, Row 4:			
1. Measure	(G.P.)	1	$425.00
2. Measure	(G.P.)	4	$295.00
3. Measure	(G.P.)	1	$595.00
4. Measure	(M)	4	$795.00
5. Measure	(N.M.)	4	$120.00
Plate 3, Row 1:			
1. Meaure	(N.M.)		$180.00
2. Measure	(M)		$195.00
3. Seamless vinegar measure	(G.P.)	5,6	$190.00
4. Seamless vinegar measure	(G.P.)	5,6	$190.00
5. Agate "Favorite" measure	(G.P.)	5	$200.00
6. Seamless vinegar measure	(N.M.)	5,6	$190.00
Plate 3, Row 2:			
1. One cup measure	(M)	3	$225.00
2. Measure	(M)	6	$195.00
3. Measure	(M)	6	$195.00
4. Measure	(M)		$250.00
5. Measure	(G.P.)		$160.00
6. Measure	(M)		$375.00
7. Measure	(G.P.)	6	$195.00
Plate 3, Row 3:			
1. Measure	(M)	6	$195.00
2. Measure	(N.M.)		$145.00
3. Measuring cup	(N.M.)		$110.00
4. Measure	(N.M.)		$195.00
5. Measure	(G.P.)		$130.00
6. Measuring cup	(M)		$125.00
7. Measure	(N.M.)	6	$185.00
Plate 3, Row 4:			
1. Four-cup graduated lipped dry measure	(M)		$110.00
2. Graduated lipped dry measure	(M)		$195.00
3. Graduated lipped dry measure	(M)		$185.00
4. Graduated lipped dry measure	(N.M.)		$170.00
5. Graduated lipped dry measure	(N.M.)		$185.00
Plate 4, Row 1:			
1. Colander	(M)	4	$395.00
2. Colander	(G.P.)	4	$295.00
3. Colander	(M)	4	$395.00
Plate 4, Row 2:			
1. Colander	(M)		$75.00
2. Handled gravy or soup strainer	(G.P.)	5,6	$155.00
3. Colander	(G.P.)	5	$125.00

Item	Condition	Rarity	Price
Plate 4, Row 3:			
1. Strainer	(M)		$95.00
2. Teardrop sink strainer	(G.P.)	5	$195.00
3. Round strainer	(M)		$110.00
Plate 4, Row 4:			
1. Colander	(N.M.)	1	$395.00
2. Handled gravy or soup strainer	(N.M.)	5	$195.00
3. Colander	(M)	4	$395.00
Plate 5, Row 1:			
1. Colander	(G.P.)	4	$185.00
2. Handled strainer	(G.P.)		$55.00
3. Colander	(N.M.)	4	$200.00
Plate 5, Row 2:			
1. Colander	(G.P.)	4	$295.00
2. Sink strainer	(N.M.)	5	$95.00
3. Colander	(M)	4	$295.00
Plate 5, Row 3:			
1. Colander	(N.M.)	4	$135.00
2. Handled strainer	(G.P.)	4	$130.00
3. Colander	(M)		$55.00
Plate 5, Row 4:			
1. Colander	(M)	4,6	$395.00
2. Square sink strainer	(N.M.)	5	$295.00
3. Colander	(M)	4	$285.00
Plate 6, Row 1:			
1. Gravy strainer	(G.P.)	5	$130.00
2. Colander	(M)	4	$295.00
3. Handled strainer	(N.M.)		$45.00
Plate 6, Row 2:			
1. Triangular sink strainer	(N.M.)		$175.00
2. Triangular sink strainer	(N.M.)		$125.00
3. Teardrop sink strainer	(G.P.)	5	$295.00
Plate 6, Row 3:			
1. Colander	(M)	4	$395.00
2. Handled strainer	(G.P.)	4	$95.00
3. Colander	(M)	4	$310.00
Plate 6, Row 4:			
1. Colander	(N.M.)		$45.00
2. Colander	(N.M.)		$55.00
3. Colander	(G.P.)	4	$235.00
Plate 7, Row 1:			
1. Colander	(G.P.)	4	$310.00
2. Colander	(N.M.)	4	$295.00
3. Strainer	(G.P.)	5	$195.00
Plate 7, Row 2:			
1. Handled strainer	(G.P.)	4,5	$310.00
2. Triangular wire footed strainer	(G.P.)	5	$200.00
3. Covered sink strainer	(N.M.)	5	$125.00
Plate 7, Row 3:			
1. Eight-sided strainer	(G.P.)	5	$295.00
2. Triangular sink strainer	(N.M.)	5	$185.00
3. Handled strainer	(G.P.)	4	$160.00
Plate 7, Row 4:			
1. Colander	(M)	4	$125.00
2. Handled gravy strainer	(N.M.)		$165.00
3. Colander	(G.P.)		$145.00

Item	Condition	Rarity	Price
Plate 8, Row 1:			
1. Covered strainer	(G.P.)	5	$135.00
2. Handled strainer	(M)	5	$165.00
3. Covered strainer	(N.M.)	5	$165.00
Plate 8, Row 2:			
1. Strainer insert	(M)		$115.00
2. Rice ball	(G.P.)	2	$375.00
3. Rice ball	(G.P.)	2,3	$525.00
Plate 8, Row 3:			
Egg poacher w/tin cover	(N.M.)	2	$295.00
Plate 8, Row 4:			
1. Upcooker	(N.M.)	5	$255.00
2,3 Asparagus boiler w/insert	(N.M.)	4,5,6	3 pc.$295.00
4. Upcooker with funnel	(N.M.)	5	3 pc.$295.00
Plate 9, Row 1:			
1. Fish kettle or poacher with insert	(G.P.)	4,6	$265.00
2. Double saucepan	(G.P.)	4,5	$125.00
Plate 9, Row 2:			
1. Double saucepan set	(G.P.)	4,5	set$295.00
2. Fish kettle or poacher with insert	(N.M.)		$235.00
Plate 9, Row 3:			
1. Fish kettle or poacher with insert	(N.M.)	4	$265.00
2. Triple saucepan set	(G.P.)	4,5	partial set$325.00
Plate 9, Row 4:			
1. Fish kettle or poacher with insert	(N.M.)	4	$325.00
2. Fish kettle or poacher	(G.P.)		$165.00

Section 21

Item	Condition	Rarity	Price
Plate 1, Row 1:			
1. Double boiler	(N.M.)	4	$575.00
2. Double boiler	(G.P.)	4,5	$245.00
Plate 1, Row 2:			
1. Double boiler	(M)	5	$295.00
2. Double boiler	(N.M.)		$325.00
Plate 1, Row 3:			
1. Double boiler	(M)		$275.00
2. Double boiler	(M)	6	$265.00
3. Double boiler	(M)	4	$210.00
Plate 1, Row 4:			
1. Double boiler	(M)	4,5	$525.00
2. Double boiler	(M)	5	$295.00
Plate 2, Row 1:			
1. Double boiler	(N.M.)	4,6	$310.00
2. Double boiler	(N.M.)	1	$435.00
Plate 2, Row 2:			
1. Double boiler	(N.M.)	4,5	$425.00
2. Double boiler	(M)		$75.00
3. Double boiler	(M)	4	$495.00
Plate 2, Row 3:			
1. Double boiler	(M)	1,2	$395.00
2. Double boiler	(M)	4	$535.00

Item	Condition	Rarity	Price
Plate 2, Row 4:			
1. Double boiler	(G.P.)	1	$395.00
2. Double boiler	(G.P.)	4	$495.00
Plate 3, Row 1:			
1. Convex kettle or sauce pan	(M)	5,6	$295.00
2. Lipped preserving kettle	(M)	4	$295.00
Plate 3, Row 2:			
1. Covered Berlin-style kettle	(N.M.)	4	$310.00
2. Covered Berlin-style kettle	(M)	5,6	$245.00
3. Covered Berlin-style kettle	(N.M.)	4	$325.00
Plate 3, Row 3:			
1. Covered small kettle	(M)	5,6	$85.00
2. Oval shirred egg plate	(G.P.)	4,5	$135.00
3. Lipped sauce pan	(G.P.)	4	$115.00
Plate 3, Row 4:			
1. Oval shirred egg plate	(G.P.)	5	$130.00
2. Covered Berlin-style sauce pan	(N.M.)	4,5	$325.00
3. Covered convex sauce pan	(G.P.)	4	$265.00
4. Oval shirred egg plate	(M)		$45.00
Plate 4, Row 1:			
1. Lipped preserving kettle	(N.M.)		$265.00
2. Two-handled pan	(G.P.)	1	$225.00
3. Lipped Preserving kettle	(M)	4	$295.00
Plate 4, Row 2:			
1. Covered Berlin-style kettle	(M)	4	$325.00
2. Covered two-handled kettle	(G.P.)	5	$120.00
3. Covered Berlin-style kettle	(N.M.)	4	$180.00
Plate 4, Row 3:			
1. Lipped preserving kettle	(M)		$145.00
2. Covered Berlin-style kettle or bean pot	(N.M.)	4,5,6	$310.00
3. Lipped sauce pan	(M)	5	$160.00
Plate 4, Row 4:			
1. Covered Berlin-style kettle	(M)	4	$310.00
2. Covered Berlin-style kettle	(M)	4,5,6	$425.00
3. Covered convex kettle	(N.M.)	1,5	$295.00
Plate 5, Row 1:			
1. Lipped preserving kettle	(G.P.)	4	$295.00
2. Covered Berlin-style kettle	(M)	5,6	$410.00
3. Lipped preserving kettle	(G.P.)	4	$295.00
Plate 5, Row 2:			
1. Oblong deep stove pan	(G.P.)		$30.00
2. Covered Berlin-style kettle	(G.P.)	5,6	$220.00
3. Oblong shallow stove pan	(M)	4	$195.00
Plate 5, Row 3:			
1. Maslin-style kettle	(M)	1	$265.00
2. Small covered kettle	(M)	5,6	$95.00
3. Covered Berlin-style kettle	(N.M.)	4	$215.00
Plate 5, Row 4:			
1. Berlin-style sauce pan	(G.P.)	5	$165.00
2. Convex sauce pan	(G.P.)	5	$160.00
Plate 6, Row 1:			
1. Deep stove kettle	(M)	2	$265.00
2. Spaghetti or potato kettle Berlin-style	(G.P.)	2	$295.00
Plate 6, Row 2:			
1. Spaghetti or potato kettle Berlin-style	(G.P.)	2	$295.00
2. Berlin-style kettle	(G.P.)	1,5	$285.00
3. Spaghetti or potato kettle convex-style	(N.M.)	2	$265.00
Plate 6, Row 3:			
1. Spaghetti or potato kettle Windsor style	(N.M.)	2	$195.00
2. Lipped preserving kettle	(N.M.)	5,6	$135.00
3. Spaghetti or potato kettle straight-style	(N.M.)	2,4	$325.00
Plate 6, Row 4:			
1. Covered stove pot	(G.P.)	5	$195.00
2. Covered stove pot	(G.P.)	4,5,6	$155.00
3. Covered stove pot	(G.P.)	5	$195.00
Plate 7, Row 1:			
1. Covered convex-style kettle	(N.M.)	4,5	$325.00
2. Covered Berlin-style kettle	(G.P.)	4	$295.00
3. Covered Berlin-style kettle	(N.M.)	4	$310.00
Plate 7, Row 2:			
1. Covered Berlin-style kettle	(M)		$125.00
2. Lipped preserving kettle	(N.M.)	4,6	$145.00
3. Lipped preserving kettle	(N.M.)	4	$135.00
Plate 7, Row 3:			
1. Covered Berlin-style kettle	(N.M.)	4	$180.00
2. Lipped handle sauce pan	(G.P.)	4	$80.00
3. Covered shallow two-handled pan	(M)	4,5	$195.00
Plate 7, Row 4:			
1. Covered Berlin-style kettle	(M)	4	$325.00
2. Mush mug or camp mug	(G.P.)	4,5	$140.00
3. Mush mug or camp mug	(M)	4,5	$235.00
Plate 8, Row 1:			
1. Cruller or potato frier	(G.P.)	2	$265.00
2. Agate cruller or potato frier	(N.M.)	2	$325.00
Plate 8, Row 2:			
1. Covered convex-style kettle	(M)	4	$275.00
2. Covered Berlin-style kettle	(M)	4,5,6	$350.00
3. Covered Berlin-style kettle or bean pot	(N.M.)	4	$175.00
Plate 8, Row 3:			
1. Lipped preserving kettle	(M)	4,6	$145.00
2. Lipped preserving kettle	(N.M.)		$75.00
3. Lipped preserving kettle	(M)	4	$145.00
4. Lipped preserving kettle	(N.M.)	4	$120.00
Plate 8, Row 4:			
1. Maslin-style kettle	(M)	4	$210.00
2. Covered Berlin-style kettle	(M)	4	$265.00
3. Agate seamless flaring preserving kettle	(G.P.)	5	$225.00

Item	Condition	Rarity	Price
Plate 9, Row 1:			
1. Dome-shaped cover	(G.P.)		$10.00
2. Dome-shaped cover	(G.P.)		$25.00
3. Lid	(G.P.)	4,5	$30.00
Plate 9, Row 2:			
Dome-shaped cover	(G.P.)	4	$25.00
Plate 9, Row 3:			
1. Cover	(G.P.)	4,5	$45.00
2. Dome-shaped cover	(G.P.)	4	$25.00
3. Lid	(G.P.)	4,5	$35.00
Plate 9. Row 4:			
Dome-shaped cover	(M)	4	$30.00
Plate 9, Row 5:			
1. Grooved lid with hook wire handle	(N.M.)	5	$85.00
2. Small handihook lid	(M)		$70.00
Plate 9, Row 6:			
1. Large handihook lid	(M)		$75.00
2. Lid rack	(G.P.)	4,5	$195.00

Section 22

Item	Condition	Rarity	Price
Plate 1, Row 1:			
1. Round miner's dinner bucket	(N.M.)	4	$325.00
2. Round miner's dinner bucket	(G.P.)	4	$255.00
3. Round miner's dinner bucket	(N.M.)	1,2	$595.00
Plate 1, Row 2:			
1. Round miner's dinner bucket	(N.M.)	5	$285.00
2. Chestnut roaster	(G.P.)	2	$285.00
3. Round miner's dinner bucket	(M)	5	$295.00
Plate 1, Row 3:			
1. Oval dinner bucket	(N.M.)	1,2	$475.00
2. Oval dinner bucket	(G.P.)	1,2	$615.00
3. Oval dinner bucket	(N.M.)	1,2	$535.00
Plate 1, Row 4:			
1. Stack dinner carrier	(G.P.)	1,2	$395.00
2. Stack dinner carrier	(M)		$95.00
3. Stack dinner carrier	(N.M.)	1,2	$525.00
Plate 2, Row 1:			
Round miner's dinner bucket	(N.M.)	1,2	complete $595.00
Plate 2, Row 2:			
Oblong dinner bucket	(M)		complete $350.00
Plate 2, Row 3:			
Oval dinner bucket	(N.M.)	1,2	complete $575.00
Plate 2, Row 4:			
Round miner's dinner bucket	(M)	5	complete $295.00

Item	Condition	Rarity	Price
Plate 3, Row 1:			
1. Oval dinner bucket	(N.M.)	5	complete $395.00
2. Oblong dinner bucket	(G.P.)	1,2	complete $625.00
3. Oblong dinner bucket	(M)		complete $350.00
Plate 3, Row 2:			
1. Covered bucket or berry bucket	(G.P.)	1	$325.00
2. Covered bucket	(N.M.)	1	$395.00
3. Covered bucket	(N.M.)	1,3	$525.00
Plate 3, Row 3:			
1. Covered bucket	(N.M.)		$165.00
2. Covered bucket	(N.M.)	4	$185.00
3. Covered bucket	(M)		$85.00
4. Covered bucket	(M)		$245.00
Plate 3, Row 4:			
1. Covered bucket	(M)	4	$185.00
2. Covered bucket	(G.P.)	6	$130.00
3. Covered bucket	(G.P.)		$90.00
4. Covered bucket	(N.M.)	6	$70.00
5. Covered bucket	(G.P.)	1	$475.00
Plate 4, Row 1:			
Oblong dinner bucket - dessert tray - coffee flask	(G.P.)	1,2	complete $625.00
Plate 4, Row 2:			
Oval dinner bucket	(N.M.)	5	complete $395.00
Plate 4, Row 3:			
1. Stack dinner carrier	(N.M.)	1,2	complete $525.00
2. Oval dinner bucket	(N.M.)	1,2	complete $535.00
Plate 4, Row 4:			
1. Covered bucket	(M)	4	$200.00
2. Covered bucket	(N.M.)	6	$140.00
2. Covered bucket	(M)	4	$195.00
4. Covered bucket	(G.P.)	6	$135.00
5. Covered bucket	(M)	4	$175.00
Plate 5, Row 1:			
1. Covered bucket	(M)	1	$495.00
2. Covered bucket	(G.P.)	5	$185.00
3. Covered bucket	(N.M.)		$195.00
Plate 5, Row 2:			
1. Covered bucket	(M)	4	$525.00
2. Covered bucket	(G.P.)	4	$310.00
3. Covered bucket	(N.M.)	4	$265.00
4. Covered bucket	(G.P.)	4	$295.00
Plate 5, Row 3:			
1. Covered bucket	(N.M.)	4	$285.00
2. Covered bucket	(M)	6	$115.00
3. Covered bucket	(G.P.)	4	$295.00
4. Covered bucket	(G.P.)	6	$120.00
5. Covered bucket	(M)	1	$475.00
Plate 5, Row 4:			
1. Covered bucket	(N.M.)		$245.00
2. Covered bucket	(M)		$275.00
3. Covered bucket	(G.P.)	4	$395.00
4. Covered bucket	(M)	4,5	$425.00

Item	Condition	Rarity	Price
Plate 6, Row 1:			
1. Covered bucket	(M)	1,6	$455.00
2. Covered bucket	(N.M.)	6	$140.00
3. Covered bucket	(M)	4	$285.00
4. Covered bucket	(M)	4	$275.00
Plate 6, Row 2:			
1. Covered bucket	(G.P.)	4	$295.00
2. Covered bucket	(M)	4	$275.00
3. Covered bucket	(M)	4	$465.00
4. Covered bucket	(G.P.)	1	$310.00
5. Covered bucket	(G.P.)	4	$295.00
Plate 6, Row 3:			
1. Covered bucket	(G.P.)		$275.00
2. Covered bucket	(N.M.)	6	$125.00
3. Covered bucket	(N.M.)		$95.00
4. Covered bucket	(G.P.)	2	$230.00
5. Covered bucket	(M)	4	$395.00
Plate 6, Row 4:			
1. Covered bucket	(G.P.)		$225.00
2. Covered bucket	(G.P.)	4	$295.00
3. Covered bucket	(N.M.)		$245.00
4. Covered bucket	(N.M.)	4,5	$285.00
5. Covered bucket	(N.M.)	4	$185.00

Section 23

Item	Condition	Rarity	Price
Plate 1, Row 1:			
Clock, school house style	(M)	1,2	$395.00
Plate 1, Row 2:			
1. Clock	(M)	1,2	$325.00
2. Clock	(M)	1,2	$325.00
Plate 1, Row 3:			
Alarm clock	(M)	2,4	$415.00
Plate 1, Row 4:			
1. Clock	(M)	1,2	$395.00
2. Clock	(M)	1,2	$375.00
Plate 1, Row 5:			
Clock	(M)	1,2	$325.00
Plate 2, Row 1:			
1. Candlestick or chamberstick	(G.P.)	4,5	$135.00
2. "Gone With The Wind" style oil lamp	(M)	1,2	$2,350.00
3. Candlesticks, pair	(M)	2,3	pr.$495.00
Plate 2, Row 2:			
1. Candlestick	(G.P.)		$75.00
2. Candlestick	(M)	4	$175.00
3. Match holder	(M)	1,2	$495.00
4. Candlestick	(N.M.)	5	$195.00
5. Candlestick	(G.P.)	4	$155.00
Plate 2, Row 3:			
1. Candlestick	(M)	4	$195.00
2. Match box	(N.M.)	4,5	$265.00
3. Candlestick	(M)	5	$295.00
4. Match box	(N.M.)	1,5	$385.00
5. Candlestsick	(G.P.)	1,2	$985.00

Item	Condition	Rarity	Price
Plate 3, Row 1:			
1. Candlestick	(M)	5	$185.00
2. Table lamp, electric	(G.P.)	2,4	$350.00
3. Oil lamp	(N.M.)	1,2	$425.00
4. Candlestick	(N.M.)	5	$225.00
Plate 3, Row 2:			
1. Candlestick	(G.P.)	2	$295.00
2. Candlestick	(N.M.)	1	$625.00
3. Double pocket match holder	(M)	1,2	$495.00
4. Twin pocket match holder	(N.M.)	2	$525.00
5. Candlestick	(N.M.)		$195.00
6. Candlestick	(N.M.)	1	$950.00
Plate 3, Row 3:			
1. Petroleum jug	(G.P.)	2	$295.00
2. Candlestick	(N.M.)	1	$625.00
3. Candlestick	(N.M.)	1	$425.00
4. Match box	(N.M.)	4,5	$285.00
Plate 4, Row 1:			
Combination wood and gas kitchen range	(N.M.)	1,2	$1,950.00
Plate 5, Row 1:			
Oil or kerosene stove	Restored	1,2	$1,275.00
Plate 6, Row 1:			
1. Twin table top oil stove	(M)	1,2,3	$795.00
Plate 6, Row 2:			
1. Table top oil stove	(N.M.)	5	$315.00
2. Hot plate	(N.M.)	6	$145.00
3. Table top oil stove, single burner	(N.M.)	5	$215.00
Plate 6, Row 3:			
1. New Perfection toaster	(N.M.)	5	$165.00
2. New Perfection toaster	(N.M.)	4,5	$155.00
Plate 7, Row 1:			
1. Oven thermometer	(N.M.)		$55.00
2. Table top oil stove with matching pit-bottom teakettle	(N.M.)	5	$375.00
3. Table top oil stove with matching pit-bottom teakettle	(N.M.)	4,5	$625.00
4. Oven thermometer	(N.M.)		$55.00
Plate 7, Row 2:			
1. Armstrong electric table top stove	(N.M.)		$185.00
2. Oven thermometer	(M)	4	$70.00
3. Table top oil stove and pit-bottom teakettle	(N.M.)	5	$495.00
Plate 7, Row 3:			
1. Hot plate, electric	(N.M.)		$65.00
2. Oven thermometer	(M)		$65.00
3. Oven thermometer	(M)	4	$60.00
4. Hot plate, electric	(N.M.)		$75.00
Plate 8, Row 1:			
1. Floor model gas heater	(M)	5	$295.00

Item	Condition	Rarity	Price
Plate 8, Row 2:			
1. Floor model oil stove	(N.M.)	2	$395.00
2. Coal scuttle	(N.M.)	2,4	$310.00
3. Coal scuttle	(N.M.)	2	$295.00
Plate 8, Row 3:			
1. Whistling tea kettle	(M)	5	$160.00
2. Handled sauce pan	(M)		$30.00
3. Twin electric hot plate	(G.P.)	4	$195.00
4. Coffee biggin	(N.M.)	5	$195.00
5. Double boiler	(M)	1	$325.00
6. Twin electric hot plate	(M)	4	$245.00
Plate 9, Row 1:			
1. Trivet	(M)		$75.00
2. Trivet	(M)	5	$85.00
3. Handled trivet	(N.M.)		$75.00
Plate 9, Row 2:			
1. Insert for No. 3 on this row	(N.M.)		$125.00
2. Trivet	(G.P.)		$60.00
3. Food warmer	(N.M.)	2	$425.00
Plate 9, Row 3:			
1. Foot warmer	(G.P.)	5	$285.00
2. Trivet	(M)	5	$95.00
3. Foot warmer	(G.P.)	5	$285.00
Plate 9, Row 4:			
1. Food warmer	(N.M.)	1,2	$425.00
2. Foot warmer	(G.P.)	5	$265.00
3. Handled trivet	(G.P.)	5	$90.00

Section 24

Item	Condition	Rarity	Price
Plate 1, Row 1:			
1. Washboard	(G.P.)	5	$165.00
2. Washboard	(N.M.)	5	$195.00
Plate 1, Row 2:			
1. Enamel cleanser	(M)		$45.00
2. Electric dishwasher and wire drainer	(G.P.)	2	$295.00
3. Soap for cleaning enamel ware	(M)		$25.00
Plate 1, Row 3:			
1. Washboard	(N.M.)	5	$195.00
2. Washboard	(M)	3,5	$325.00
Plate 1, Row 4:			
1. Covered clothes boiler	(N.M.)	4,5,6	$215.00
2. Covered oblong clothes boiler	(G.P.)	1,5,6	$465.00
Plate 2, Row 1:			
1. Suds dipper	(G.P.)	5	$95.00
2. Clothes boiler	(G.P.)	5	$175.00
3. Powder cannister	(G.P.)	5	$165.00
Plate 2, Row 2:			
1. Coffee flask			No value
2. Coffee flask	(N.M.)		$225.00
3. Flask	(G.P.)		$155.00
4. Flask	(M)		$165.00
5. Coffee flask	(N.M.)		$295.00
6. Coffee flask	(N.M.)	4	$285.00

Item	Condition	Rarity	Price
Plate 2, Row 3:			
1. Electric toaster	(N.M.)	2	$485.00
2. Dog nut cracker	(N.M.)	2,4	$365.00
3. Starch cannister	(N.M.)		$75.00
4. Soap saver	(N.M.)	2	$295.00
Plate 2, Row 4:			
1. Stack refrigerator containers	(G.P.)	4	3pc.$155.00
2. Cat spoon rest	(G.P.)	2	$185.00
3. Horse spoon rest	(M)	2	$295.00
4. Nut cracker	(N.M.)	5	$95.00
5. Handled griddle cleaner	(N.M.)	5	$110.00
6. Thermos	(G.P.)	5	$130.00
Plate 3, Row 1:			
1. Dust pan	(N.M.)	2,4	$225.00
2. Coleman gas iron	(N.M.)		$85.00
3. Dust pan	(G.P.)	2,4	$125.00
Plate 3, Row 2:			
1. Dust pan	(G.P.)	2	$145.00
2. Electric iron	(N.M.)	1,2	$140.00
3. Ant cup	(M)	2	$475.00
4. Dust pan	(G.P.)	2,3	$185.00
Plate 3, Row 3:			
1. Dust pan	(G.P.)	2,4	$195.00
2. Dust pan	(G.P.)	2	$135.00
3. Electric iron	(N.M.)	1,2	$130.00
4. Dust pan	(G.P.)	2	$175.00
Plate 4, Row 1:			
1. Cuspidor	(N.M.)	4	$450.00
2. Cuspidor	(M)	4,5	$385.00
3. Cuspidor	(N.M.)	1	$415.00
Plate 4, Row 2:			
1. Cuspidor	(N.M.)	5	$310.00
2. Comb case	(N.M.)	2	$695.00
3. Cuspidor	(G.P.)		$295.00
Plate 4, Row 3:			
1. Cuspidor	(M)	4	$475.00
2. Spit cup	(G.P.)	2,3	$215.00
3. Cuspidor	(M)		$135.00
4. Cuspidor	(G.P.)	4	$255.00
Plate 4, Row 4:			
1. Cuspidor	(G.P.)	1,2	$425.00
2. Comb case	(G.P.)	2	$595.00
3. Cuspidor	(G.P.)	1,2	$425.00
Plate 5, Row 1:			
Handled advertising dishpan	(G.P.)	1	$325.00
Plate 5, Row 2:			
1. Handled dishpan	(G.P.)	1	$155.00
2. Handled dishpan	(G.P.)		$125.00
Plate 5, Row 3:			
Oval foot tub	(G.P.)	2,4	$225.00
Plate 6, Row 1:			
1. Handled dishpan	(N.M.)	4	$135.00
2. Handled dishpan	(N.M.)	4,5	$155.00

Item	Condition	Rarity	Price
Plate 6, Row 2			
1. Handled dishpan	(N.M.)	4	$185.00
2. Dishpan	(N.M.)	4	$75.00
Plate 6, Row 3:			
1. Dishpan	(M)		$55.00
2. Handled dishpan	(G.P.)	4	$195.00

Section 25

Item	Condition	Rarity	Price
Plate 1, Row 1:			
Checkerboard	(M)	1,2,3	$3850.00
Plate 2, Row 2:			
Wicker picnic basket (Contents continued on row 2 & 3)	(G.P.)	1,2	complete $875.00
Plate 2, Row 2:			
1. Salt shaker			
2. Tumbler			
3. Granite saucer			
4. Granite cup			
5. Granite plate			
6. Granite plate			
7. Granite cup & saucer			
8. Tin insert			
Plate 2, Row 3:			
1. Cream flask			
2. Butter dish			
3. Fuel can			
4. Teakettle			
5. Stove with alcohol burner			
6. Covered container	(G.P.)	1,2	complete $750.00
Plate 3, Row 1:			
1. Pedestal vase	(G.P.)	2,4	$285.00
2. Vase	(N.M.)	2,4	$255.00
3. Pedestal vase	(N.M.)	2,4	$315.00
Plate 3, Row 2:			
1. Wine cooler or pedestal vase	(M)	4,5	$185.00
2. Hanging wall vase	(N.M.)	1,2,3	$365.00
3. Vase	(M)	5	$325.00
Plate 3, Row 3:			
1. Ashtray and cigar nipper	(N.M.)	2	$185.00
2. Ashtray	(G.P.)	1	$165.00
3. License plate	(G.P.)	2	$185.00

Section 26

Item	Condition	Rarity	Price
Plate 1, Row 1:			
1. Child's two-piece feeding set	(G.P.)	5	2 pcs.$65.00
2. Child's feeding dish	(G.P.)		$25.00
3. Child's two-piece feeding set	(G.P.)		2 pc.$55.00
4. Child's cup	(G.P.)		$25.00
5. Child's plate	(G.P.)		$55.00

Item	Condition	Rarity	Price
Plate 1, Row 2:			
1. Child's two-piece feeding set	(G.P.)		2 pc.$55.00
2. Child's plate	(G.P.)		$25.00
3. Child's mug	(N.M.)		$30.00
4. Child's feeding dish	(N.M.)	4	$30.00
5. Child's two-piece feeding set	(G.P.)		2 pc.$55.00
Plate 1, Row 3:			
Child's table and two chairs	(G.P.)	5	3 pc.$285.00
Plate 2, Row 1:			
1. Child's starter plate	(N.M.)		$140.00
2. Salesman's sample "hearth style" wood-burning stove	(G.P.)	2,4	$2200.00
3. Child's starter plate	(N.M.)		$100.00
Plate 2, Row 2:			
1. Child's miniature electric toy stove	(G.P.)	4,5,6	$485.00
2. Child's starter plate	(G.P.)		$45.00
3. Child's starter mug	(M)		$40.00
4. Child's starter plate	(M)		$60.00
Plate 2, Row 3:			
1. Child's three-piece starter set	(M)	4	3 pc.$185.00
2. Child's miniature toy stove	(N.M.)	1,2,3	$1,175.00
Plate 3, Row 1:			
1. Miniature electric range	(N.M.)	2	$1,025.00
2. Advertising booklet for No. 1 on this page	(N.M.)		$35.00
Plate 3, Row 2:			
1. Child's potty	(N.M.)	4	$235.00
2. Child's sectioned tray	(N.M.)	2	$285.00
3. Child's covered potty	(M)		$65.00
Plate 3, Row 3:			
1. Child's feeding dish	(G.P.)		$25.00
2. Child's tray	(M)	4,6	$225.00
3. Child's two-piece starter set	(M)	4	set$295.00
Plate 4, Row 1:			
1. Child's cup and saucer	(N.M.)		set$55.00
2. Child's miniature toy stove	(N.M.)	1,2,3	$2,500.00
3. Embossed alphabet plate	(M)	2	$1,250.00
4. Child's mug	(G.P.)	4,6	$85.00
Plate 4, Row 2:			
1. Thirteen-piece tea set	(N.M.)		set$460.00
2. Child's plate	(M)		$45.00
Plate 4, Row 3:			
1. Child's three-piece starter set	(G.P.)		3 pc.$125.00
2. Child's three-piece starter set	(G.P.)		3 pc.$125.00

Item	Condition	Rarity	Price
Plate 5, Row 1:			
1. Handled skimmer	(G.P.)	5	$65.00
2. Handled skimmer	(G.P.)	5	$65.00
3. Grater	(G.P.)	5	$135.00
4. Dust pan	(M)	5	$175.00
5. Spoon	(G.P.)	5	$65.00
6. Spatula or turner	(G.P.)	5	$125.00
7. Ladle	(G.P.)	5	$65.00
8. Grater	(N.M.)	4,5	$175.00
9. Colander	(G.P.)	1,2,3	$395.00
10. Handled strainer	(N.M.)	5	$125.00
Plate 5, Row 2:			
Tea set	(N.M.)		set$345.00
Plate 5, Row 3:			
1. Teakettle	(N.M.)	2,3,4	$595.00
2. Salesman's sample plate	(M)	3,4	$135.00
3. Miniature candlestick	(G.P.)	2,3	$275.00
4. 13-piece tea set (continued on row 4)	(G.P.)		set$325.00
Plate 6, Row 1:			
1. Child's fry pan	(M)	4	$95.00
2. Cooking set (continued on row 2)	(M)		5pc.$250.00
Plate 6, Row 3:			
1. Roaster	(M)	2,3	$195.00
2,3 Roaster insert and covered roaster	(N.M.)	1,2,3	$1,850.00
Plate 6, Row 4:			
1. Covered roaster and handled insert, salesman's sample	(M)	1,2,3	$795.00
2,3 Insert and covered roaster, salesman's sample	(M)	1,2,3	$1,100.00
Plate 7, Row 1:			
1. Covered handled sauce pan	(N.M.)	1	$110.00
2. Teakettle	(M)	1,2,3	$625.00
3. Lipped preserve kettle	(M)	1,2,3	$295.00
4. Salesman's sample water pail	(G.P.)	2,3	$275.00
Plate 7, Row 2:			
1. Covered sugar	(G.P.)	5,6	$145.00
2. Long-handled strainer	(N.M.)	5	$70.00
3. Preserve kettle	(G.P.)		$80.00
4. Covered, handled sauce pan	(M)	4	$140.00
Plate 7, Row 3:			
1. Child's electric iron	(M)		*$135.00
2. Cuspidor, salesman's sample	(M)	1,2,3	$950.00
3. Child's electric iron	(M)		*$135.00
4. Miniature coffee pot	(G.P.)	2,3	$325.00
Plate 7, Row 4:			
Domestic Science cook set	(G.P.)		5 pc.$395.00

* in working condition

Item	Condition	Rarity	Price
Plate 8, Row 1:			
1. Cup and saucer	(N.M.)		2pc.$55.00
2. Plate	(M)		$25.00
3. Cup and saucer	(N.M.)		2pc.$55.00
4. Coffee pot	(N.M.)	1,2,3	$495.00
5. Oval platter	(N.M.)	5	$70.00
6. Pudding pan	(N.M.)	1,2,3	$180.00
7. Percolator funnel	(G.P.)	1,2,3	$325.00
8. Wash basin salesman's sample	(M)	4	$75.00
Plate 8, Row 2:			
1. Partial tea set, large size	(N.M.)		6pc.$275.00
2. 13-piece tea set (continued on row 3)	(N.M.)		set$525.00
Plate 8, Row 3:			
1. Salesman's sample wash basin	(M)		$45.00
2. Partial tea set (part of a 13-piece set)	(G.P.)	4	6 pc.$410.00
3. Wash basin	(M)		$65.00
Plate 8, Row 4:			
1. Partial tea set (part of a 12-piece set)	(G.P.)		4 pc.$375.00
2. Cup	(G.P.)	1	$75.00
3. Pitcher	(G.P.)	5	$135.00
4. Tube mold	(N.M.)	2,3	$395.00
5. Funnel	(N.M.)	6	$35.00
6. Cup and saucer	(G.P.)	3	2 pc.$75.00
7. Oblong teapot	(G.P.)	2,3	$185.00
Plate 9, Row 1:			
1. Handled skimmer	(G.P.)	5	$75.00
2. Perforated spatula or turner	(G.P.)	5	$125.00
3. Ladle	(G.P.)	5	$65.00
4. Grater	(N.M.)	4,5	$175.00
5. Grater	(N.M.)	4,5	$165.00
6. Grater	(M)	4,5	$180.00
7. Perforated spatula or turner	(G.P.)	5,6	$120.00
8. Spatula or turner	(N.M.)	5	$130.00
9. Perforated spatula or turner	(G.P.)	5	$120.00
Plate 9, Row 2:			
1. Partial tea set	(G.P.)		11pc.$485.00
2. Coffee pot	(N.M.)	2,3	$395.00
3. Covered sugar	(G.P.)	5,6	$125.00
4. Creamer	(G.P.)	5	$110.00
5. Wash basin, salesman's sample	(M)	1	$295.00
6. Wash basin, salesman's sample	(M)	1	$295.00
Plate 9, Row 3:			
1. Preserve kettle	(G.P.)	6	$115.00
2. Covered stew pan	(G.P.)		$25.00
3. Mug	(G.P.)		$35.00
4. Plate	(M)		$20.00
5. Egg fry pan	(G.P.)	5	$125.00
6. Fluted mold	(G.P.)	5	$95.00
7. Crumb tray	(G.P.)	5	$145.00
8. Fry pan	(G.P.)		$70.00

Item		Condition	Rarity	Price
Plate 9, Row 4:				
1.	Oblong roasting pan	(G.P.)	4	$75.00
2.	Two-handled sauce pan	(M)		$55.00
3.	Covered mush mug	(N.M.)		$135.00
4.	Creamer	(G.P.)	5	$85.00
5.	Fry pan	(N M)	6	$65.00
6/	Plate	(M)		$20.00
7.	Teakettle	(G.P.)	1,2,3	$210.00
Plate 10, Row 1:				
1.	Creamer	(N.M.)	5	$125.00
2.	Handled sauce pan	(G.P.)		$155.00
3.	Handled, divided vegetable dish	(N.M.)	5	$175.00
4.	Two-handled sauce pan	(G.P.)		$55.00
5.	Small wash basin	(M)	5,6	$85.00
6.	Funnel	(G.P.)	6	$55.00
7.	Oblong roasting pan	(N.M.)		$65.00
8.	Large wash basin	(M)	5	$60.00
9.	Egg fry pan	(G.P.)	5	$160.00
10.	Two-handled roasting pan	(G.P.)		$60.00
11.	Plate	(N.M.)		$20.00
Plate 10, Row 2:				
1.	Creamer	(G.P.)	5	$115.00
2.	Platter	(M)		$75.00
3.	Teapot	(M)	5,6	$395.00
4.	Open sugar	(M)	5	$125.00
5.	Large platter	(G.P.)		$55.00
6.	Pieced scoop	(N.M.)	5,6	$165.00
7.	Fry pan	(M)	5	$110.00
8.	Gravy or sauce bowl	(M)	5	$195.00
Plate 10, Row 3:				
1.	Covered sauce pan	(N.M.)		$75.00
2.	Fry pan	(G.P.)	5	$95.00
3.	Mug	(G.P.)		$55.00
4.	Fluted mold	(N.M.)	5	$115.00
5.	Funnel	(N.M.)	6	$70.00
6.	Pail	(G.P.)	2	$165.00
7.	Two-handled sauce pan	(N.M.)		$65.00
Plate 10, Row 4:				
1.	Two-handled sauce pan	(N.M.)		$65.00
2.	Fry pan	(G.P.)		$95.00
3.	Wash basin	(N.M.)		$45.00
4.	Oblong roasting pan	(G.P.)		$65.00
5.	Creamer	(G.P.)	5	$115.00
6.	Mug	(M)		$60.00
7.	Fluted mold	(M)	5	$115.00
8.	Fry pan	(G.P.)	4	$95.00
9.	Stew pan	(M)	5,6	$125.00
10.	Pail	(M)	2	$165.00
Plate 11, Row 1:				
1.	Cup and saucer	(N.M.)		2 pc.$55.00
2.	13-piece tea set (continued on row 2)	(N.M.)		set$500.00
Plate 11, Row 2:				
1.	(continued from row 1)			
2.	Pr. of place card holders	(M)	1,2,3	pr.$250.00
3.	Pr. of place card holders	(N.M.)	1,2,3	pr.$225.00
4.	Creamer and saucer	(M)	5	2 pc.$140.00

Item		Condition	Rarity	Price
Plate 11, Row 3:				
1.	Grater	(N.M.)	4,5	$165.00
2.	Cup and saucer	(G.P.)		$35.00
3.	Plate	(M)	4	$25.00
4.	Cup and saucer	(G.P.)		$35.00
5.	Cup and saucer	(G.P.)		$35.00
6.	Creamer	(G.P.)	5	$115.00
7.	Partial tea set	(G.P.)		6 pc.$215.00
Plate 11, Row 4:				
1.	13-piece tea st	(N.M.)		set$525.00
Plate 12, Row 1:				
1.	13-piece tea set (continued on row 2)	(N.M.)	4,5,6	set$550.00
Plate 12, Row 2:				
1.	(continued from row 1)			
2.	Partial serving set	(G.P.)	5	set$510.00
Plate 12, Row 3:				
	13-piece tea set (continued on row 4)	(N.M.)	4	set$725.00
Plate 12, Row 4:				
1.	(continued from row 3)			
2.	Partial tea set	(G.P.)	4,5	7 pc.$330.00
Plate 13, Row 1:				
	13-piece serving set	(G.P.)	4	set$285.00
Plate 13, Row 2:				
	12-piece doll's tea set	(G.P.)	3	set$575.00
Plate 13, Row 3:				
1.	Salesman's sample wash basin	(M)	4	$75.00
2.	Salesman's sample wash basin	(M)		$65.00
3.	12-piece tea set	(G.P.)		set$485.00
4.	Salesman's sample wash basin	(M)		$75.00
5.	Salesman's sample wash basin	(M)	4	$75.00
Plate 13, Row 4:				
1.	Saucer	(M)	4	$25.00
2.	Plate	(M)	4	$25.00
3.	Plate	(M)	4	$25.00
4.	Saucer	(M)	4	$25.00
5.	Two-handled sauce pan	(M)	4	$95.00
6.	Covered mush mug	(M)	4	$165.00
7.	Oblong roasting pan	(M)	4	$75.00
8.	Handled sauce pan	(M)	4	$75.00
Plate 14, Row 1:				
1.	Salesman's sample advertising cuspidor	(M)	1,2,3	$895.00
2.	Miniature "Red Riding Hood" clock	(M)	1,2,3	*$425.00
3.	Fluted mold	(M)	5	$95.00
4.	Miniature mountain scene clock	(M)	1,2,3	*$285.00
5.	Child's coffee pot	(N.M.)	3	$495.00

*running condition

413

Item	Condition	Rarity	Price
Plate 14, Row 2:			
1. Two-handled sauce pan	(M)		$55.00
2. Melon-shape mold or patty pan	(M)	2,6	$165.00
3. "Heart" fluted mold or patty pan	(M)	2,6	$195.00
4. "Lobster" fluted mold or patty pan	(M)	2,6	$195.00
5. Two-handled bean pot	(G.P.)	1,2	$195.00
Plate 14, Row 3:			
1. 13-piece tea set	(G.P.)		set $495.00
Plate 14, Row 4:			
1. Advertising salesman's sample wash basin	(G.P.)	5	$105.00
2. Advertising salesman's sample wash basin	(M)	5	$150.00
3. Two-handled egg plate	(G.P.)	4,5	$135.00
4. Advertising salesman's sample wash basin	(G.P.)	5	$115.00
5. Advertising salesman's sample wash basin	(M)	5	$125.00
Plate 15, Row 1:			
1. Fry pan	(N.M.)	1	$210.00
2. Pitcher	(N.M.)	1,2	$265.00
3. Handled strainer	(N.M.)	1,2	$220.00
4. Mixing bowl	(M)	1	$195.00
Plate 15, Row 2:			
1. Scalloped soap dish	(M)	1,2	$210.00
2. Water dipper	(M)	1,2	$295.00
3. Covered sugar	(N.M.)	1,2	$295.00
4. Covered sauce pan	(M)	1	$200.00

Item	Condition	Rarity	Price
Plate 15, Row 3:			
1. Oval platter	(N.M.)	1	$195.00
2. Pudding pan	(M)	1	$195.00
3. Cup and saucer	(G.P.)	1	$125.00
4. Cup and saucer	(G.P.)	1	$125.00
Plate 15, Row 4:			
1. Pitcher and bowl	(G.P.)	4,5	$245.00
2. Partial wash set	(G.P.)	1,2,3	4 pc. $525.00

Section 27

Item	Condition	Rarity	Price
Plate 1, Row 1:			
1. Oil stove teakettle	(G.P.)	2	$295.00
2. Small bucket	(M)	3	$295.00
3. Coffee biggin, 4 pcs.	(G.P.)	1,5	$410.00
4. Oyster measure	(M)	2	$345.00
5. Rice or farina boiler	(M)	2	$495.00
Plate 1, Row 2:			
1. Teapot	(M)	3	$195.00
2. Teapot	(N.M.)	6	$165.00
3. Cake safe	(G.P.)	2	$225.00
4. Electric percolator	(M)	5	$175.00
Plate 1, Row 3:			
1. Molasses pitcher	(G.P.)	1,2	$975.00
2. Chocolate or coffee pot	(N.M.)	5	$295.00
3. Small tumbler	(N.M.)	3	$95.00
4. Bread pan	(N.M.)	1	$325.00
5. Partial set of spice cannisters	(N.M.)	4,6	$165.00
6. Coffee pot	(G.P.)		$195.00

Schroeder's Antiques Price Guide

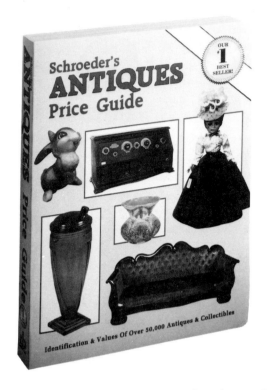

Schroeder's Antiques Price Guide has become THE household name in the antiques & collectibles field. Our team of editors work year-round with more than 200 contributors to bring you our #1 best-selling book on antiques & collectibles.

With more than 50,000 items identified & priced, Schroeder's is a must for the collector & dealer alike. If it merits the interest of today's collector, you'll find it in Schroeder's. Each subject is represented with histories and background information. In addition, hundreds of sharp original photos are used each year to illustrate not only the rare and unusual, but the everyday "fun-type" collectibles as well -- not postage stamp pictures, but large close-up shots that show important details clearly.

Our editors compile a new book each year. Never do we merely change prices. Accuracy is our primary aim. Prices are gathered over the entire year previous to publication, from ads and personal contacts. Then each category is thoroughly checked to spot inconsistencies, listings that may not be entirely reflective of actual market dealings, and lines too vague to be of merit. Only the best of the lot remains for publication. You'll find Schroeder's Antiques Price Guide the one to buy for factual information and quality.

No dealer, collector or investor can afford not to own this book. It is available from your favorite bookseller or antiques dealer at the low price of $12.95. If you are unable to find this price guide in your area, it's available from Collector Books, P.O. Box 3009, Paducah, KY 42002-3009 at $12.95 plus $2.00 for postage and handling.

8½ x 11", 608 Pages   **$12.95**

COLLECTOR BOOKS

A Division of Schroeder Publishing Co., Inc.